JN062024

A Short Introduction to the Structure of English

A Short Introduction to the Structure of English

Kazuo Nakazawa

KAITAKUSHA

Kaitakusha Co., Ltd.
22–16, Otowa 1-chome
Bunkyo-ku, Tokyo 112–0013
Japan

A Short Introduction to the Structure of English

Published in Japan
by Kaitakusha Publishing Co., Ltd., Tokyo

First published 2024

Printed and bound in Japan
by Hinode Printing Co., Ltd.

Cover design by Shihoko Nakamura

Preface

The present book is intended to be an introductory course book to the structure of English, and at the same time it is hoped that readers will gradually get familiar with the ways linguists analyze the sentences in English. In other words, the book is primarily concerned with what English is like and how it is structured. For that end, the book introduces fundamental notions prevalent in linguistic analyses, which is the second aim of this book. The reason this book is meant to serve to introduce basic notions in linguistics is that the author believes that understanding English is not simply learning English but that it also involves studying the structure of English. With this in mind, we introduce grammatical notions and explain how English is structured.

English can be seen from a number of perspectives. Because of this, we have chapters in this book that will cover from "Sound and Spelling" to "Pragmatics." Each chapter focuses on the very field in which one of these areas of study enjoys regularities and systematicity. For example, the chapter on Phonetics and Phonology deals with the English sound system and the regularities found in the English phonological phenomena. Also, the one on Syntax deals with syntactic regularities and these regularities, as a whole, constitute systematicity. And other chapters go in the same fashion. But as for Pragmatics, we must say a few more words. Strictly speaking, Pragmatics is the type of study that is not part of the structure of

English, but rather, the study of the structure of English is one of the prerequisites for the study of Pragmatics. Pragmatics shows how humans use language as a means to convey their intentions. It is due to this affinity to the language use, particularly use of English, that we have included Pragmatics in this book.

The book presupposes no knowledge about linguistics or about any grammatical notions. Every notion is explained when it appears for the first time. So, the author hopes and believes that readers will eventually find themselves confident that after going through the pages down to the last, they have gained the general, if not overall, understanding of both the structure of English and the basics of linguistics.

For the rest of the preface, let me continue in a personal note. I have been teaching English and linguistics at several universities in Japan for a long time; it's over three decades now. It is true that there is an increasing number of introductory books to linguistics, phonology, morphology, syntax, and so on, but those that are already on the market are either too general or too specialized for the course book I use in my class. The title of the class I regularly teach is "Introduction to English and linguistics." The course is for the freshmen at the English department, and their majors include English and American literature, linguistics, communication stud-ies, and TEFL (Teaching English as a Foreign Language). I have long wanted to use a textbook that is concisely rich but not superfluous for the general interest of the students in the department. This book is written for these students, as well as for the general readers outside colleges and universities who are also interested in English and linguistics. I hope this book, partly a grammar book and partly a linguistics book, will serve these purposes.

I acknowledge, finally, that I owe much to Kaitakusha Publishing, in particular to Masaru Kawata's editorship, for the publication of this book.

December 2023

Kazuo Nakazawa
Tokyo, Japan

Table of Contents

Chapter I

Introduction

1.1　Why Study Linguistics and the Structure of English?

When you drive a car, you don't need to know the entire mechanism of the vital parts of the car, but you only need to know the minimum technique of how to start the engine, how to steer the wheel, how to control the accelerator and the brake pedal, etc. But when you want to be a good driver, which means a safe, skillful, comfort-giving, environment-conscious driver, you need a lot more to learn. Once you know the system of the internal combustion engine, that of the power transmission train, that of the road stability-shock absorbing equipment, and that of all other hardware stuff, you deserve a good mechanic and at the same time you will make a good driver.

By the same token, if you want to be a good writer of English, a good listener of English, a good communicator in English, and a good teacher of English, you need to know the structure of English and also need to understand the linguistic analyses applied to the components of the language. So we study linguistics and the structure of English.

Furthermore, there is a second reason to study linguistics and the structure of English. We know the fact that there are great many species living on the planet, from humans to birds to fish and sea urchins, for example, and that they use the 'language' of their own, but it sometimes goes unnoticed that studying the language itself is a highly intellectual activity that only humans can get engaged in. And a highly intellectual activity really pays. For example, progress in linguistics makes possible an in-depth analysis of our verbal behaviors and, accordingly, a deeper understanding of our unconscious state of mind. Understanding our unconscious state of mind will be the prerequisite both fundamental and indispensable in other areas of research such as psychology, pedagogy, sociology, politics, and so on. Thus there is no denying that linguistics is the most challenging field of study regarding all human activities, and this is simply because of the fact that linguistics is one of the empirically sound probes into mind.

As a third reason for us to study linguistics and the structure of English, we may point to pragmatic motivations. Now we live in the real world, and here we are involved in so many kinds of relations that range from international to interpersonal. We are striving for the better understanding of all these relations. And we should point out that as far as the international and the interpersonal relationships are concerned, culture and language play an essential part. We firmly believe that in order to promote these relationships, we need to know more about culture and language. But no culture is without language. Therefore, if you wish to promote the kind of cultural relationship you are engaged in, you need to know more about language. Studying language is an ever new threshold to all sorts of human relationships. Thus, studying linguistics is the most effective, if not only, way to the goal you would set in leading your own life if you wish to keep good terms with others.

1.2   Approaches to the Study of English

Contemporary disciplines and methods designed to study human languages are so diverse that it is extremely a hard job to get the full picture, let alone the full understanding, of the whole enterprises. So in this section, we will confine ourselves to the very general idea of what constitutes the study of English. In other words, let us note the variety of approaches to the study of English.

First, there is the structural approach to the study of English. It comprises such fields as Phonetics, Phonology, Morphology, Syntax and Semantics. Phonetics is sometimes regarded as the physical study of human speech sounds, so it often finds its place outside of linguistics. But since our concern here is about the investigations into the structure of English, we lay as much emphasis on Phonetics as we do on other fields.

Second, there is the cognitive perspective in the study of language. Cognitive studies are concerned with the idea of how human thinking is structured, the linguistic behavior being part of it. Goals and methods of these studies are fairly diverse that it is virtually impossible to delimit the field of survey. A glimpse of the nomenclature will help to understand the diversity of the field: philosophy of language, acquisition of a first (or a second/foreign) language, pragmatics (or the study of speech acts), error analysis, sign language, mental lexicon, mental logic, and aphasia, to give a few key terms.

Thirdly, there is the social perspective, which includes pragmatics (again! Pragmatics covers so wide an area that it may be part of cognitive studies, and at the same time it may be part of sociolinguistics), discourse studies, and communication theories. Communication theorists work on interpersonal communication and intercultural communication, while sociolinguists study the languages in advertisement, business and commerce, journalism, legal matters, gender issues, and so on.

Geographical differences are another subject of linguistics, which is called dialectology. Lexicology is the study about words (especially about their form, history and meaning) and has much to do with lexicography, which we recognize as dictionary making.

Literary perspective in the linguistic studies provides views on metaphor, poetic license, and the prosody of verses, among others.

Last but not least, there is the historical perspective on language, which is often called diachronic linguistics or philology.

There is so wide a variety of disciplines and approaches, indeed. But we cannot cover all these topics in a single book like this. And our main concern is in the structure of English, as the title of the book shows. So, you will find topics related to the structural properties of the English language in the chapters that follow.

Let us quickly preview the targets of study contained in the book. We will start with a rather conventional issue, the sound-spelling relationship. We then study the smallest units of the language, i.e. phones and phonemes, and gradually go up to larger units such as words and sentences. Objects we are manipulating up until here are all formal, or they have concrete and tangible structural forms. After studying formal structural properties, we step forward to rather abstract entities, something we call meaning. Finally, we will focus on the issue of how we use the language as a tool to convey our intentions. That way, you will find answers to the questions "What is English?" and "What is it that is called the structure of English?" And, on the way, you may probably find somewhere in the book many unanswered questions and unsolved problems that would help lead to an advanced study, and also to a deeper understanding, of the English language. Now, let's get started!

EXERCISES

1.   What kinds of associations do you have with the word "structure"? What kinds of parts make up the construct that has a "structure"? (*Hint*: Physical objects like a house, a bridge, and an animal's body have a "structure." For example, a house has the base, pillars, walls, floors, a roof, etc. Are there any abstract objects that have a "structure"? How about music, poems, stories, etc.?)

2.   What do the parts of a structure do? In other words, what are the functions of these parts? (*Hint*: In the case of a house, the base is something on which the house is built, walls keep a room protected from heat, cold, or noises, and a roof keeps the interior of a house dry when it rains. What about the parts in the abstract objects?)

3.   How are the parts of a structure jointly related to the cause of the existence of the object in question? (*Hint*: The parts of a house are related to people's way of living. They contribute to the quality of our life. What about the parts in the abstract objects?)

4.   If you have guessed that a sentence has a structure and, for that matter, so does a language, then it is a good guess. Have you? (*Hint*: The author believes that you have. For the details, see the chapters that follow.)

Chapter II

Sound and Spelling

2.1 English Orthography

Basically, human languages are transmitted by air waves, i.e. they are spoken, and, thus, have sounds as a means of communication. A large number of languages, on the other hand, have some sort of writing systems as a means of communication, which we will call orthography. Human languages have a variety of types of orthography. It may well be the case that there is a scale along which types of orthography are aligned: one extreme point of the scale is the phonetic type of orthography, and the other the logo-ideational type of it. In other words, one extremity is sound-oriented, and the other meaning-oriented. English orthography is of the former type, employing the Roman alphabet, and Chinese is of the latter type, employing Chinese characters. What is it that is in-between? It is Japanese, which employs both the Japanese syllabary, or syllable-based alphabet, and Chinese characters.

English orthography is sound-oriented, but this does not immediately mean that the relationship between the English sounds and the corresponding spellings is anything that is simple and straightforward. It is true that lots of sound-spelling regularities are observed in English orthography, but there are nevertheless not a few irregularities that are to be classified, explicated and analyzed. And we should point out that English orthographical regularities and irregularities are a rich source of introductory topics relating to the history of English, English phonology, loan word morphology, and so on. In what follows, it is shown that there are a whole variety of regularities and irregularities in English orthography that are part of the structure of English.

Before going into the descriptions of regularities and irregularities, we should note that the notions of "regular" and "irregular" are never static or absolute ones: from one point of view, such and such cases are "regular," but from another point of view, they may be "irregular." Thus, it happens that there are cases where regularities and irregularities overlap with each other, and, furthermore, we see in §2.3 that certain irregularities are classified into more than one category, i.e. there is an area that covers two types of irregularity. See Yasui (1962) for the various types of consonant patterning in English.

2.2   Regularities

English employs the Roman alphabet in writing, and the Roman alphabet is a phonetic (or, to be precise, "phonemic") means to fix the sounds in the air onto the paper. Thus, as a first regularity between sound and spelling, we have (1) below:

(1)   When a vowel letter is in the environment [#C___C#], it is a stressed short vowel with the phonetic value of this very letter.

N.B.1 # is a word boundary, which marks the extent of a word on either side.
N.B.2 Our general practice is that C means a consonant sound, or segment, but C in the cases (1) through (3) in this section represents a consonant letter.

Examples of this regularity include *pat, pet, pit, pot,* and *put*. Each vowel letter in these examples has as its phonetic value the one that corresponds to its respective letter, i.e. [æ], [e], [i], [ɔ], and [u], respectively.

As a second case of regularity, we have (2), which is minimally distinct from (1).

(2)   When a vowel letter is in the environment [#C___Ce#], it is a stressed long vowel or a stressed diphthong (roughly, a combina-

tion of two vowels), with the phonetic value of the name of this very letter.

Examples of this regularity include *pane, gene, pine, tone,* and *mute.* Each vowel letter in these examples has as its phonetic value the one that corresponds to the name of its respective letter, i.e. [ei], [i:], [ai], [ou], and [ju:], respectively. This is a regularity between spelling and sound, but it may also be a case of irregularity from a viewpoint of the previous regularity (1), in that the letter *a* is not [æ] but [ei]. This type of phenomena is largely due to the historical change on the part of English phonology, to which we will turn in §2.3.2.1.

As a third type, we have (3) below:

(3)   When a vowel letter *i* is in the environment [#(C)C___gh(C)#], it is invariably a stressed diphthong with the phonetic value of the name of this very letter, i.e. [ai].

Examples of this type include *high, thigh, bright, right, fight, light, knight, night, might, sigh, sight, slight* and *tight.*

The fourth regularity that we will introduce below is a slightly different type than those above. In the regularities (1) through (3), we have noted that a specific letter has the specified phonetic value when it is in the specified environment. This is one type of regularity. But there is another. As a fourth illustration of regularity, we have English phonotactics: particularly in the following cases, it is the regularity regarding the word-initial combinations of consonants. In general terms, phonotactics studies the possible combinations of sounds in a given language. Every language has its own unique regularities about the combinations of phones, or for that matter, "phonemes." English has its own phonotactics. According to English phonotactics, we have the following patterns regarding the word-initial consonant combinations:

(4)   a.   When there are two word-initial consonants, i.e. [#C_1C_2V...], C_1 is either [p], [t], [k], [b], [d], [g], [f], [θ], [s], [ʃ], [h], [v], [m], [n] or [l], and C_2 is either [l], [r], [w] or [j]. But only when C_1 is [s], C_2 can be, besides [l], [r], [w] and [j], one from among [p], [t], [k], [f], [θ], [m] and [n].
      b.   When there are three word-initial consonants, i.e. [#$C_1C_2C_3$V...], C_1 is [s], C_2 is either [p], [t] or [k], and C_3 is

either [l], [r], [w] or [j].

N.B.1 C represents a consonant sound, or segment, and V a vowel sound, or segment.

N.B.2 If we use the feature specifications that are introduced in Chapter III, the second half of the regularity, i.e. (4b), will be neatly phrased as follows:

When there are three word-initial consonants, i.e. [#$C_1C_2C_3$V...], C_1 is [s], C_2 is a voiceless stop, and C_3 is either a liquid or a glide.

The first half of the regularity, i.e. (4a), is shown graphically as below:

(5)   Table of English phonotactics (4a): word-initial combinations of two consonants

#	C_1	C_2	V...
#	[p], [t], [k], [b], [d], [g], [f], [θ], [ʃ], [h], [v], [m], [n] or [l]	[l], [r], [w] or [j]	Vowel...
#	[s]	[p], [t], [k], [f], [θ], [m], [n], [l], [r], [w] or [j]	Vowel...

Examples of (5), i.e. the regularities of (4a), are listed below:

(6)   #[pl]: *play*; #[pr]: *pray*; #[pj]: *pew, pupil*; #[tr]: *tree*; #[tw]: *twin*; #[tj]: *tune*; #[kl]: *clean, Kleenex*; #[kr]: *cry, Kremlin*; #[kw]: *quake, queen, quick, quilt*; #[kj]: *cue, queue, Kewpie*; #[bl]: *blue*; #[br]: *brew*; #[bj]: *beauty*; #[dr]: *dry*; #[dw]: *dwarf, dwell, dwindle, Dwight*; #[dj]: *deuce, dew, due, duet, duke*; #[gl]: *glad; gleam, glean, glimpse, glitter, globe*; #[gr]: *green*; #[gw]: *Gwendolen*; #[gj]: *gewgaw*; #[fl]: *flower*; #[fr]: *free, frown*; #[fj]: *few, feud, fuel, fugitive*; #[θr]: *three, threat, thrill*; #[θw]: *thwaite, thwart*; #[θj]: *thew(s)*; #[sp]: *spin*; #[st]: *stay*; #[sk]: *skate, ski, sky*; #[sf]: *sphere, sphinx*; #[sθ]: *sthenia, Stheno*; #[sm]: *smack, small, smart*; #[sn]: *snack, snake, snap, snow*; #[sl]: *slam, slim, slum*; #[sr]: *Sri Lanka*; #[sw]: *sweat, sweet*; #[sj]: *sewer, sewage, sewen*; #[ʃl]: *schlep, schlock, Schliemann*; #[ʃr]: *shred, shrimp*; #[ʃw]: *schwa, Schwartz, Schweitzer*; #[hw]: *whale, what*; #[hj]: *heuristic, hue, huge*; #[vj]: *view*; #[mj]: *mew, mule, museum, mute*; #[nj]: *new, neutral, nuisance*; #[lj]: *lieu*

Among the possible combinations of two word-initial consonants that would have to be allowed by the stipulation of (4a), i.e. (5), English has no such word-initial consonants as follows:

(7)   *#[pw]V, *#[tl]V, *#[bw]V, *#[dl]V, *#[fw]V, *#[θl]V, *#[ʃj]V,
      *#[hl]V, *#[hr]V, *#[vl]V, *#[vr]V, *#[vw]V, *#[ml]V, *#[mr]V,
      *#[mw]V, *#[nl]V, *#[nr]V, *#[nw]V, *#[ll]V, *#[lr]V, *#[lw]V

N.B. The asterisk "*" marks the expression that follows as ungrammatical.

Of the possible word-initial combinations given above, some have a 'foreign note,' or, they ring 'foreign.' For example, words like *schlep*, *schlock*, and *Schliemann* of the type #[ʃl] and those like *schwa* and *Schweitzer* of the type #[ʃw] are all loanwords from German or a related language. The words of the type #[sf], i.e. *sphere* and *sphinx*, and those of the type #[sθ], i.e. *sthenia* and *Stheno*, all sound Greek. The only example of the type #[sr] is the name of a country in Asia, Sri Lanka. So, the word-initial combinations of the types #[ʃl], #[ʃw], #[sf], #[sθ] and #[sr] have an exotic flavor and have their origins outside the kingdom of English phonology. In addition, we may cite other word-initial combinations that begin with #[ʃ] that are not listed above that ring 'foreign.' They include *Stuttgart* of the type #[ʃt], *schmaltz*, *schmoe* and *Schmidt* of the type #[ʃm], *schnitzel* and *Schneider* of the type #[ʃn], and *Schwarzwald* and *Schweitzer* of the type #[ʃv]. It is true that they are now part of the English vocabulary, but they are definitely of German origin.

Now, let us turn to the cases of three word-initial consonants. The second half of the regularity, i.e. (4b), is shown graphically as below:

(8)   Table of English phonotactics (4b): word-initial combinations of three consonants

#	C₁	C₂	C₃	V...
#	[s]	[p], [t] or [k]	[l], [r], [w] or [j]	Vowel...

Examples of (8), i.e. the regularities of (4b), are listed below:

(9)   #[spl]: *splash*, *splint*, *split*; #[spr]: *sprite*, *spring*, *sprint*; #[spj]: *spew*; #[str]: *street*, *strict*, *structure*, *strong*; #[stj]: *stew*, *steward*;

#[skl]: *sclaff, sclerosis*; #[skr]: *scratch, scrawl, scroll, script, screw*; #[skw]: *square, squad, squid*, #[skj]: *skew, skewer*;

Among the possible combinations of three word-initial consonants that would have to be allowed by the stipulation of (4b), i.e. (8), English has no such word-initial consonants as follows:

(10)   *#[spw]V, *#[stl]V, *#[stw]V

Now, if we go back to the note of N.B. 2 in (4), we now know that in the word-initial combinations of three consonants of the form [#$C_1C_2C_3$V...], C_1 is invariably [s], C_2 is restricted to a voiceless stop, i.e. either [p], [t] or [k], and C_3 is a liquid or a glide, i.e. either [l], [r], [w] or [j]. Regarding this word-initial structure of [#$C_1C_2C_3$V...], we will see a notable fact below such that the sequences "C_1C_2" and "C_2C_3" independently stand as word-initial combinations on their own right. In other words, if there is a two-consonant combination that is not allowed word-initially, it cannot appear as "C_1C_2" nor as "C_2C_3" in the structure of [#$C_1C_2C_3$V...]. To use the terminology to be introduced in Chapter III, the sequence that can occur as "C_1C_2" is "[s] + [voiceless stop]," and the one that can occur as "C_2C_3" is "[voiceless stop] + [liquid / glide]." Both "[s] + [voiceless stop]" and "[voiceless stop] + [liquid / glide]" are possible word-initial consonantal combinations. Let us illustrate this.

First, we examine the cases where "C_1C_2" taken from the structure [#$C_1C_2C_3$V...] is involved. Since in the word-initial structure of [#$C_1C_2C_3$V...], C_1 is invariably [s] and C_2 is one from among [p], [t] and [k], we find three instances of word-initial #C_1C_2 combinations:

(11)   #C_1C_2V...: #[sp]V..., #[st]V..., #[sk]V...

Examples of (11) include *span, stop* and *skip*. Now it is clear that the two-consonant sequences in (11) are in fact all possible sequences of "C_1C_2" even in the structure of [#$C_1C_2C_3$V...]. And needless to say, those sequences that are impossible as *[#C_1C_2V...], e.g. those in (12) below, do not appear as "C_1C_2" in the structure of [#$C_1C_2C_3$V...].

(12)   *# C_1C_2V...: *#[sb]V..., *#[sd]V..., *#[sg]V..., etc.

Next, we examine the cases where "C_2C_3" taken from the structure [#$C_1C_2C_3$V...] is involved. Since in the word-initial structure of

[#$C_1C_2C_3$V...], C_2 is [p], [t] or [k], and C_3 is [l], [r], [w] or [j], we find two groups of "C_2C_3" combinations: one group is such that #C_2C_3 is word-initially possible, and the other is such that *#C_2C_3 is word-initially impossible. The former group is:

(13)   #C_2C_3V...: #[pl]V..., #[pr]V..., #[pj]V..., #[tr]V..., #[tw]V..., #[tj]V..., #[kl]V..., #[kr]V..., #[kw]V..., #[kj]V...

Examples of (13) include *plan, prince, pure, trip, twenty, tulip, click, creature, quality* and *cute*. And the latter impossible group is:

(14)   *#C_2C_3V...: *#[pw]V..., *#[tl]V...

Now it is clear that the two-consonant sequences in (13), except for [tw], are all possible sequences of "C_2C_3" in the structure of [#$C_1C_2C_3$V...], but that those in (14) are all impossible sequences of "C_2C_3" in the structure of [#$C_1C_2C_3$V...].

Thus, we have shown that in the word-initial structure of [#$C_1C_2C_3$V...], the sequences "C_1C_2" and "C_2C_3" independently stand as word-initial combinations on their own right. In other words, we have shown that if there is a two-consonant combination that is not allowed word-initially, it cannot appear as "C_1C_2" or as "C_2C_3" in the structure of [#$C_1C_2C_3$V...].

N.B. From the discussion above, it seems reasonable to assume that the word-initial sequence of the three consonants "*#[stw]V..." is in fact theoretically possible, but it is, by chance, nonexistent in contemporary English. This type of nonexistence, we call "accidental gap." And the type of nonexistence that is not allowed on structural or theoretical grounds, e.g. "*#[spw]V...," and "*#[stl]V...," is what we call "structural gap."

2.3   Irregularities

2.3.1   Irregularities of Idiosyncrasy

As the first and foremost case of irregularity in English orthography, we may point to the somewhat odd example (1), which is ascribed to Bernard Shaw's satirical coinage.

(1)   *ghoti (= 'fish') cf. rou<u>gh</u>, w<u>o</u>men, sta<u>ti</u>on

George Bernard Shaw is said to have blamed the English orthography for its inconsistency: the spelling "gh" could be for [f] as in *rough*, the spelling "o" for [i] as in *women*, and the spelling "ti" for [ʃ] as in *station*. Therefore, according to him, 'fish' could well be spelled *"ghoti." He has shown that the English orthography is that far inconsistent. He is quite right, in a sense, for we can add to the list a number of words that have irregularities between sound and spelling: the former, i.e. sound, ought to be represented by means of the latter, i.e. spelling. Examples of this type of irregularity are in (2):

> (2) a. <u>bo</u>mb, <u>co</u>mb, <u>to</u>mb
>   b. c<u>augh</u>t, d<u>augh</u>ter, sl<u>augh</u>ter, t<u>augh</u>t: l<u>augh</u>, l<u>augh</u>ter
>   c. th<u>ough</u>, thr<u>ough</u>, t<u>ough</u>, c<u>ough</u>
>   d. n<u>ine</u>, n<u>ine</u>teen, n<u>ine</u>ty: n<u>in</u>th

In (2a), the underlined parts have one and the same form of spelling but they have a different phonetic value from each other. Thus, *bomb*, *comb* and *tomb* are pronounced as [bɔm], [koum] and [tu:m], respectively.

> **N.B.1** Etymological studies tell us that the words in (2a) have come to be spelled as they are now due to the different origins and histories of their own. Roughly speaking, *bomb* is originally an instance of onomatopoeia and can be traced back to French, to Italian, and ultimately to Greek. *Comb* comes from OE in the form of *comb* or *camb*. *Tomb* comes from ME *toume* or *tumbe*, which is borrowed from AF *tumbe* or (O)F *tombe*. The latter are derived from LL *tumbam*, which, in turn, is borrowed from Gk *tumbos*.
>
> **N.B.2** Abbreviations: OE stands for Old English, ME for Middle English, AF for Anglo-French, OF for Old French and F for French.

In (2b), the underlined part 'augh' reads not only as [ɔ:] but also as [æf]. In this case, too, the relationship between sound and spelling is not straightforward.

In (2c), the underlined part 'ough' reads either [ou], [u:], [ʌf], or [ɔ:f]. In this case, again, the relationship between sound and spelling is erratic.

In (2d), though all words are derived from the number "nine," they nevertheless have inconsistency as to whether to keep the letter *e* or to leave it out.

Another type of irregularity comes from (3):

> (3) When a vowel letter is in the environment [#C___Ce#], where C

represents a consonant letter, this vowel letter is pronounced as a stressed short vowel.

Examples of this irregularity include *have, live, love, come, give, done, dove, some* and *none*. The phenomenon of (3) is irregular in that it is in sharp contrast to the regularities of (1) and (2) of the last section, i.e. §2.2. It is true that words of the type of (3) are of high irregularity, but they have a noteworthy property in common, i.e., that they are words of high frequency. This means that these words are part of everyday usage in the overall English vocabulary. The notion "everyday usage" is related to our observation such that certain words are functionally central in the paradigm of verbal inflections, some words are essential in human's life and thought, and certain other words are quite common in everyday communications. And it is a general property of language that highly frequent words tend to retain irregular forms, e.g. irregular inflections, while infrequent ones tend to become regularized. Readers are invited to recall the irregular and the regular forms of past tense verbs, past participial verbs, and plural nouns. The general tendency is that irregular forms are rather common and frequent, and that regular ones are less common and less frequent. Needless to say, there are counter cases to this tendency, as is the case with any type of generalizations.

In §2.2, we have regarded the English phonotactics as a window through which we can view the regular types of word-initial consonant combinations. By the same token, or to turn the table around, the types of word-initial combinations we failed to observe are those that we regard as irregular, if not impossible, types of word-initial consonant combinations. Thus we have the type of irregularity between sound and spelling as in (4):

(4) If an English word begins with the two consonant letters that are not allowed by the first half of the regularity (4a) in §2.2, then the first consonant letter should be phonetically "ignored," i.e., the word should begin with the phone that corresponds to the second consonant letter.

Examples of the type (4) include the words in (5):

(5) #*gn*- should be read as #[n]-: *gnarl, gnat, gnaw, gnosis*
     #*kn*- should be read as #[n]-: *knave, knead, knee, knife, knight, knob, knock, knot, know*

#*mn*- should be read as #[n]-: *mnemonic*

#*pn*- should be read as #[n]-: *pneumatic, pneumatometer, pneu-monia*

#*ps*- should be read as #[s]-: *Psyche, psychology*

#*pt*- should be read as #[t]-: *Ptolemy, ptomaine*

#*x*- should be read as #[z]-: *xenophile, xenophobe, xenophobia, Xenophon, Xerox, xylophone*

N.B. Regarding the last examples of the type #*x*-, the prefixes *xeno-, xero-* and *xylo-* are all morphemes of Greek origin. If the English letter *X(x)* is to be pronounced as [gz] in these Greek-related words, the first sound should be ignored and the entire cluster should become [z]. This is what things are in these examples. Alternatively, if the English letter *X(x)* is to be pronounced as [ks] in these Greek-related words, the first sound should be ignored and the entire cluster should have become [s]. But this [s] in fact becomes voiced and ends up as [z]. This voicing may presumably be the result of the mechanism called Blocking: the letters *s* and *c* block the process of the letter *x*'s having the phonetic value [s], because the phonetic value [s] is almost invariably reserved for the letters *s* and *c* and no other letter should assume this phonetic value. Thus, the letter *x* fails to assume the phonetic value [s] but, instead, assumes the voiced counterpart of [s], i.e. [z].

So far, we have observed cases of irregularity that are more or less idiosyncratic in nature. But in the section that follows, we focus on the cases of irregularity that are somewhat systematic.

2.3.2   Four Types of Discrepancy between Sound and Spelling

Irregularities are irregularities because we cannot make systematic predictions about certain sound-spelling correspondences. There are, however, some distinct types of irregularities in English orthography, and within each of these types fall certain systematic behaviors. Irregularity in English orthography means discrepancy between sound and spelling. In what follows, we introduce four types of discrepancy between sound and spelling, and describe and analyze them in detail with illustrations.

But a few words are in order here regarding the way the four types are categorized. The four types that we will see below are by no means strict or rigid ones. Some types may have a vague demarcation and items on the periphery may be accounted for by principles of other types. So, we ask readers to think of the four types simply as four general tendencies in the area of sound-spelling discrepancy.

2.3.2.1   Historical Change

The English language has a long history of over 1,300 years to date. In the course of the development of the language, there is one significant change in the phonological system that is remarkably unique to English: it has undergone the Great Vowel Shift (sometimes abbreviated as GVS). The Great Vowel Shift is a phonological change in the history of English and it is one of the prominent features that mark the transition from Middle English (ME) to Modern English (ModE). The phonological change was slow but drastic and it lasted about 200 years roughly from the 15th century to the 17th century. Notice that the change was slow from one perspective because it took about 200 years, but from another perspective, it was quick and abrupt because the process has completed just in 200 years in the long span of 1,300 years of the history of English.

Before we go into the detail, let us have a quick historical overview of the language. Observe the chart below:

European History and the History of English

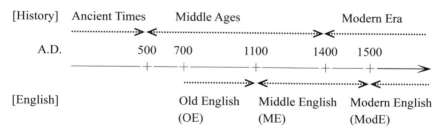

It is very important to note the terminological difference that we have between the history of Europe and English historical linguistics. In European history, there are three major eras: Ancient Times, the first era being up to around A.D. 500, Middle Ages, the second being from around A.D. 500 to around 1400, and Modern Era, the last being from around 1400 up to the present. In English historical linguistics, however, we should be cautious about the terms "Middle" and "Modern," the usage of which is distinct from the practice of that in the European history. In linguistics, there are also three major divisions in the history of English:

Old English (OE), the first and oldest documented type of English being from around A.D. 700 to around 1100, Middle English (ME), the second being from around 1100 to around 1500, and Modern English (ModE), the last and latest being from around 1500 up to the present. And The Great Vowel Shift is one of the key features that distinguish ME from ModE.

> **N.B.** The English that characterizes the 20th and 21st centuries are often called Present-Day English, abbreviated as PE.

Now let us see how the Great Vowel Shift has caused what change on the part of the English phonology. In general terms, GVS has had the following effects on the phonology and the sound-spelling correspondences in English. First, a stressed long vowel was "raised" one-degree higher. In other words, the articulatory position of the tongue for a stressed long vowel became one-degree higher, and the "incumbent" stressed long vowel of this higher tongue position came to be articulated one-further higher, and so on. Finally, the stressed long vowel of the highest tongue position got diphthongized. Second, the letters for the vowels that used to retain the phonetic value of their own right, e.g. the letter *e* for [e:], and *i* for [i:], are now the letters that carry with them, as a result of GVS, the phonetic value of their names, e.g. the letter *e* for [i:], and *i* for [ai]. Note that this is an extremely simplified description of the entire process of GVS, and there is indeed much room of indeterminacy as to the exact nature of the whole processes and motivations for GVS.

But, now, for the purpose of this section, we need some illustrations. Below are some typical examples of GVS:

(1)   The Great Vowel Shift (GVS)
       [i:]→[ai]: child, light, mine, wife
       [e:]→[i:]: feet, meet, see, belief
       [ɛ:]→[e:]→[i:]: dream, meat, sea
       [ɛ:]→[e:]→[ei]: break, great, steak, yea (cf. Shea (Stadium),
                        (Ronald) Reagan)
       [a:]→ [ɛ:]→[e:]→[ei]: haste, mate, name, take
       [u:]→[ou]→[au]: cow, mouse, house, tower
       [o:]→[u:]: food, moon, tooth
       [ɔ:]→[ou]: boat, home, stone
       [ai]→[ɛi]→[ɛ:]→[e:]→[ei]: maid

[au]➔[ɔ:]: laud

Now, it is clear that we have had a gross vowel change in the history of English phonology. Notice that although the vowel system has changed, the spelling has remained almost essentially the same. This is due to such an extralinguistic fact that William Caxton, the first English printer, began publishing many printed books in the 15th century and the words printed in the books are spelled as they were spelled when GVS did not take place. Thus, in this post-GVS period today, we have cases of discrepancy between sound and spelling as illustrated above. This is clearly the result of the historical change in the phonology of English, which we now call the Great Vowel Shift.

There is another type of historical change in English phonology that deserves mention in relation to sound-spelling correspondences. It is Verner's Law in English. Verner's Law itself explains the systematic voicing of certain Proto-Germanic consonants that had been voiceless in Proto-Indo-European.

> **N.B.** Proto-Indo-European is what the historical linguists assume to be the source of the language families that roughly cover the huge geographical areas of the western half of the Eurasia continent, i.e. from Europe to India, and Proto-Germanic is one among all these families. Proto-Germanic is what the historical linguists assume to be the oldest form of language from which many Germanic languages, English being one of them, are derived.

Verner's Law in English is a rule to explain the similar phonological change that took place in English during the period of 15th century through 17th century. Verner's Law in English is roughly stated as follows:

(2)   [C, −voice] ➔ [+voice] / [−stress] _____

The phonological description (2) means that a voiceless consonant becomes voiced if it follows an unstressed vowel. Examples of this phonological change include words like (3) through (5):

(3)   [ʧ] ➔ [ʤ]: Greenwich, Norwich, spinach; knowleche (ME) ➔ knowledge (PE), partriche (ME) ➔ partridge (PE), cabach (ME) ➔ cabbage (PE)

(4) [s] → [z]: di*ss*[z]olve (cf. di*ss*[s]olution, di*ss*[s]olute), a*s*, i*s*, wa*s*, ha*s*, hi*s*

(5) [ks] → [gz]: e*x*ert (cf. e*x*ercise), an*x*iety (cf. an*x*ious), e*x*ecutive (cf. e*x*ecute), e*xh*ibit (cf. e*xh*ibition), lu*x*urious (cf. lu*x*ury)

Thus, in (3) we have [dʒ] for the letters 'ch,' in (4) we have [z] for the letters 's' and 'ss,' and in (5) we have [gz] for the letter 'x.' Here we observe another case of sound-spelling discrepancy in that the letters employed as representing voiceless consonants, i.e. 'ch,' 's,' 'ss,' and 'x,' have, in fact, all assumed the voiced sounds in the specified phonological environment. And there is a notable piece of orthographical change in the course of development: the words in ME period 'knowle*che*,' 'partri*che*,' and 'caba*ch*' are now spelled as 'knowle*dge*,' 'partri*dge*,' and 'cabba*ge*,' respectively, perhaps due to an unconscious effort to drive away the sound-spelling anomaly. So, in PE, we no longer have this type of irregularity in the cases of *knowledge*, *partridge*, and *cabbage*.

As a final remark to this subsection, let us comment on some words that appear to be exceptions to the regularity of the Great Vowel Shift. In the history of English, GVS marks the transition from ME to ModE. This means that chances are that the loan words that entered the English vocabulary in the 17th century or afterwards are basically immune from the phonological influence caused by GVS. And this is the case. Observe the words below that are loan words in the ModE period.

(6) [iː]: antique, chemise, critique, elite, liter, machine, naïve, police, prestige, routine, suite, unique

(7) [uː]: group, routine, soup

(8) [ɑː]: camouflage, garage, mirage, plaque ([plæk] is also possible)

Each of these words has a stressed long vowel and thus appears to be a good target of GVS. But the fact is that the stressed long vowels in these words, i.e. [iː], [uː], and [ɑː], did not undergo the phonological change prescribed by GVS. This is because the magic of GVS had already been away when these words set foot in the English language vocabulary. Thus, for example, *liter* is not *[laitə] but [liːtə].

N.B. The word *courier* has the spelling 'ou' just as the ones in (7) do. It was brought into English from French in the 14th century but the vowel corresponding to 'ou' was not a stressed long vowel. So, it was immune from the GVS. There is another loan word from French with the sequence 'ou.' It is *rouge*. Though the adjective *rouge* is said to have entered the English language in the 15th century, the word characteristically had a strong French flavor and, therefore, it is highly likely that the 'French' word was immune from GVS: the latter is peculiarly of English nature. On the other hand, the noun *rouge*, as a name of a cosmetic, actually joined the English vocabulary in the 18th century. As a result, it still has a French accent [ru:ʒ], but not the Anglicized one *[rauʒ].

2.3.2.2   Borrowing

English has borrowed many words from many languages around the world. As a result, English has specific types of sound-spelling irregularity that are ultimately due to borrowing. One type is such that English has borrowed specific forms of spelling from the original 'ancestor' language. The other type is such that the borrowed English words, i.e. loan words, are pronounced the English phonological way: they are pronounced in conformity with the English phonological patterns but their English pronunciations are against the sound-spelling regularities observed in the original languages.

As a first type of example, observe the word *indict*. The 'ancestors' of the word *indict* are roughly shown in (1):

(1)   PE indict < ME endite(n) < AF enditer < L indictāre

N.B. PE stands for Present-Day English (the type of English of the 20th and the 21st centuries), ME for Middle English, AF for Anglo-French, and L for Latin.

PE *indict* has developed from ME *endite(n)*, but the letter *c* was borrowed from L *indictāre*. Thus the word *indict* with the pronunciation [indait] shows the type of sound-spelling discrepancy that no phonological rules can predict. Likewise, we have words like *debt* [det], *doubt* [daut], and *subtle* [sʌtl], and their respective ancestors are shown in (2), (3), and (4):

(2)   PE debt < ME dette < (O)F dette < L dēbitum
(3)   PE doubt (v.) < ME doute(n) < (O)F douter < L dubitāre
(4)   PE subtle < ME sutil < OF sutil, soutil < L subtīlis

The letter *b* in the PE word *debt* is the result of Borrowing from L *dēbitum*, though the PE word *debt* itself, or its pronunciation, has directly developed from ME *dette*. The same explanation applies to the cases of (3) and (4). In these cases, the letter *b* borrowed from Latin is the source of sound-spelling discrepancy.

N.B. There are some PE words which have the word final letter *b* that remains silent. They are *limb*, *numb*, and *thumb*. Note that the letter *b* in these words is not due to borrowing from a certain ancestor or foreign language, but rather it is the result of some kind of analogy.

Other instances include (5) and (6):

(5)   PE receipt < ME receit(e) < AF receite < ML recepta

N.B. ML stands for Medieval Latin.

(6)   PE salmon < ME sa(l)moun < AF sa(u)moun = (O)F saumon < L salmōnem

Next, let us observe another type of irregularity. This type of irregularity is meant to be such that once a word has been borrowed from a foreign language, the pronunciation of the word gets inevitably Anglicized, or conformed to the English phonological patterns. Some examples are shown below:

(7)   From German to English
Stuttgart: [ʃtutgɑ:t] → [stʌtgɑɚt]
Hamburg: [hamburk] → [hæmbɚ:g]
Goethe: [gø:tə] → [gə:tə] [geitə]
Volkswagen: [folksva:gn] → [fɔ:lksva:gən] [voukswægən]

In the cases of (7), we see that German accents are transformed into the English phonological templates. German initial consonants [ʃt] are sometimes converted to [st] in English. With the words *Hamburg* and *Goethe*, vowels are totally different between German and English. The word *Volkswagen* carries distinctly different pronunciations between German and English. In addition to the English loan words from German, there are other loan words from other languages and they include the following:

(8)   From French to English
Paris: [pari] → [pæris]
(Tour) Eiffel: [(tur) ɛfɛl] → Eiffel (Tower) [aifl (tauɚ)]

     Seine: [sɛn] → [sein]
     champagne: [ʃɑ̃paɲ] → [ʃæmpein]
(9)   From Italian to English
     pizza: [piʔtsa] → [pi:tsə]
     pianissimo: [pjaniʔsimo] → [pi:ənisəmou]
     spaghetti: [spageʔti] → [spəgeti]
     Michelangelo: [mikelandʒelo] → [maikəlændʒəlou]

In the case of (8), we observe that French pronunciations have been conformed to the English phonological patterns. In the case of (9), we also see that Italian accents are transformed into the English phonological templates. Italian geminate consonants are pronounced as glottal stop [ʔ] followed by the very consonant itself. Observe the words *pizza*, *pianissimo*, and *spaghetti*. But English does not have such a way of pronouncing geminate consonants: geminates are pronounced as if they were a single consonant. *Michelangelo* is pronounced the English way as if it is made of two names "Michael" and "Angelo."

> **N.B.** The glottal stop is the 'sound' produced by the closure of the vocal cords, the phonetic representation of which is [ʔ]. In plain English, [ʔ] is a piece of silence.

Finally, let us see the words from outside Indo-European languages, e.g. those from Japanese:

(10)   From Japanese to English
     Aoki (proper name):   [aoki] → [eiəki]
     Ryukyu ("Okinawa"): [rju:kju:] → [riu:kju:] [riju:kju:]
     Hakone (place name): [hakone] → [həkouni]
     tsunami: [tsunami] → [tsu:nɑ:mi] [su:nɑ:mi]

In English, the first letter of *Aoki* is stressed and diphthongized and this is not what happens in Japanese. With *Ryukyu*, the first two consonants in Japanese are [rj] followed by a vowel, but this type of word-initial consonant cluster is not allowed in English, hence Anglicized as [ri]. In the case of Anglicized pronunciation of *Hakone*, we observe destressing in the first and the last syllable, hence [ə] and [i], respectively. And the syllable for the letter *o* gets stressed and diphthongized, hence [ou]. The word-initial consonant cluster [ts] in *tsunami* is common in Japanese, but this cluster virtually never happens word-initially in English. So, in an Anglicized form, the word-initial consonant cluster becomes, more often than not, a single consonant with [t] omitted, hence [su:nɑ:mi]. All of these show that the original Japanese pronunciations have been altered the Anglicized way.

Now, we have seen that Borrowing is the source of sound-spelling irregularity: in one case of Borrowing, etymological *c*, *b* and other consonant letters disturb the sound-spelling regularity; in the other case, i.e. the case of loan words, the original phonological regularities are cumbersome to the English language, hence the words are adapted the English phonological way.

2.3.2.3   Spelling Pronunciation

Broadly speaking, 'Spelling pronunciation' means a type of pronunciation whereby words are pronounced exactly as they are spelled. In light of the general theme of the section "Four Types of Discrepancy between Sound and Spelling," we believe we need this subsection "Spelling Pronunciation." This is the right place to take up such cases as those where the "irregularities" observed originally in certain words have become "regularized" in the sense that they are now pronounced in the way we call 'Spelling pronunciation.'

Now, let us see some examples. In a number of cases, British English has many words with "irregular" pronunciations that deserve cultural, linguistic or phonological inquiries from a historical perspective. Once these words are carried across the Atlantic, they may be pronounced the American way, i.e. exactly as they are spelled. Observe below:

	British	American
Birmingham	[bə́:miŋəm]	[bə́:miŋhæm] ;
Greenwich	[grínidʒ] [grénidʒ]	[grí:nitʃ] [grénitʃ]
Thames	[temz] (in London, UK)	[θeimz] (in Connecticut, US)
forehead	[fɔ́rid]	[fɔ́ɚhèd]
spinach	[spínidʒ]	[spínitʃ]
lieutenant	[lefténənt]	[lu:ténənt]
nephew	[névju:]	[néfju:]

In the case of *Birmingham*, British pronunciation retains no 'h' in the last syllable, but American pronunciation does retain it. With *Greenwich*, we see Verner's Law in English operative in British pronunciation: [ʧ] for the letters *ch* becomes [ʤ] after an unstressed vowel, hence [grínidʒ] or [grénidʒ] in British English. But, the combination of the letters *ch* essentially represents [ʧ] in the spirit of 'Spelling pronunciation,' thus the word is [grí:niʧ] or [gréniʧ] in American English. The same story goes with the word *spinach*. American pronunciations of the words like *Thames*, *forehead* and *nephew* have almost literal correspondence with their spellings, respectively. In the case of the word *lieutenant*, it is obvious that the American counterpart comes much closer to 'Spelling pronunciation' than the British one does.

Next, observe the word below:

boatswain: [bousn] [boutswein]

Both British English and American English have essentially the same two pronunciations for the word *boatswain*, i.e. either [bousn] or [boutswein]. It is clear that the latter pronunciation keeps track of the form of spelling but the former does not. In this sense, the latter pronunciation is of the type 'Spelling pronunciation.'

Finally, we will see some sophisticated cases of 'Spelling pronunciation.' Let us confine our discussion to the American English pronunciations. It is a common practice in American English that when the letter 'o' carries a short stressed vowel with it, it is pronounced as [ɑ]. Examples abound. They include *pot, top, cot, bob, dog, God, chop, jot, mop, not, lot, rock, hot,* and many others. We may call this '[ɑ]' a 'Spelling pronunciation' of the letter *o* when it bears a short stressed vowel. But there is always a bunch of exceptions: words like *front* and *money* have a letter *o* that carries a short stressed vowel but this very letter is never pronounced as [ɑ] but as [ʌ], instead. Exceptional words like *front* and *money* are thus the offenders of the 'Spelling pronunciation' principle. However, the interesting point is that when these words undergo some derivative processes, i.e., when we derive words from these words, surprising facts emerge as shown below:

(1) a. front: [frʌnt]
     b. frontier: [frʌntiɚ] [frɑntiɚ]
(2) a. money: [mʌni]
     b. monetary: [mɑnətɛri] [mʌnətɛri]

   c. monetarily: [mɑnətɛrəli] [mʌnətɛrəli]
   d. monetize: [mɑnətaiz] [mʌnətaiz]

In (1a), the word *front* only allows the vowel [ʌ] and never allows others like [ɑ], but as shown in (1b), the word *frontier* permits either [frʌntiɚ] or [frɑntiɚ]. We may rightly interpret this phenomenon as an indication of the emergence of 'Spelling pronunciation' principle. Let us see how this emergence takes place. In a sense, 'Spelling pronunciation' can be a normal state of the affairs. When derivations go away from the marked, i.e. special, cases, it means that derivations may arrive in the unmarked, i.e. general and common, areas. It is in these unmarked areas that a normal state of affairs will prevail. The normal state of affairs in this case means 'Spelling pronunciation.' For example, the word *frontier* is a derivative from the marked case of *front*, and it is to the very word *frontier* that 'Spelling pronunciation' principle may apply. Thus, *frontier* may be either [frʌntiɚ] or [frɑntiɚ]. Therefore, we may plausibly regard the vowel [ɑ] in *frontier* as an instantiation of 'Spelling pronunciation' principle. The same line of explanation applies to the sharp contrast that we have between (2a) and (2b–d): the former is the marked case, and the latter the unmarked case where 'Spelling pronunciation' principle prevails.

N.B. There are cases where even when we derive a word from a marked case, the derived word still retains a marked characteristic and does not conform to a general principle. For example, we have words like below:

  (i) London [lʌndən] / *[lɑndən] → Londoner [lʌndənɚ] / *[lɑndənɚ]
      comfort [kʌmfɚt] / *[kɑmfɚt] → comfortable [kʌmfɚtəbl] / *[kɑmfɚtəbl]

A stressed short vowel for the letter 'o' in these words is invariably [ʌ] but not *[ɑ].

2.3.2.4 'Economy'

By the term 'Economy,' we mean the motivation we have when we try to pronounce words with less effort without any failure of mutual understandings. Put simply, 'economized' pronunciations are much easier for us to produce than the original ones. There are a variety of cases of phonological simplification induced by 'Economy,' which process in turn results in sound-spelling discrepancy. Now let us see these cases one by one.

First, observe the words below:

(1)   clothes, cupboard, shepherd, chestnut, handkerchief

The word *clothes* should be pronounced as [klouðz], but it also has a variant form [klouz]. The latter pronunciation is made possible by omitting the consonant [ð], thereby requiring less effort on the part of the speaker. In other words, the sequence of consonants [ðz] is rather a tongue-twisting combination of voiced fricative sounds, so that we find an easier way to go, simply by suppressing one of them, i.e. [ð]. Thus, while *clothes* of [klouðz] retains the sound-spelling correspondence, *clothes* of [klouz] does not. Hence, the latter shows sound-spelling discrepancy. With the word *cupboard*, the pronunciation should be [kʌpbɔəd], but in reality it is [kʌbəd]. Here, the sequence [pb] is reduced to a simple [b], and the second syllable is destressed to become [bəd]. Note that both [p] and [b] are characterized as [bilabial, stop] and the first occurrence of [bilabial, stop], i.e. [p], gets unreleased. (For the phonological terms employed in this section, readers are referred to the chapter on Phonetics and Phonology.) In other words, the phonological reduction of [p] is induced by the 'less-effort' principle, and this principle we label as 'Economy.' Thus, *cupboard* illustrates another case of sound-spelling discrepancy in that the letter 'p' finds no counterpart in the pronunciation. Likewise, the word *shepherd* should be [ʃéphəd], but in reality it is [ʃépəd] because it is a common reduction in English to suppress [h] when it is followed by an unstressed vowel. Here, again, we have another case of sound-spelling discrepancy, since the letter 'h' has no counterpart in the pronunciation. In the case of *chestnut*, too, its pronunciation should be [tʃestnʌt] or [tʃestnət], but in reality forms like [tʃesnʌt] and [tʃesnət] are possible, with [t] left out. Hence, sound-spelling discrepancy, again. In the case of *handkerchief*, since this word is a compound noun, the pronunciation should be composed of [hænd] and [kəːtʃif]. But, in reality, the pronunciation is [hæŋkətʃif]. So, the question is twofold: "Where has the sound corresponding to the letter 'd' gone?" and "Where does the consonant [ŋ] come from?" The answer is a bit long story. First, the sequence [dk] in the 'original' pronunciation [hændkətʃif] consists of two consonants that have the feature [stop] in common. (Note that the vowel in the second syllable in this 'original' pronunciation is destressed and has ended up as [ə] rather than [ɚː]. This is due to the independent reasons, the exact characterization of which does not concern us here.) When a stop consonant is followed by another stop consonant, the first stop gets unreleased. Thus, [d] is suppressed and the 'original' pronunciation becomes [hænkɚ-ʧif]. Or, it may be the case that in the sequence of [ndk], [d] in the middle should be decomposed and taken into the consonants on both sides. In other words, since those features that define [d] are [voiced, alveolar] and [stop] (if you employ the features introduced in the next chapter), and they are the very features that are part of the defining features of [n] and [k], respectively, it is reasonable to assume here that the phonetic value of [d] is absorbed into the consecutive [n] and [k]. Or, for that matter, we may say that [d] should be entirely absorbed into [n], because [n] already has such features as [voiced, alveolar, stop], which also define [d]. In any event, [d] drops. Now, we have a new sequence of consonants [nk]. It is at this stage that the process called 'assimilation' takes place. Assimilation is a process where a segment, i.e. a single sound, gets influenced by the surrounding phono-logical environment. In the case of [nk], the left-hand nasal [n], which is a [nasal, alveolar] consonant, gets influenced by the following [k], which is a [stop, velar] consonant. The result is such that the place of articulation of [n] has been changed from [alveolar] to [velar] but the manner of articula-tion is intact, i.e., it remains as [nasal]. Thus, [n] has now been transformed, or assimilated, to a [nasal, velar] consonant and this is in fact the very consonant [ŋ]. This is the story of why [ŋ] emerged and how it did. So, the word *handkerchief* shows another type of sound-spelling discrepancy in that the letter *d* has no counterpart in the pronunciation and that [ŋ] has no counterpart in the spelling. Note that we observe the same process of alteration from [nk] to [ŋk] in many other words: words like *bank, tank, ink, link, pink, punk* and *funk* should all have [nk] at the end, but, instead, they do have [ŋk], there. The production of [ŋk] requires less effort than that of [nk]. Hence, this type of assimilation is regarded as a case of 'Economy.'

Examples of 'Economy' above are cases where the 'original' forms are getting shorter in the sense that certain segments are suppressed for some reason or other. But there are cases where processes of 'Economy' make the original forms somewhat longer. As a first type, we have words like below:

(2)   length, strength, warmth

Here, *length* and *strength* should be [leŋθ] and [streŋθ], respectively. But, in reality, their respective pronunciations, more often than not, are [leŋkθ] and [streŋkθ]. In both pronunciations, they have become longer because of the [k] that is inserted. Why is it the case that a longer pronunciation is the pronunciation of 'Economy'? The answer lies in a very simple fact: the longer pronunciation is easier to produce than the shorter one. Notice that the consonant [ŋ] is [velar, nasal] and the consonant [θ] is a type of fricative, where air from the lung goes through the oral cavity. At the very moment of transition from the segment [ŋ] to that of [θ], the closure at the velar position suddenly gets released with airflow, which articulation is nothing but the production of [k]. Thus, we have [k] in *length* and *strength*, and even though the pronunciation with [k] is longer than the one without, that pronunciation with [k] is of 'Economy' in the sense that it is a natural process of articulation and it requires less effort. In the case of *warmth*, the same line of argument applies. What is at stake is the string of two consonants at the end, i.e. [mθ]. Notice that the consonant [m] is [bilabial, nasal] and the consonant [θ] is a type of fricative, where air from the lung goes through the oral cavity. At the very moment of transition from the segment [m] to that of [θ], the closure at the bilabial position suddenly gets released with airflow, which articulation is nothing but the production of [p]. Thus, we hear [p] in *warmth* [wɔːmpθ], and even though the pronunciation with [p] is longer than the one without, that pronunciation with [p] is of 'Economy' principle in the sense that it is a natural process of articulation and it requires less effort. In addition to the words in (2), there is another word of interest, a word of both historical and orthographical interest: it is *glimpse*. The PE word *glimpse* comes from ME *glymse(n)*. The ME word *glymse(n)* acquired 'economical' [p] just between the consonants [m] and [s]. The word later has survived an orthographical innovation and now is spelled *glimpse*, which form is the evidence that the 'Spelling pronunciation' principle has been at work ever since the genesis of orthography.

> **N.B.** There is a phenomenon called Epenthesis, by which we mean such a case where a segment intervenes into an already existing sequence of segments. Note that 'Economy' principle does not always work out the same way. In the context of the consonants "[m] + [voiceless, fricative]," the 'Economy' principle sometimes induces Epenthesis, as we have observed above, in cases like *warmth*, but it does not in other cases. For

example, the word *comfort* has the string [mf] in its pronunciation, but it does not become *[kʌmpfɚt]. Rather, the pronunciation of the string is such that [m] is assimilated to the following [f], which is [labio-dental, fricative], and [m] itself becomes [labio-dental, nasal], with the resulting string "[labio-dental, nasal] + [f]." Here, we observe another case of assimilation: the place of articulation of [m] is assimilated to that of the following [f]. This assimilation is another manifestation of the principle 'Economy.'

As a second type of the cases where processes of 'Economy' make the original forms somewhat longer, we consider the words in (3):

(3)   sense, answer, mansion, tenth, else, Welsh, health

Let us take the word *sense* for example. The pronunciation of *sense* should be [sens], but we sometimes have an 'Excrescent' [t] between the consonants [n] and [s]: the pronunciation of *sense* becomes [sents], which happens to be identical to *cents* [sents]. Thus, the pronunciation of *sense* [sents] is longer than the 'original' [sens] because of the excrescent [t] that is inserted in between. Though the pronunciation becomes longer, it is still due to the 'Economy' principle. Let us see why and how it is economical to insert an 'Excrescent' [t]. The 'original' pronunciation of *sense* should be [sens], the last two consonants of which are the target of the analysis. Notice that the consonant [n] is [alveolar, nasal] and the consonant [s] is a type of fricative, where air from the lung goes through the oral cavity. At the very moment of transition from the segment [n] to that of [s], the closure at the alveolar position suddenly gets released with airflow, which articulation is nothing but the production of [t]. Thus, we have [t] in *sense* [sents], and even though the pronunciation with [t] is longer than the one without, that pronunciation with [t] is of 'Economy' in the sense that it is a natural process of articulation and it requires less effort. With the rest of the words in (3), the same line of argument will apply. The words *answer* [ænsɚ], *mansion* [mænʃən], *tenth* [tenθ], *else* [els], *Welsh* [welʃ] and *health* [helθ] may all have longer pronunciations with an 'Excrescent' /t/ inserted in between, i.e. [æntsɚ], [mænʧən], [tentθ], [elts], [welʧ] and [heltθ], respectively. Thus, we have another case of sound-spelling discrepancy in the sense that an 'Excrescent' [t] has no counterpart in the spelling, and this insertion of a segment, which we call Epenthesis, is due to the principle of 'Economy.'

N.B.1 Notice that the 'Economy' principle does not, and should not, go too far. There are cases where the forms with 'less effort' might conceivably make sense, but these 'easier' forms are in fact not used in the language. For example, in pronouncing the word *sense*, there are two reasons for us to believe that it should be easier, or more economical, to replace the part [en] with a single nasalized vowel [ẽ]. For one thing, in pronouncing the string "[ẽ] + [s]," the tip of the tongue need not, and in fact does not, travel the round trip to and from the alveolar ridge as it does when we pronounce the string "[en] + [s]." To travel a shorter route means 'less effort,' i.e. it is more economical. And for another, the string "[ẽ] + [s]" consists of two segments, while that of "[en] + [s]" does of three segments. To pronounce fewer segments means 'less effort,' i.e. it is more economical. With all these economical conditions met, however, English does not employ the pronunciation of *sense* in the form *[sẽs]: *sense* is [sen(t)s]. This is the point where the English grammar rules.

N.B.2 From a historical point of view, the variant pronunciations in PE of the plural ending -*(e)s* and the third person singular ending -*(e)s* can possibly be described in economical terms. For example, the ancestor of PE *books* is ME *bokes*, and the history of phonological alterations is a series of economical steps. Roughly speaking, ME [bu:kəs] becomes [bu:kəz] due to Verner's Law in English, which explains the consonant voicing in the environment where the very consonant follows an unstressed vowel, and the latter form becomes [bukz] due to the principle of economical simplification, with the long vowel shortened and the unstressed short vowel, schwa [ə], suppressed. The form [bukz] finally becomes [buks] because of the process of assimilation, with the final [z] assimilated to the preceding voiceless segment [k]. Assimilation is obviously an instantiation of the principle of 'Economy.' Similarly, PE *comes* has developed roughly from ME [kuməs], which in turn becomes [kuməz]. The latter has then been transformed to [kumz], and finally has become [kʌmz].

N.B.3 Verner's Law in English can also be explained in economical terms. As was shown in N.B.2 above, the voiceless consonant [s] becomes voiced when it follows an unstressed short vowel: [əs] becomes [əz]. Note that, phonetically speaking, the voiceless [s] is more strenuous than the voiced [z], which fact means that [s] requires stronger muscle movements than [z] does. In other words, [s] requires more effort and [z] less effort in producing respective sounds. And note also that the entire syllable [əs] is an unstressed weak syllable. Therefore, it is a natural consequence that the weak syllable [əs] should become a 'further weak' syllable [əz] with less effort. That way, we find that Verner's Law in English is another case for the 'Economy' principle.

EXERCISES

---

1. What is the pronunciation of the initial consonant of *Celtic*? Why do you think it is so?

2. What is the pronunciation of the second vowel of *facade* (or *façade*)? Why do you think it is so?

Chapter III

Phonetics and Phonology

3.1 Phonetics vs. Phonology

Human speech is a string of sound waves. Phonetics and Phonology both study human speech sounds but they are different disciplines from each other. In this section, we are concerned about the question of what phonetics and phonology are. To answer this question, we will briefly show how they are alike and how they are different from each other.

Phonetics and phonology are the areas of studies whose primary source of empirical data is human linguistic voices, or phones. This is the first and foremost characterization of phonetics and phonology. So, they are alike in that they study all the phones available to human languages.

Next, regarding the difference between phonetics and phonology, they are to be characterized as follows:

(1) Phonetics is the study of phones used by humans as physical entities.

(2) Phonology is the study of phones used by humans as psychological (or language-particular) entities that constitute a system.

And we have to note the notational difference there is between "phones" and "phonemes," which notions we will turn to with illustrations in the section on phoneme, §3.3.

(3)   Notation for "phone" and "phoneme"
       The standard practice is such that (allo)phones are enclosed in
       brackets like [p], whereas phonemes are enclosed in slashes like
       /p/.

N.B. Phone or allophone is practically a physical sound, whereas phoneme is an abstract notion for a set of certain sounds. Details are explained in §3.3.

Now, according to (1), phonetics accommodates all possible phones observed in all human languages, whereas according to (2), phonology
studies the regularities, or the system of the phones, found in the target
language, i.e. a certain particular language. For example, phonetics
describes the articulatory differences observed in the pair of [s] and [ʃ].
English phonology is responsible for the systematic contrast found in such
a minimal pair as *sip* and *ship*, which contrast is due to the contrast found
in the phonemes /s/ and /ʃ/. Note that the phonemic difference between the
English /s/ and /ʃ/ is ultimately due to the phonetic difference between [s]
and [ʃ]. Japanese phonology, on the other hand, has a different system of
regularities of phones than that of English phonology. For example, in
Japanese, [s] and [ʃ] are noncontrastive in that there is no such minimal
pair as [saru] ("monkey") and *[ʃaru], nor is there a minimal pair like
*[sima] and [ʃima] ("island"). [s] and [ʃ] are, therefore, allophones of the
same phoneme /s/ in Japanese.

N.B. There are sounds (phones) that are contrastive in English but
noncontrastive in Japanese. Below is a list of pairs, members of which are
noncontrastive in Japanese, but contrastive in English.
[s] vs. [ʃ] as in *sip* and *ship*
[s] vs. [θ] as in *sin* and *thin*
[z] vs. [ð] as in *close* and *clothe*; *breeze* and *breathe*
[b] vs. [v] as in *berry* and *very*; *bet* and *vet*
[l] vs. [r] as in *light* and *right*; *long* and *wrong*, *belly* and *berry*

3.2   English Consonants and Vowels: Articulatory Definitions

English consonants are defined in terms 'place of articulation' and
'manner of articulation.' Place of articulation includes such features as
bilabial, labiodental, interdental, alveolar, palato-alveolar, palatal, velar,

and glottal. Manner of articulation includes such features as voiceless, voiced, stop (or plosive), fricative, affricate, nasal, liquid, lateral, and glide (or approximant). As for the features of place of articulation, see the figure below:

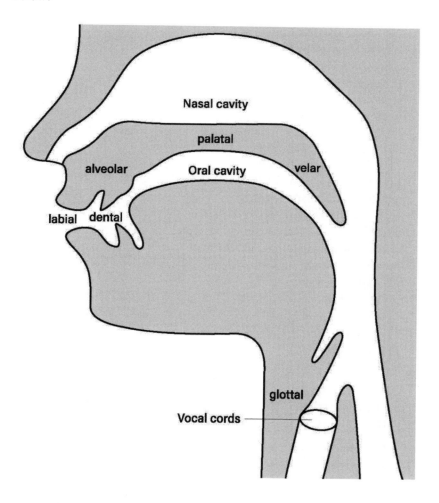

Figure: Places of Articulation Illustrated (grossly simplified)

Thus, English consonants are defined by the combinations of the features of place of articulation and the features of manner of articulation.

/p/: voiceless bilabial stop
/b/: voiced bilabial stop
/t/: voiceless alveolar stop
/d/: voiced alveolar stop
/k/: voiceless velar stop
/g/: voiced velar stop
/f/: voiceless labio-dental fricative
/v/: voiced labio-dental fricative
/θ/: voiceless interdental fricative
/ð/: voiced interdental fricative
/s/: voiceless alveolar fricative
/z/: voiced alveolar fricative
/ʃ (š)/: voiceless palatal fricative
/ʒ (ž)/: voiced palatal fricative
/h/: glottal fricative
/ʧ (č)/: voiceless palato-alveolar affricate
/ʤ (ǰ)/: voiced palato-alveolar affricate
/m/: bilabial nasal
/n/: alveolar nasal
/ŋ/: velar nasal
/l/: alveolar lateral liquid
/r/: alveolar liquid
/j/: palatal glide
/w/: (bilabial) velar glide

N.B. The two symbols like 'ʃ (š)' mean that the two are equivalent: you can use either symbol. The same story applies to 'ʃ (š),' 'ʒ (ž),' 'ʧ (č),' and 'ʤ (ǰ).'

See the table below:

Table of English consonants

manner of articulation	place of articulation	bilabial	labio-dental	interdental	alveolar	palato-alveolar	palatal	velar	glottal
stop	voiceless	p			t			k	(ʔ)
	voiced	b			d			g	
fricative	voiceless		f	θ	s		ʃ		h
	voiced		v	ð	z		ʒ		
affricate	voiceless					tʃ			
	voiced					dʒ			
nasal		m			n			ŋ	
liquid					l (lateral), r				
glide		(w)					j	w	

N.B.1 '?' is a symbol called "glottal stop," which means closure of the glottis (i.e. a narrow space between the vocal cords). It thus stops airstream entirely and causes no sound. A glottal stop is phonetically significant, but it plays no role in the distinction of meanings of words. Therefore, we do not count a glottal stop as a phoneme. This is why ? is enclosed in parentheses in the table (as "(?)"). As to the notion "phoneme," see the next section. (Notice incidentally that the closure of glottal stop is sometimes released as in one of the possible forms of *garden*, i.e. [gɑɚʔn].)

N.B.2 The two symbols 'w' and '(w)' mean that this consonant is produced by way of double-articulation, which is characterized by two places of articulation.

N.B.3 The definitions made above of English consonants and the phonetic (or phonemic) symbols employed here are not always in line with those of the International Phonetic Alphabet (IPA), which the International Phonetic Association (also IPA) defines. IPA phonetic symbols are meant to be used to describe all human sounds of the world languages, while the symbols and definitions above are to represent the specificities and regularities observed in the English phonetic and phonological system. The same remark applies to the definitions below of the English vowels.

N.B.4 Some differences between our notation and IPA (revised to 2015) are: our symbol "r" is a trill in IPA, and IPA's "ɹ" stands for our "r"; our "ʃ" and "ʒ" are palatal, but IPA's "ʃ" and "ʒ" are postalveolar.

N.B.5 According to the definitions above, consonants /s/, /ʧ/ and /ʃ/ are aligned from more 'front' to more 'back' with respect to the place of articulation dimension. This is due to the observation of how we pronounce the word-initial consonants in the following words: *s*eas, *ch*eese and *sh*e's; *S*ue's, *ch*oose and *sh*oes. The consonants /s/, /ʧ/ and /ʃ/ appear in [# __ iːz] and in [# __ uːz]. In either case, the author's observation is such that the places of articulation for the consonants /s/, /ʧ/ and /ʃ/, or for that matter, [s], [ʧ] and [ʃ], go backward one by one.

English vowels, on the other hand, are defined solely in terms of place of articulation. This is because vowels are phonetically distinct from consonants. Note that vowels are always voiced and they are a natural, spontaneous flow of breath, or air stream, without any constriction or any total closure throughout the vocal tract. Vocal tract is, as it were, a long sound-producing pipe that extends from glottis (i.e. where vocal cords are) through the lips or through the nostrils. Therefore, in the analysis of vowels, there is no need to specify any features of closure or constriction, i.e. of manner of articulation. Accordingly, English vowels are defined in terms of two-dimensional geometry applied to the oral cavity: one dimension is front-central-back, and the other high-mid-low. See the chart below:

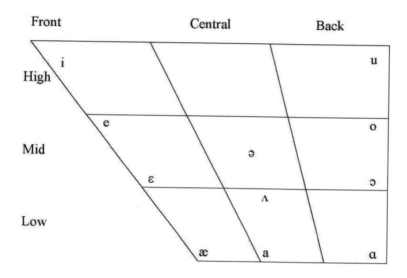

Schematic two-dimensional chart of English vowels

Thus the vowels are given the following definitions:
   /i/: high-front
   /e/: higher mid-front
   /ɛ/: lower mid-front
   /æ/: low-front
   /a/: low-central advanced
   /ɑ/: low-back
   /ɔ/: lower mid-back
   /o/: higher mid-back
   /u/: high-back
   /ə/: mid-central
   /ʌ/: low-central

N.B.1 The vowels above are a typical set of English vowels. English has other kinds of vowels, i.e. long vowels and diphthongs. We have shown above how vowels are characterized, as distinct from consonants.

N.B.2 Some words are in order here regarding the vowel /a/. Daniel Jones, a distinguished British phonetician, proposed a trapezoidal system of cardinal vowels (Vowel Quadrilateral), on the chart of which every vowel of any language should have its own place of articulation spotted. The Jonesian vowel [a], one of the cardinal vowels, is defined as "low-front," but in our vowel system given above, we do not, in fact, employ [a] as a single segmental vowel. Rather, English has such diphthongs as [ai], e.g. in *pile*, and [au], e.g. in *bout*. In the diphthongs like these, the initial vowel [a] (or /a/) should be characterized as "low-central advanced." Cf. Jones (1960[9]).

3.3   The Notion 'Phoneme'

A sentence is basically a stream of sounds. So, our first question in this section is: What are the building blocks of the stream of sounds? The answer is "phonemes." A phoneme is defined by a group of articulatory (or phonetic) features, but it sometimes has a number of different forms of appearance depending on the environment in which it appears. Technically speaking, the variant appearances of one phoneme are called allophones. The standard practice for representing phoneme and (allo)phone is such that phonemes are enclosed in slashes like /p/, whereas (allo)phones are enclosed in brackets like [p]. Allophones of a phoneme are, from a rigorously scientific point of view, distinctly different physical entities from each other. So our next question is: How can we conceive of all those distinctly different physical entities as the members of the same class, i.e. the allophones of one and the same phoneme? As a first approximation, we might have the following scheme:

(1)   Scheme 1
      Physically identical phones are of the identical category, i.e. the same phoneme. Likewise, phones that are not physically identical are of the distinct categories.

Scheme 1 goes well with the phones like [p], [t] and [k], since they are physically different from each other; therefore they belong to the distinct phonemes /p/, /t/ and /k/, respectively. But at the same time Scheme 1 makes wrong predictions such that [p] (released, unaspirated /p/), [pʰ] (aspirated /p/) and [p˺] (unreleased /p/) should belong to distinct phonemes

since they are physically distinct from each other. This prediction is clearly
wrong in English phonology, and is definitely against the intuitions of the
native speakers of English. For example, as for the pair like *pin* and *spin*,
though the former has the pronunciation [pʰ]*in* and the latter s[p]*in*, the
native intuition is that they have one and the same phone 'p': in phonological terms, [pʰ] and [p] are variant appearances of the same phoneme /p/, i.e.
allophones. Also, as for another illustration, observe the utterance "Stop!"
"Stop!" can be pronounced either as *sto*[p] or *sto*[pʭ]. Though [p] and [pʭ]
are physically distinct phones, the native intuition is that *sto*[p] and *sto*[pʭ]
are simply repetitions of the same word "stop." Thus, in this case, too, [p]
and [pʭ] should not be classed into the distinct phonemes, but rather be
classed into one and the same phoneme /p/. Therefore, it should be clear
that Scheme 1 fails.

   As an alternative to Scheme 1, we have Scheme 2 as shown below:

(2) Scheme 2
     A phoneme is a class of noncontrastive (or nondistinctive)
     phones: the noncontrastive phones of the same phoneme are
     called allophones. Phone *x* and phone *y* are noncontrastive if they
     satisfy both (A) and (B):
     (A) Phones *x* and *y* are in the relation called either "Comple-
          mentary distribution" or "Free variation".
     (B) Phones *x* and *y* are "Phonetically similar."

First, we look at the condition (A) of Scheme 2. Let us now see what the
notions of "Complementary distribution" and "Free variation" mean. Suppose that an item *x* appears in the environment P___Q, i.e., P_*x*_Q is a
grammatical sequence, and that an item *y* does not appear in the same
environment, i.e., *P_*y*_Q is not a grammatical sequence. Suppose further
that *x* does not appear in the environment R___S, i.e., *R_*x*_S is
ungrammatical, and that *y* appears in the same environment, i.e., R_*y*_S is
grammatical. In this case, we say that *x* and *y* are in the relation called
Complementary distribution. (Needless to say, P ≠ R nor Q ≠ S.) For
example, assuming that # stands for "word boundary," [pʰ] appears in the
environment #___[V, +stress], i.e., [pʰ]*in* is grammatical, but [p] does not
appear in the same environment, i.e., *[p]*in* is ungrammatical. Furthermore,
[pʰ] does not appear in the environment #s___[V, +stress], i.e., *s[pʰ]*in* is
ungrammatical, but [p] appears in the same environment, i.e. s[p]*in* is

grammatical. In this case, [pʰ] and [p] are in the relation called Complementary distribution.

Suppose that *x* appears in the environment M___N, i.e., M *x* N is grammatical, and that *y* does appear in the same environment, too, i.e., M *y* N is also grammatical. Suppose further that M *x* N and M *y* N are regarded by the native speakers of a certain language, e.g. English, as the repetitions of the same word or phrase. In this case, we say that *x* and *y* are in the relation called Free variation, or alternatively, *x* and *y* are Free variants. For example, [p] appears in the environment V___#, i.e., *sto*[p] is grammatical (as in "Stop it!"), and [pˀ] also appears in the same environment, i.e., *sto*[pˀ] is grammatical (as in "Stop peeling!"). Also, native English speakers regard *sto*[p] and *sto*[pˀ] simply as repetitions of the same word 'stop.' In this case, [p] and [pˀ] are in the relation called Free variation, or alternatively, [p] and [pˀ] are Free variants.

Next, we look at the condition (B) of Scheme 2. Let us see what "Phonetic similarity" means. The condition of Phonetic similarity is necessary because there are cases where even though phones *x* and *y* satisfy condition (A), it happens that *x* and *y* can hardly be regarded as allophones of a single phoneme. For example, [h] and [ŋ] are in Complementary distribution in the sense that # [h] V is possible, e.g. *hat*, but *# [ŋ] V is impossible, and that *V [h] # is impossible but V [ŋ] # is possible, e.g. *hang*. In this case, it is true that [h] and [ŋ] are in Complementary distribution, but they can hardly be regarded as allophones of such a single phoneme as, e.g., /H/. In order to avoid this implausible supposition of the phoneme /H/, we look to the condition Phonetic similarity. [h] has the distinctive set of features of [(voiceless), glottal, fricative], and [ŋ] the set of [(voiced), velar, nasal]. In terms of the definition by the distinctive features, it is evidently clear that [h] and [ŋ] are not phonetically similar. This means that [h] and [ŋ] do not satisfy the condition (B) of Scheme 2, which leads one to conclude that [h] and [ŋ] are not allophones of a single phoneme. Needless to say, [pʰ], [p], and [pˀ] are all characterized as [voiceless, bilabial, stop], and, therefore, they are phonetically similar. Thus, [pʰ], [p] and [pˀ] satisfy the condition (B) of Scheme 2, as well as the condition (A). Therefore, [pʰ], [p] and [pˀ] are noncontrastive with each other, so we conclude they are allophones of a single phoneme /p/.

As for another illustration of the need for the condition of Phonetic similarity, let us observe the case where items *x* and *y* are in Free variation but are nevertheless not the allophones of a single phoneme. [p] is possible in the environment V___#, e.g. *po*[p], and [t] is also possible in the same environment V___#, e.g. *po*[t]. In this case, from a strict distributional point of view, [p] and [t] appear to be Free variants, but in fact they can hardly be regarded as allophones of a single phoneme. This is simply because [p] and [t] have places of articulation that are far away from each other. Recall that [p] is [voiceless, bilabial, stop] and [t], [voiceless, alveolar, stop]. Thus, [p] and [t] are not phonetically similar, and they cannot be allophones of a single phoneme. Or, if we take into account the fact that *po*[p] and *po*[t] are not the repetitions of one and the same word, we could immediately conclude that [p] and [t] are not the Free variants.

N.B. There is another way of blocking the grouping of [p] and [t] as members of a single phoneme. You might want to say, for example, something like (a) below:

> (a)   Since we have the distributional fact such that [pʰ]*ill* is possible but *[t]*ill* is impossible and that **s*[pʰ]*ill* is impossible but *s*[t]*ill* is possible, we could conclude that [pʰ] and [t] are in Complementary distribution.

The assertion of (a) is quite right in its strict distributional sense. It is true that [pʰ] and [t] are in Complementary distribution, but this fact does not suffice to say that they are the allophones of one and the same phoneme. This observation misses one of the important requirements of the phonemeship stated in Scheme 2, i.e. "Phonetic similarity." Recall that [pʰ] is [voiceless, bilabial, stop] and [t], [voiceless, alveolar, stop]. Thus, [pʰ] and [t] are not phonetically similar. Therefore, they are not the allophones of a single phoneme.

Now, we believe it is clear that phonemes can be said to have a psychological status in our mind: it is not simply that they are merely patterns of sound-wave entities but that they are psychological realities for the native speakers of a given language. Cf. §3.1.

3.4   English Phonological Rules

Phonological rules are intended to describe the phonological phenomena of a particular target language, e.g. English. Thus, English phonological rules are proposed to describe the regularities observed in the

English phonological phenomena. The fact that English phonological rules represent the system of regularities hidden behind the English phonological behaviors means that English phonological rules 'predict' the English phonological phenomena irrespective of whether the phenomena are already known to us or they are totally new to us. In other words, English phonological rules represent the part of psychological reality that English speakers share that is responsible for the processing of everyday oral-aural interactions.

In the analysis of phonology, distinctive features play an important role in formulating the phonological rules. In what follows, we see a variety of English phonological rules that serve to shed light on the systematic patterns of English vocal activities.

3.4.1   Aspiration

First, observe the alternation of unaspirated /p/, i.e.[p], and aspirated /p/, i.e. [pʰ]. Now, we know that [p] and [pʰ] are allophones of the phoneme /p/, and this type of alternation, observed for example in the pair of *spin* and *pin*, can be predicted by the rule (1):

(1)   [p] → [pʰ] / #___ [V, +stress]

N.B. The rule (1) is an informal formulation. Formally, the phonological rule of the form 'A → B / X ___ Y' means "the segment A assumes the feature(s) B when it occurs in the environment X ___ Y." The informal formulation like the one in (1) is occasionally employed where confusion does not arise.

Note that the /p/ in "*p*erhaps" is unaspirated but the /p/ in "*p*erfect" aspirated. Both /p/'s stand before a vowel, but the stress levels on these vowels are not the same: unstressed in "*p*ĕrhaps," and stressed in "*p*érfect." Thus, we have [p] in the former but [pʰ] in the latter. This fact about "*p*ĕrhaps" and "*p*érfect" simply results from (1).

N.B. If we take into consideration the type of words like "repeat" and "impersonal," (1) would have to be revised as:

(i)   [p] → [pʰ] / $___ [V, +stress], where $ represents a syllable boundary

If we employ the rule (1) as it is, the medial /p/ in "re*p*eat" and "im*p*ersonal" fails to get aspirated. This is contrary to the fact. The fact is it gets aspirated. And the revised (i) correctly predicts this since the aspirated [pʰ] in "re*p*eat" and "im*p*ersonal" is a syllable-initial /p/ followed by a stressed vowel.

Now, regarding aspiration in English, there are two points of interest that are worth mentioning. One is the fact that /t/ and /k/, as well as /p/, undergo the process of aspiration under the same condition as that in (1). Thus, we have [t] in "s*t*all" but not in "*t*all"; [tʰ] is impossible in "s*t*all" but obligatory in "*t*all." Likewise, we have [k] in "s*k*in" but not in "*k*in"; [kʰ] is impossible in "s*k*in" but obligatory in "*k*in."

The other point is that voiced counterparts of /p/, /t/ and /k/, i.e. /b/, /d/ and /g/, respectively, do not induce the aspiration process. Thus, *bin* is [bin] but is never *[bʰin]; *dim* is [dim] but is never *[dʰim]; *gill* is [gil] but is never *[gʰil].

N.B. The facts about aspiration above are, for the most part, based on the observation of American English. British English, on the other hand, tends to have aspirated [pʰ], [tʰ] and [kʰ] even when American English usually does not: e.g. *writer* [$rai$$tʰə$].

3.4.2   "Clear" /l/ vs. "Dark" /l/
Next, we take up the contrast observed between the two types of /l/ as in (1) and (2).

(1) *l*eap   *l*ick   *l*et   *l*ate   tai*l*or   *l*oot
(2) pee*l*(s)   ki*ll*(ed)   ki*l*t   te*ll*(s)   tai*l*   too*l*

The /l/ in (1) is called "clear" /l/ and the one in (2) is called "dark" /l/. The two /l/'s are distinctly different from each other in two respects: first, in pronouncing clear /l/, the tip of the tongue is firmly pressed against the alveolar ridge, i.e. the hard ridge right behind the upper teeth, and then the contact is subsequently released, while dark /l/ does not necessarily induce such tongue-apical movements; secondly, in pronouncing dark /l/, the back of the tongue is slightly raised as compared with the case of clear /l/. And these differences are predictable from the phonological environment of the respective /l/'s. Thus, clear /l/ occurs when followed by a vowel, and so does dark /l/ when followed by a consonant or a word boundary. Note that in distributional terms, clear /l/ and dark /l/ are in Complementary distribution, and this type of distributional properties prove that clear /l/, i.e. [l], and dark /l/, i.e. [ɫ], are allophones of the same phoneme /l/. If we put this phenomenon into the formulation of phonological rules, we may have a rule like (3) below:

(3)   [l] → [ɫ] / ___ $\left\{ \begin{array}{c} C \\ \# \end{array} \right\}$

Informally, the rule (3) reads as "clear /l/ becomes dark /l/ when it occurs before a consonant or a word boundary."

N.B. "A$\left\{ \begin{array}{c} B \\ C \end{array} \right\}$D" means either "ABD" or "ACD."

3.4.3   Flap [D]

We often see, or for that matter "hear," /t/ pronounced as a voiced flapped alveolar consonant. This happens characteristically in American English. This phone is the so-called Flap [D] (or [ɾ] in IPA (the International Phonetic Alphabet)). Flap [D] is observed in such words as in (1), and this phonological process is represented by the rule (2).

(1)   wri*t*er   wri*t*ing   wa*t*er   be*tt*er   bu*tt*er   thir*t*y   for*t*y
(2)   [t] → [D] / [V, +stress] ___ [V, −stress]

Rule (2) accommodates all instances of (1) and, furthermore, such imaginary or nonsense words as "flei*t*er," "sproo*t*ing," and "repur*t*antly," and it also accommodates even non-English words like "Yamamo*t*o," which is originally a Japanese proper name. This fact is quite significant in two respects: one is that alternation of [t] and [D] is possible irrespective of the morphological environment of the target segment /t/. Rule (2) simply prescribes the phonological environment that induces the process, paying no attention at all to whether the morpheme after [D] is agentive *-er*, participial *-ing*, *-ty* with the meaning "ten," or whatsoever. Thus, (2) is called a 'phonological' rule. The other respect in which Rule (2) is significant is that it applies not only to the existing English words but also to the words that have never existed in the English language. In this sense, we claim that Rule (2) is psychologically real and that it makes predictions as to the possible cases in the given language.

A few more words are in order here regarding Flap [D]. As a first fact, Flap [D] alternates with [d] as it does with [t]. The words in (3) have [D] on the segment indicated by the italic *d*.

(3)   ri*d*er   ri*d*ing   fee*d*er   so*d*a   Fri*d*ay   Tu*d*or   Yama*d*a

There is another fact worth mentioning. Flap [D] is also observed 'across word boundaries,' in the sense that it occurs in the word final position. See, for example, the phrases below, where the italicized *t*, i.e. [t], can be replaced by [D]. This process is represented as in (5).

(4)   Ge*t* away!
      Ge*t* ou*t* of here!
      Ge*t* up!
      Shu*t* up!
      No, no*t* a*t* all.
      Ou*t* of sight, ou*t* of mind.

(5)   [t] → [D] / [V] ___ # # [V]

N.B. The first # signals the right-hand boundary of the word that ends with [t]. The second # signals the left-hand boundary of the word that follows.

3.4.4   Epenthesis

Epenthesis is a term for the phonological phenomena where a segment intrudes, as a newcomer, between the old segments in the phonological representation of a word. As a special case of Epenthesis, let us observe the case of /t/-intrusion: the intrusive /t/ may also be called an 'Excrescent' /t/. Some examples of this alternation are shown below:

(1)   answer: [ǽnsə] → [ǽntsə]
      since: [síns] → [sínts]
      fancy: [fǽnsi] → [fǽntsi]
      Minsk: [mínsk] → [míntsk]
      minstrel: [mínstrəl] → [míntstrəl]

An excrescent /t/ intrudes into the sequence /ns/ when a stressed vowel precedes this sequence /ns/ and either (a) a string of both optional consonants and an unstressed vowel follows it, or (b) the sequence of [/ns/ + C_0] is word-final. Alternatively, this process can be described as [s] becoming [c] under the condition just noted, [c] being equivalent to [ts]. Thus, we have the Rule (2) for this type of Epenthesis.

(2)   [s] → [c] / [V, +stress]n ___ C_0 ([V, −stress] X) #

N.B. C₀ means a sequence of consonants, the number of which ranges from zero to any indefinite number. X is a variable that represents any sequence of segments. The rule schema employing parentheses means the two rules such that the longer rule applies first and subsequently does the shorter one: the rule schema A(B)C, for example, means the two rules ABC and AC that apply in this order. # designates a word boundary.

Rule (2) correctly accounts for the facts in (1) as well as the facts such that the words in (3) below do not undergo the epenthetic alternation simply because Rule (2) does not stipulate that the segment [z] be affected, though the environment surrounding [z] in the words of (3) is identical to that of [s] in the representation of (2).

(3)   Keynes kinsman lens Windsor

Furthermore, (2) is responsible for the contrast observed in the pairs of words in (4), where the left-hand words allow for the alternation between [ns] and [nts], or [s] and [c], while the right-hand words do not.

(4)   cóncentràte—concéntric
       cònsolátion—consóle, consólatory
       cònspirátion—conspíre
       cónstitùte, cònstitútion—constítuent
       cònsultátion—consúlt

N.B. The primary stress and the secondary stress are both specified as positive regarding the feature [stress].

This is precisely the result that Rule (2) predicts.

N.B.1 If we take into consideration the fact that we have Epenthesis in words like *relevance* but not in words like *relevancy*, the rule (2) above should look like (i) below:

(i)   [s] → [c] / <[V, +stress]> n ___ C₀ <[V, −stress] X> #

Note that the rule schema "<A> B <C>" is an abbreviation of the two rules "ABC" and "B" that apply in this order. Elements enclosed in angled brackets are chosen or dismissed simultaneously.

N.B.2 Excrescent /t/ can also be observed in such words as *mansion* [mænʧən], *tenth* [tentθ], *else* [elts], *Welsh* [welʧ] and *health* [heltθ]. Cf. Nakazawa (2002).

N.B.3 In §2.3.2.4, the section on "Economy," we touched upon *length*, *strength, warmth,* and *glimpse.* These words each have an epenthetic segment inserted into their original sequence of sounds.

3.4.5   Stress Assignment
3.4.5.1   Stress Assignment in Nouns

English word-stress assignment is somewhat erratic, but if we look at the areas of high systematicity, regularity surfaces. In this subsection, we look into the systematic patterns of stress assignment in English nouns. But, before that, we should note two things. One is about where stress falls: the assumption is that stress falls on a vowel. The other is about the notion "syllable": syllable consists of a vowel and possibly consonants on either side of the vowel. Now, we see below how and where the primary stress falls in English nouns.

First of all, let us see the case of monosyllabic nouns, i.e. nouns that have only one vowel in them. In this case, the primary stress falls on this one and only vowel. Examples of this type are *pin, book, cat, view, God,* and many others.

Second, when nouns are disyllabic (or bisyllabic), i.e., nouns have two syllables, the basic type of stress assignment is such that the first syllable receives the primary stress. Examples include *father, mother, brother, sister, diva, widow, window, hobby, motto, monkey, forty, story, sofa, April, August, Europe, language, China, Cuba, Russia, Paris, London, Moscow, Venus, Saturn, Pluto,* and *Xerox.* But there are a number of counterexamples where the second syllable receives the stress. Some of them are *canal, device, guitar, hotel, police, taboo, shampoo, July, Detroit, Brazil,* and *Japan.*

Next, we consider the trisyllabic (i.e. three-syllabic) nouns and the nouns with more than three syllables. Before we go into the discussion of stress assignment in this type of nouns, we must introduce two notions that are part and parcel of the analysis. One is the notion "strong cluster," and the other "weak cluster." They are characterized as follows:

(1)   Strong cluster: $[\overline{V}C_0]$ or $[\breve{V}C_2]$
       Strong cluster consists of either (a) a long vowel or a diphthong followed by an indefinite number of consonants, or (b) a short vowel followed by at least two consonants.

(2) Weak cluster: [$\breve{V}C^1$]
Weak cluster consists of a short vowel followed by at most one consonant.

N.B.1 $\bar{V}$ means either a long vowel or a diphthong. For example, the long vowel [i:] in *beat* is $\bar{V}$, and the diphthong [ai] in *bite* is also $\bar{V}$. $\breve{V}$ means a short vowel. For example, the short vowel [i] in *bit* is $\breve{V}$. C^x means a string of at most x-consonants. C_y means a string of at least y-consonants.
N.B.2 Here, the notion "cluster" differs from the notion "syllable" that is noted in the text above.

Now, the stress assignment rule for English nouns with three or more syllables is (3):

(3) a. If the penultimate cluster is a strong cluster, then the stress falls on this penult.
b. If the penultimate cluster is a weak cluster, then the stress falls on the antepenult.

N.B.1 Penultimate cluster, or the penult, means the second cluster from the word final cluster. Antepenultimate cluster, or the antepenult, means the third cluster from the word final cluster.
N.B.2 Subrules formulated as (3a, b) can be formalized as (3a)' and (3b)', respectively:

(3a)' [V] → [+primary stress] / $\begin{Bmatrix} [\bar{v}\underline{\quad}] \, C_0 \\ [\breve{v}\underline{\quad}] \, C_2 \end{Bmatrix}$ V C_0 #

(3b)' [V] → [+primary stress] / $\underline{\quad}$ C_0 $\breve{V}$ C^1 V C_0 #

As an illustration of how Rule (3) predicts the correct stress assignment patterns in English nouns, let us observe the contrast between *diploma* and *diplomat*. But before that, we have to make clear how we 'clusterize' the given phonological sequence in a word. The 'clusterizing' process goes like (4) below:

(4) Clusterization
The "clusterizing" process goes from the word final toward the word initial cluster and each cluster should have the form [VC_0] except for the word initial cluster, which may have consonants on the left to the vowel, i.e., only the word initial cluster may

look like [C_0VC_0].

N.B. "Cluster" and "syllable" are different notions, and accordingly "clusterization" and "syllabication (or hyphenation)" are not the identical processes.

Note that Rule (3) applies only to the phonological representation of the word but not to the form of English orthography. For ease of exposition, however, we will draw on the English orthography in the description below. Now, *diploma* and *diplomat* are "clusterized" as shown in (5), where hyphens indicate the cluster boundaries.

(5) a. dipl-om-a: [CVCC]-[V̄C]-[V]
     b. dipl-om-at: [CVCC]-[V̆C]-[VC]

In (5a), the penultimate cluster has a diphthong; therefore, it is a strong cluster. Thus the stress falls on the vowel in this penult. Hence, *diplóma*. In (5b), however, the penultimate cluster has a short vowel followed by a single consonant; therefore, it is a weak cluster. Thus the stress falls on the vowel in the antepenult. Hence, *díplomat*. Other instances with the stress on the penult, i.e. ones to which (3a) applies, include those in (6). The other group of instances with the stress on the antepenult, i.e. ones to which (3b) applies, include those in (7).

(6) abracadabra alameda ameba anaconda alfalfa bambino enigma onomatopoeia veranda Arizona Oklahoma Francisco Nebraska Ticonderoga Nabisco UNESCO

(7) acrobat anemone apostrophe balcony comedy gondola opera institute America Alamo Idaho Florida Canada Italy Portugal UNICEF

Finally, let us see an interesting group of "exceptional" English nouns. They are "exceptional" in that it is true that they have the very environment specified in Rule (3b) and we expect them to have the stress on the antepenult but the fact is that they have the stress on the penult. Such "exceptional" nouns are shown below:

(8) antenna bandanna committee dilemma gorilla guerilla operetta spaghetti tomorrow umbrella vanilla Cinderella Madonna Mississippi Morocco Piccadilly Rebecca Ulysses

Notice that there is something noteworthy in the "exceptional" words in (8). All words in (8) have the stress on the penult, and the orthography, i.e. spelling, of this very penult has the form [VCC]. It seems fairly likely that the spelling form of [VCC] has had an analogical force on the application of Rule (3a). Thus, on the analogy of the orthographical form of [VCC], Rule (3a) is induced to apply to the words in (8).

Lastly, let us take a quick look at another type of exceptions. There might remain 'pure' exceptions like *Indiana, Louisiana, Montana* and *Nevada*, in which case the stress is on the penult though the penult is a weak cluster in the sense of both phonological form, i.e. /æn/ and /æd/, and orthographical spelling, i.e. "*an*" and "*ad*." But, it may well be the case that 'pure' exceptions of this type are only exceptions when seen solely from a phonological viewpoint. When we take into consideration the acoustic phonetic facts about the vowel [æ], these 'exceptions' should rather be regarded as normal. Thus, American [æ] is acoustically rather long especially when it is stressed, compared with such vowels as [i], [e], [ɑ], [ɔ] and [ʌ]. So, the penult in the examples above should be regarded as a 'stronger' cluster than a simple weak one. In fact, British counterparts of these nouns have [ɑ:] as the vowel of this penult cluster, and the cluster with a long vowel [ɑ:] is indeed a strong cluster. The interchangeability of [æ] and [ɑ:] between American and British pronunciations is best observed in the words like *can't* and *castle*: Americans say [kænt] and [kæsl], but the British [kɑ:nt] and [kɑ:sl]. Therefore, we may rightly assume that even in American English, too, the penult of the above nouns can be taken to be a strong (or stronger) cluster and it thus receives the primary stress.

N.B. Words like *photograph, telegraph, autopsy, necropsy, albatross*, and *algebra* might be claimed to constitute a group of "true" exceptions. It might be, since they actually have a primary stress on the first cluster, or the antepenult, of their phonological representations, contrary to the expectation that it should have fallen on the penult. But they could be analyzed in such a way that *photograph*, for example, is a compound noun derived from the constituents *photo-* and *-graph*, and it is indeed the case. Notice that compound nouns are left-stressed as exemplified in such cases as *gréenhòuse* and *bláckbòard*. Similarly, we have a compound structure like [ₙ *auto-* + *-opsy*] or [ₙ *al-* + *-batross*] for other words mentioned above.

3.4.5.2   Stress Assignment in Verbs

In this subsection, we look into the systematic patterns of stress assignment in English verbs. We see below how and where the primary stress falls in English verbs.

First of all, let us see the case of monosyllabic verbs. In this case, the primary stress falls on this one and only vowel. Examples of this type are *eat, find, get, take, walk, write,* and many others.

Next, we consider the disyllabic (or bisyllabic) verbs, i.e., verbs that have two syllables. A general tendency of the stress assignment in verbs is such that the primary stress goes rightward. Therefore, disyllabic verbs generally have the primary stress on the right. But there are some that do not confirm to this tendency. So we need some rules here. When we are to show how the primary stress is assigned in disyllabic verbs, we need to employ the two notions that we have already introduced in the previous section: they are "strong cluster" and "weak cluster." Now, the stress assignment rule for English verbs with two syllables is (1):

(1) a. If the ultimate cluster is a strong cluster, then the stress falls on this ultima.

  b. If the ultimate cluster is a weak cluster, then the stress falls on the penult.

N.B.1 Ultimate cluster, or the ultima, means the word final cluster.
N.B.2 Subrules formulated as (1a, b) can be formalized as (1a)' and (1b)', respectively:

(1a)' $[V] \rightarrow [\text{+primary stress}] / \begin{Bmatrix} [\bar{v}\underline{\quad}] \, C_0 \\ [\check{v}\underline{\quad}] \, C_2 \end{Bmatrix} \#$

(1b)' $[V] \rightarrow [\text{+primary stress}] / \underline{\quad} C_0 \, \check{V} \, C^1 \#$

As an illustration of how Rule (1) predicts the correct stress assignment patterns in English verbs, let us observe the contrast between *conceal* and *cancel*. But before that, we need to "clusterize" these words. The 'clusterizing' process is defined in the previous section. Also, note that the 'clusterizing' process applies to the phonological representation of the word but not to the form of orthography. For ease of exposition, however, we will draw on the orthography in the description below. Now, *conceal* and *cancel* are "clusterized" as shown in (2), where hyphens indicate the cluster boundaries.

(2) a. conc-eal: [CVCC]-[V̄C]
     b. canc-el: [CVCC]-[V̆C]

In (2a), the ultimate cluster has a long vowel; therefore, it is a strong cluster. Thus the stress falls on the vowel in this ultima. Hence, *concéal*. In (2b), however, the ultimate cluster has a short vowel followed by a single consonant; therefore, it is a weak cluster. Thus the stress falls on the vowel in the penult. Hence, *cáncel*. Other instances with the stress on the ultima, i.e. ones to which (1a) applies, include those in (3). The other group of instances with the stress on the penult, i.e. ones to which (1b) applies, include those in (4).

(3) believe complain complete consist contain convert decide delay deny digest describe enjoy esteem expect protest pursue select suggest torment

(4) banish bury carry copy ferry furnish punish vanish

A few words are in order here about the disyllabic verbs. It is true that words like *forgo* and *forsake* rightly receive the primary stress on the ultima due to (1a), but those like *forbid*, *forget* and *forgive* behave rather exceptionally. The latter three are exceptional in that they have primary stress on the ultima, although we would expect them to have primary stress on the penult through the application of (1b). What to do with this case? It may well be the case that the latter three verbs are simply in line with the general tendency of stress assignment in disyllabic verbs such that the primary stress goes rightward. Or it may well be the case as far as the five verbs mentioned above are concerned, the prefix *for-* ought to be phonologically transparent: in other words, *for-* is disregarded when we consider the stress assignment in these verbs, which means that all these verbs are monosyllabic when in the process of stress assignment. If this is the case, *forgo, forsake, forbid, forget,* and *forgive* receive main stress just like the way the verbs *go, sake* (etymologically, a verb), *bid, get,* and *give* do so.

Thirdly, we consider the trisyllabic verbs and the verbs with more than three syllables. In this type of verbs, we see there are at least three subtypes of stress assignment. One is the suffix-dependent type, the second the prefix-dependent type, and the last the exceptional type. We will see them in detail below.

(5)   Stress assignment in verbs with three syllables or more

(a) Suffix-dependent type	
suffix	examples
-ate	accentuate contemplate formulate graduate integrate interrogate
-ify	clarify exemplify identify purify solidify
-ize	apologize authorize characterize emphasize organize realize specialize recognize
-ee	guarantee referee
(b) Prefix-dependent type	
prefix	examples
over-	overcome overestimate overlook oversee overshadow overthrow
under-	underestimate undermine underscore understand undertake underwrite
(c) Exceptional type	
prefix	examples
inter-	(i) intervene interact intercept interfere intersperse
inter-	(ii) interview intercourse
inter-	(iii) interpret interrupt intersect
con-	(iv) continue

In (5a), we have verbs whose main stress is determined by each of the suffixes attached to them. Thus verbs with *-ate* attached to them have main stress on the antepenult and at the same time, they have secondary stress on the ultima, i.e. the cluster that comprises *-ate*. Verbs with *-ify* attached to them have main stress on the antepenult, and at the same time, they have secondary stress on the ultima, i.e. the cluster that comprises *-y*. Verbs with *-ize* attached to them have main stress on the same cluster as that of the 'original' noun/adjective that would eventually end up having *-ize* attached to it. But the exception in this case is *recognize*. It seems that the main stress of the verb *recognize* would rather be the result of the process below:

(6)   a.   First, apply the rule (1a) above, i.e., "If the ultimate cluster is a strong cluster, then the stress falls on this ultima."

b.   Next, copy and move leftward this main stress unto the penultimate cluster.

c.   Finally, destress the main stress on the ultima to secondary stress.

Note that the process in (6) is in fact at work in the cases of verbs with *-ate* or *-ify* attached to them. Verbs with *-ee* attached to them have a somewhat different story than the verbs we have just mentioned, i.e. verbs with *-ate*, *-ify*, or *-ize*. There are nouns with the suffix *-ee* attached to them, e.g. *employee, examinee, nominee, refugee,* and *standee,* and they invariably have main stress on this suffix. We also have nouns *guarantee* and *referee* and they are converted to verbs with phonetic structure intact, i.e. with main stress on the ultima. Thus verbs like *guarantee* and *referee* have main stress on the ultima.

In (5b), we disregard prefixes *over-* and *under-* and seek for main stress in the 'remainder' verbs. This procedure correctly leads to the correct main stress assignment in these verbs, and the suffixes *over-* and *under-* subsequently receive secondary stress.

Finally, in (5c), we have certain miscellaneous types of verbs here. First, in (5ci), we disregard the prefix *inter-*, take the 'remainder' as a verb (even when the 'remainder' does not look like a Present-Day English verb), and decide where main stress is. In these verbs of (5ci), the prefix *inter-* receives secondary stress. In (5cii), the words *interview* and *intercourse* are originally nouns and we take them to be compound nouns. Compound nouns have main stress on the left-branch constituent. Thus they have main stress on *inter-* and secondary stress on *-view/-course*. Then, these nouns get converted to verbs. This is what they are now as verbs, their phonetic structure being the same as that of nouns. In (5ciii), the verbs *interpret*, *interrupt*, and *intersect* are all assigned main stress as if they were simple verbs: stress assignment in these verbs follow the steps we have already employed, i.e. the way the rule in (1) applies. Note that in the verbs *interrupt* and *intersect*, secondary stress falls on *inter-*. In (5civ), placement of main stress in the verb *continue* is purely exceptional. (As for the notions "compound noun" and "conversion," see Chapter IV. Morphology.)

3.4.6   Rhythm Rule

Phonological features that constitute a word may frequently be under the influence of the accompanying phonological environment. Observe, for example, the cases of "clear" vs. "dark" /l/, aspiration of voiceless stops (i.e. /p/, /t/ and /k/), and Flap [D]. Rhythm rule is another example of the phonological alternation of the features in a word. For example, the adjective *thirtéen* has the primary stress on the ultima, i.e. the word final cluster or syllable, but when followed by a noun like *stúdents*, the primary stress of *thirtéen* moves leftward and it falls on the first syllable. Thus, we have, especially in a casual speech, *thírteen stúdents* instead of **thirtéen stúdents*. The rule of this type of effect on the stress pattern of certain phrases is called Rhythm rule, or sometimes Clash rule, and the rule is formulated as in (1):

(1)   Rhythm rule

If an adjective with the primary stress on the ultima is followed by a noun with the primary stress on the initial syllable, i.e., the two primary stresses are adjacent to each other, then the primary stress of the adjective moves leftward and falls on the syllable with the secondary stress.

It should be clear that Rhythm rule of (1) has the effect of both preventing the stress clash and rendering the clash-stricken phrases much more rhythmical. Hence, it is called Rhythm rule. The range of phrases over which the rule (1) has the effect include those in (2):

(2)   Jápanèse stúdents (cf. Jàpanése)
Chínèse pórcelain (cf. Chìnése)
Pórtuguèse lánguage (cf. Pòrtuguése)
Néw Yòrk Cíty (cf. Nèw Yórk)
Ténnessèe Válley (cf. Tènnessée)
Ténnessèe Wílliams (cf. Tènnessée)
Márcèl Próust (cf. Màrcél)

Notice that in the last four examples, "New York," "Tennessee" and "Marcel" are proper nouns but each of them in fact acts like an adjective that modifies the noun that follows.

N.B. Observe below:

   (i) Nèw Yórk Yánkees
   (ii) Nèw Yórk Méts

In these examples, we see no application of Rhythm rule to the prenominal "Nèw Yórk." This indicates a strong condition on the applicability of Rhythm rule that we have when we get into the analysis of this phenomenon. It is the condition such that the prenominal constituent must act like an adjective that modifies the noun that follows (as we have just said in the text). "Nèw Yórk" does not modify "Yánkees" or "Méts" in the same way as "Nèw Yórk" modifies "Cíty" or "Jàpanése" does "stúdents." The reason is as follows. As "Japanese students" are those students who are Japanese, i.e., the adjective "Japanese" reduces the membership of all students to only those entitled "Japanese," so the constituent "Néw Yòrk" reduces the membership of all cities to only one that is entitled "New York." But now, "Yankees" and "Mets" are proper names and their referent is already uniquely one, irrespective of the existence of the prenominal "New York." Thus "New York" in (i) and (ii) is not the kind of constituent as the "New York" in "Néw Yòrk Cíty" from the perspective of semantic modification. See Nakazawa (2006, 2014) for the detail.

3.5   Some Phonological Universals

Now, we know that phonological rules of a particular language describe the phonological behaviors of this particular language. But, phonological universals are simply not the rules of grammar: they are notions of a more abstract nature. So, we may ask what function phonological universals are supposed to assume. In discussing the notions about universals, it is very important to note that arguments should go in a careful and elaborate manner. First of all, Grammar is a theory about a language, and thus phonological rules of a particular language are statements about the sound systems of this particular language. Next, Universal Grammar (UG), or Linguistic Theory (LT), is a theory about grammars of all human languages, which means that phonological universals are statements about the sound systems of all human languages. Thus, grammatical rules, on the one hand, deal with the language particular idiosyncrasies. Universals, on the other, deal only with the general properties of grammars, and they never deal with language particular incidentals.

In other words, linguistic universals deal with abstract properties induced from all the language particular grammatical rules: they are essentially the very nature that grammars of all human languages share.

> **N.B.** So, it is reasonably claimed from the viewpoint of language acquisition that UG is an innate knowledge a newborn baby has as an initial state in his/her language learning. But we do not go further into this issue here.

It is true that there are all sorts of differences among all human languages, but these differences should be derived from the differences among the language particular grammars. And as for these language particular grammatical differences, they are within the confinement of the possible variations prescribed by UG. Hence, as is often claimed by linguists, it is not that arguments about universals can be based on the naïve empirical facts, but the truth is that they should be confirmed on the basis of the abstract properties of grammatical rules that are obtained from, or the result of, the elaborate and careful inquiries of all human languages. Therefore, grammatical rules are to a language as universals are to all grammars of human languages. In what follows in this section, we will see only a handful of the phonological universals.

But a word is in order here. As regards the descriptive levels in the study of linguistics, we need to discern four levels of abstraction: they are Data, Language, Grammar and Linguistic Theory. Linguistic Theory is a theory about Grammar, Grammar is a theory about Language, Language is a theory about Data, and Data is a solid object, both concrete and observable. Thus Linguistic Theory is the most abstract and Data is the most concrete among the four levels. Data may sometimes be conceived of as a collection of acceptable and grammatical sentences. But the latter view is mistaken. See §7.2 of Chapter VII on this point.

3.5.1 Order of Acquisition of Phonemes

As a first illustration of phonological universals, we may cite the order of acquisition of sounds, or phonemes, by children. No matter what language infants are born to be exposed to, they will eventually acquire, or come to produce, vowels and consonants roughly in the order indicated by the hierarchy below:

(1)   Vowel: Low front vowels >> High back vowels
(2)   Consonant: Bilabial stop >> Alveolar stop >> Velar stop >>

Fricative>> … >> Glide

Needless to say, the two hierarchies are gross tendencies. But the tendencies are such that the easiest come first, and then come the less easy ones. For example, the English interpretation of the hierarchy (1) may look like (3):

(3)   /a/ > /e/ > /i/ > /o/ > /u/

Physiologically speaking, or in terms of the tongue positions and other kinetic movements, /a/ is more lax than /i/ and /u/, the latter two being tense. Lax vowels require less effort to produce than tense vowels do. In fact, among the first words infants may produce, we find words like *Mama* and *Dada*. And it may be the case that infants say *cat* far earlier than they would say *cool*: the vowel in *cat* is low front, whereas the one in *cool* is high back.

The English interpretation of the hierarchy (2) may look like (4):

(4)   /m/ /b/ /p/ >> /d/ /t/ >> /g/ /k/ >> /z/ /s/ >> … >> /j/

Stop consonants require less effort to articulate than fricatives do, and front consonants are easier to articulate than back consonants. Thus, some of the first words by infants are, as noted above, *Mama* and *Dada*. And it may be the case that infants say *bell* far earlier than they would say *yell*: the first consonant in *bell* is bilabial stop, whereas the one in *yell* is glide. See Jakobson (1968, 1971) for this type of universals.

3.5.2   Articulatory Features as Distinctive Features: What It Means to Employ Phonological Features (I)

When we define phonemes, we have employed phonological distinctive features like [bilabial], [labio-dental], etc., on the one hand, and such features as [+/− voice], [stop], [fricative], etc., on the other. The former group comprises features of 'place of articulation,' and the latter those of 'manner of articulation.' Both types of features are the features we can control. This fact sometimes goes unnoticed but is fundamentally important: the distinction of meaning that we can make hinges on the value of distinctive features. To articulate sounds ultimately means to make semantic distinctions. Thus, all distinctive features are the features over which humans have free control. Therefore, we have a universal as in (1):

(1)   Phonological articulatory features are controllable distinctive
       features.

The universal (1) has two kinds of implications: one is such that every one
of the articulatory features has the effect of serving to differentiate the
meanings in a given language, and the other is such that features other than
phonological distinctive features do not contribute to the human linguistic
faculty. Let us illustrate the first implication. The features [+/− voice], for
example, have the effect of differentiating the phonemes /p/ and /b/ in
English. Thus, (2) and (3) have distinct meanings from each other.

(2)   English: par
(3)   English: bar

In terms of the feature specifications, *par* begins with the consonant
[voiceless bilabial stop], and *bar* does with the consonant [voiced bilabial
stop]. The only difference between the two is [+/− voice]. In Mandarin
Chinese, however, the features [+/− aspirated], i.e. having [ʰ] or not, have
the effect of differentiating the phonemes /p/ and /b/. Thus, (4) and (5)
have distinct meanings from each other in Mandarin Chinese.

(4)   Chinese: pā [pʰa] "to lie down on one's face"
(5)   Chinese: bā [pa] "eight"

In terms of the phonetic representations, *pa* begins with the consonant [pʰ],
and *ba* does with the consonant [p]. The only difference between the two is
[+/− aspirated]. Thus, in Mandarin Chinese, these features are distinctive
and, of course, they are controllable by humans. Notice that while the
features [+/− aspirated] are distinctive in Mandarin Chinese, they are not in
English. Every language has its own system of distinctive features that are
drawn from the repertoire of the universal set of articulatory features. And
each language has a phonological system that is unique and peculiar to the
language itself.

Next, let us see what it means to say that as the second implication of
the universal (1), the features other than phonological distinctive features
do not contribute to the human linguistic faculty. It means the very fact that
those features over which we do not have any control should never be
employed as the phonological distinctive features. For example, such
phonetic features as hiccups, sneezing, or snoring are not phonological

distinctive features. This is because they are accidentals and, therefore, are never controllable by humans. The second implication of this effect may sound too obvious to give a serious moment of discussion to, but it is a vital reality. Linguistic universal is a key notion that characterizes what is possible as human languages, as distinct from something that is impossible. Therefore, the linguistic universal of the type (1) is important and indispensable.

3.5.3 Natural Class: What It Means to Employ Phonological Features (II)

Employment of distinctive features makes it possible for us to state the linguistically significant generalizations in phonology. Thus, we can define a natural class in terms of distinctive features; or we should say that only through the use of distinctive features can we define a natural class. This means that we have a universal as in (1) below:

(1) Distinctive features are necessary for the definition of a natural class.

Now, one may ask what the 'natural class' is. A natural class is defined as follows:

(2) A natural class is a class such that the number of the features that define the class itself is smaller than the number of the features that define each of the elements of the class.

Let us take, for example, the class that comprises /p/ /t/ and /k/, and see how we define the class itself and also each of its elements.

(3) The two features [voiceless stop] define {/p/ /t/ /k/}.
     The three features [voiceless bilabial stop] define /p/.
     The three features [voiceless alveolar stop] define /t/.
     The three features [voiceless velar stop] define /k/.
     The number of the features that define the class {/p/ /t/ /k/} is smaller than the number of the features that define either /p/ /t/ or /k/.
     Therefore, {/p/ /t/ /k/} is a natural class.

As is clearly shown in (3), the number of the features that define the class of /p/ /t/ and /k/ is two, while the number of the features that define each of its elements is three. Therefore, by definition, the class of /p/ /t/ and /k/ is a natural class. Note that the class of /p/ /t/ /k/ and /s/, for example, is not a natural class. This is because we need at least four different features to define this class: the set of features "[voiceless stop] or [voiceless alveolar fricative]" define {/p/ /t/ /k/ /s/}. Similarly, the class of /p/ and /t/ is not a natural class, either. This is because we need at least four different features to define this class: the set of features "[voiceless bilabial stop] or [voiceless alveolar stop]" define {/p/ /t/}.

Now, let us see how phonological rules state the linguistically significant generalizations in terms of the notion of natural class. First, we note the process called aspiration. Aspiration is observed on the initial segment in the words like *pole, toll* and *coal*, but not on the initial segment in the words like *bowl, dole* or *goal*. Thus, at a first glance, one may be tempted to describe the phenomena and propose rules like (4):

(4)   /p/ → [aspirated] / #___ [V, +stress]
      /t/ → [aspirated] / #___ [V, +stress]
      /k/ → [aspirated] / #___ [V, +stress]

But, theoretically speaking, the rules in (4) are all independent from each other, and are thus unrelated to each other. But this observation is wrong: English speakers "know" that the processes that we observe in all of the cases in (4) are, in fact, one and the same case of aspiration. This type of "knowledge," or intuition, can be rightly expressed in (5), where linguistically significant generalization is achieved through the use of distinctive features that define a natural class.

(5)   [voiceless stop] → [aspirated] / #___ [V, +stress]

Note that both (4) and (5) describe the same phenomena, but (5) is much closer to English speakers' intuition. Hence, we call (5) a linguistically significant generalization.

As a second case of phonological generalization through the use of distinctive features that define a natural class, we see Flap [D] is a good example. Flap [D] occurs in words like *writer* and *rider*, so one may be tempted to describe the phenomena and propose rules like (6):

(6)   /t/ → [D] / [V, + stress] _____ [V, − stress]
      /d/ → [D] / [V, + stress] _____ [V, − stress]

But, theoretically speaking, the rules in (6) are all independent from each other, and are thus unrelated to each other. But this observation is wrong: English speakers "know" that the processes that we observe in both of the cases in (6) are, in fact, one and the same case of Flapping. This type of "knowledge," or intuition, can be rightly expressed in (7), where linguistically significant generalization is achieved through the use of distinctive features that define a natural class.

(7)   [alveolar stop] → [D] / [V, + stress] _____ [V, − stress]

Note that both (6) and (7) describe the same phenomena, but (7) is much closer to English speakers' intuition. Hence, we call (7) a linguistically significant generalization.

The natural class plays a significant role in stating phonological generalizations, and distinctive features are part and parcel in giving substance to the notion of natural class. Therefore, we say that employment of phonological distinctive features is a kind of linguistic universal. And at the same time, it is reasonable to say that having the notion of natural class is a kind of linguistic universal, too.

EXERCISES

1.   There is a woman tennis player whose family name is "Navratilova." State, or write in phonetic alphabet, how you pronounce her name. Also explain how you arrive at it. (*Hint*: There is more than one possibility.)

2.   The class of {/p/ /b/ /m/} is a natural class defined by the feature [bilabial]. State what kind of phonological phenomena this class captures a significant generalization of. (*Hint*: A negative prefix attaches to, for example, *tolerable* and converts it to *intolerable*. What about other cases?)

Chapter IV

Morphology

4.1   Domain of the Study of Morphology

Human speech is a string of sound waves, specifically the type of sound waves called speech sounds. Speech sounds are grouped together to make up sequences of phonemes, which in turn make up a string of morphemes. A single morpheme or more than one morpheme will make up a word. When we study the structure of words, we say we are doing morphological investigations. Thus, the domain of the study of Morphology is word.

4.2   The Notion 'Morpheme'

Morphology studies the structure of words. In other words, it concerns the make-up of each and every word in the language. Therefore, in a broader sense, morphology is sometimes synonymous with Word Formation. In phonology, we have seen that phonemes are the 'building blocks' that we use to make up the flow of speech. In morphology, one may ask what is the 'building blocks' that we use to make up words. The answer is morpheme. Morpheme is defined as follows:

(1)   Morpheme is the smallest meaningful element.

For example, the word *book* consists of a single morpheme {Book}, which means that the word *book* means "book." But the word *books* consists of two morphemes {Book} and {Plural}, which means that the word *books* means "more than one book." Thus, the word *book* has the meaning of a single morpheme, but the word *books* has the combined meaning of two morphemes. Note that our standard practice is such that morpheme is enclosed by braces as in {Book} and it is formally represented as a sequence of phonemes like /buk/. Thus, the pluralized *books* has two morphemes {Book} and {Plural}, and is represented as /buk/ + /s/.

Let us see other instances of morpheme. The word *box* has a single morpheme {Box} and is represented as /bɑks/. And the word *boxes* has two morphemes {Box} and {Plural} and is represented as /bɑks/ + /iz/. Furthermore, the word *boys* is a pluralized word of *boy*, has two morphemes {Boy} and {Plural}, and is represented as /bɔi/ + /z/. Notice that it happens that one and the same morpheme has different guises depending on the environment in which it appears: {Plural}, when attached to {Box}, appears as /iz/, the same {Plural}, when attached to {Book}, appears as /s/, and the very same {Plural}, when attached to {Boy}, appears as /z/. We call these variant forms, i.e. /iz/, /s/, and /z/, allomorphs of the morpheme {Plural}. The forms of the allomorphs of this type are determined by the phonological environment in which they appear. This is clearly shown in (2):

(2)   Analysis of regular plural endings
    a.   If the stem ends with a sibilant (i.e. /s/, /z/, /ʃ/, /ʒ/, /ʧ/ or /dʒ/), then {Plural} becomes /iz/.
    b.   Otherwise (i.e. when the above case (a) does not hold), if the stem ends with a voiceless consonant, then {Plural} becomes /s/.
    c.   Otherwise (i.e. when the above cases (a) and (b) do not hold, which means when the stem ends with a voiced segment, excepting /z/, /ʒ/ and /dʒ/), {Plural} becomes /z/.

N.B. Stem is something to which an affix attaches. Affix is a type of morpheme to which we will turn below. We sometimes call "root" something that is the starting point of all processes of word-formation.

Therefore, we say these allomorphs of {Plural}, i.e. /iz/, /s/ and /z/, are phonologically conditioned, or we say they are phonologically conditioned allomorphs.

There are, however, another type of allomorphs: they are morphologically conditioned allomorphs, which we see in irregular plural nouns. Observe the variant forms of {Plural} in words like *oxen*, *children*, *feet*, *analyses* and *fish*, among others. Their forms are /ən/, /rən/ coupled with "de-diphthongization" in the stem, vowel mutation, vowel lengthening in the last syllable, and no change, respectively.

> **N.B.** Diphthong means two vowels combined, and diphthongization is the process such that a short vowel becomes a diphthong. "De-diphthongization" is intended here to mean for a diphthong to become a short vowel. Vowel mutation means change of quality of a vowel. Vowel lengthening means to make a short vowel long.

Morphologically conditioned allomorphs are unique in that their forms are determined not by the phonological environment but solely determined by the morphological properties of the stem to which they attach.

4.3   Types of Morpheme

4.3.1   Classification of Morphemes

In this section, we observe a variety of morphemes and their morphological functions that are more or less related to their semantic properties. Below is a table of morphemes.

Classification of morphemes

morpheme	free form	content word		N, V, A, Adv	open class
		function word		Conj, Art, Dem, P, Aux, Com	closed class
	bound form	affix	prefix	*a-*, *pre-*, *sub-*, etc.	
			suffix	*-ment*, *-ion*, *-e(s)*, etc.	
		contracted form		*'ll*, *'d*, *'ve*, etc.	
		bound base		*anim-*, *path-*, *-ology*, *cranberry* morpheme (*cran-*)	

Abbreviations: N for Noun, V for Verb, A for Adjective, Adv for Adverb, Conj for Conjunction, Art for Article, Dem for Demonstrative, P for Preposition, Aux for Auxiliary verb, and Com for Comparison.

There are two types of morpheme: one is free form and the other bound form. Free form is a type of morpheme that can stand alone; in other words, a free form itself is a word. Bound form, on the other hand, cannot stand alone, nor can it constitute a word by itself. Free form can be a content word or a function word. Content word is a word that has its own semantic content as well as its grammatical properties: *dog* is a content word that means a "four-legged canine mammal" and can take a plural form *dogs*; *peace* is also a content word that means the "state without such disturbing matters as war" and cannot take a plural form **peaces*. (The asterisk or star '*' marks the expression that follows as ungrammatical.) Other content words include the words of such categories as 'verb,' 'adjective' and 'adverb.' Function word is a word whose primary role is to make explicit the functional relations among the words that are related by it. For example, conjunction *and* is a function word that makes up a coordinate structure whose dependents are of the equal grammatical status. Article *a(n)* is another function word whose function is to indicate that the noun that follows is a countable singular indefinite noun. *This*, *these*, *that* and *those* are demonstratives and they are function words in that they function as referential deictic pointers. Preposition is another function word to specify the relationship among the words combined by it: *on* specifies the relative positions of *the book* and *the table* in the phrase "the book on the table." Auxiliary verbs are the function words that lost their semantic content, or are semantically bleached, and have only grammatical functions: progressive *be* is a progressive marker, perfective *have* a perfective marker, passive *be* a passive marker, and modals modality markers. Words of comparison are *more* and *most* and they are the function words that specify comparative and superlative degrees, respectively.

Bound form is a morpheme that cannot stand alone, or they have to be dependent on others. Hence they are called 'bound.' Bound form can be an affix, a contracted form, or a bound base. Affixes can be cross-classified as shown in the table below:

Types of affix

affix	prefix	suffix
derivational	de-, in-, pre-, sub-, re-, etc.	-able, -ion, -ity, -ment, -ness, -ly, etc.
inflectional	(No instance)	-(e)s, -(e)d, -(e)n, -ing, -er, -est, etc.

Affixes attach to their stem either on the left periphery or on the right. In terms of the relative position to the stem to which they attach, an affix can be a prefix when in a pre-stem position, or a suffix when in a post-stem position. In addition to the positional classification, affixes can be classified according to their function they assume. If an affix attaches to a stem and makes the entire construct a new category, its function is derivational. If an affix attaches to a stem and it grammatically marks the stem, its function is inflectional. Thus, we have derivational prefix, derivational suffix, and inflectional suffix, but English lacks inflectional prefix. Examples of derivational prefixes are found in words like *de*part, *in*cline, *pre*pare, *sub*marine, *re*port, and others. As to the examples of suffixes and their peculiar characteristics, we will see a lot in the subsequent section.

> **N.B.** We make a fundamental difference between free form and bound form on the structural grounds. To say that a free form, or a word, stands alone means that we may have a pause or hesitation like *hmm* or *uh* or *umm* around a word, that we may modify a word, and that we may put a sentence stress on a word. But we do not expect such properties applied to bound morphemes. Thus, the example in (a) is fine but the one in (b) is disastrous.
>
> (a) Those *umm* undergraduates must submit the final compoSItion.
> (b)*Those   undergraduate-*umm*-s   sub-must-mit   the   compo-final-siTION.
>
> In (a), hesitation occurs right before the word *undergraduate*, but it doesn't between *graduate* and a suffix -*s* in (b). A modal auxiliary verb *must* comes before the verb *submit* and an adjective *final* modifies the noun *composition* in (a), but the former does not modify the bound form -*mit*, nor does the latter come in between bound forms *compo* and *sition* in (b). The sentence stress falls on the sentence final noun in the phrase *the final compoSItion* in (a), but it doesn't on the sentence final suffix -*TION* in (b).

Contracted form can be a reduced form of an auxiliary verb: a free form *will* will become a bound form *'ll* when attached to a subject noun phrase. Other contracted forms include *'d*, *'ve*, and others. See below:

(1) I *'ll* be here. You *'ll* be there. She *'ll* be away.
(2) I *'d* like to hear from you soon.
(3) I *'ve* learned a lot today.
(4) Mary *'s* an early riser and she *'s* already finished her homework.

N.B. The form *Mary's* in (4) is short for *Mary is*, which means that the main verb *be* behaves like auxiliary verbs when in certain syntactic conditions. Such cases include the following:
  (i) Negative-contraction
     "Mary *isn't* an early riser." vs. "Mary *won't* finish her homework."
  (ii) Subject-Aux Inversion
     "*Is* Mary an early riser?" vs. "*Will* Mary finish her homework?"
  (iii) Right-most remnant after predicative-phrase deletion
     [As answers to certain interrogatives]
     "Yes, she *is*." vs. "Yes, she *will*."

Bound base is bound because it does not stand alone, but it is not an affix because it has a substantive semantic content as does a content word. Once a bound base has a certain morpheme attached to it, this structure becomes a word. Examples are: *anim*-ate, *anim*-al, *path-ology*, *psycho-path*, etc. It is true that affix and bound base are behavioral look-alikes in that they are both bound, but they are distinct from each other for the following two reasons: one is, as indicated right at the beginning of this paragraph, that bound base has a unique substantive semantic content, which affix lacks indeed, and, the other is that affix does not have an affix attached to it in order for it to become a word, whereas bound base does so for sure. Examples of 'affixed affixes' like **pre-al*, **de-ness* and **sub-ment* are all ungrammatical. *Cranberry* morpheme is another type of bound base that is defined as such that it appears attached to only one stem in the language: *cran-* is the very morpheme of this type and it attaches only to the stem *berry*. But nowadays, in fact, we see words like *cranapple* and *cransauce*, so the morpheme *cran-* is no longer a *cranberry* morpheme in its strict sense.

Content words are said to constitute an open class because the category is open to newcomers, i.e. new words. For example, the category noun is open to such entirely new words as *motel, talkathon* and *selfie*. On the other hand, function words and bound forms are said to be types of closed class because their membership is, simply, fixed. English has no new conjunction, no new article, no new prefix, and so on.

> **N.B.** It might be claimed that the word *regarding*, for example, would be a new preposition derived from the verb *regard*. Or we may take *à la* (or *a la*) as a new preposition borrowed from French. If it is the case, then we may count the category preposition as an open class.

4.3.2   Derivational vs. Inflectional Suffix

In this section, we see in detail what derivational suffixes and inflectional suffixes are, how they are alike, and how they are different from each other.

First of all, derivational suffixes and inflectional suffixes are alike in that they are suffixes and are thus attached to their stem on the right periphery. Next, as to the issues of what they are and how they are different, see the table below and the following explanations.

Comparison of derivational and inflectional suffixes

	derivational suffix	inflectional suffix
(A) items	many	small fixed number
(B) resultant category	same or different	same
(C) meaning	irregular	regular
(D) stem	irregular	regular
(E) order	derivational suffix > inflectional suffix	
(F) class	open	closed
(G) number	multiple	one (cf. *children's*)
(H) concord	no	yes

(A) Items. There are abundantly many derivational suffixes in English. Words with derivational suffixes attached to their stems include: wash-*able*, lyric-*al*, appear-*ance*, pleas-*ant*, planet-*ary*, activ-*ate*, pesti-*cide*, demo-*crat*, king-*dom*, employ-*ee*, writ-*er*, hand-*ful*, child-*hood*, Dickens-*ian*, econom-*ic*, class-*ify*, elect-*ion*, fool-*ish*, real-*ism*, national-*ist*, regular-*ity*, mass-*ive*, American-*ize*, harm-*less*, slow-*ly*, develop-*ment*, loud-*ness*, danger-*ous*, member-*ship*, trouble-*some*, trick-*ster*, tru-*th*, gran-*ule*, home-*ward*, clock-*wise*, and witt-*y*, among others. On the other hand, there are a small finite number of inflectional suffixes in English. First, there is a Case marking suffix, but it only affects the forms of pronouns as in, for example, *I* (nominative case), which is analyzed as the combination of {1st Person, Singular} and {Nominative}. Similarly, *my* and *me* are the result of combining {1st Person, Singular} and {Genitive} on the one hand, and {1st person, Singular} and {Accusative/Dative} on the other, respectively. But note that full nouns are exceptionally affected only by the suffix {Genitive}, which will show up as -*'s*, as in *the witch's*, *the President's*, and *John's*. The allomorphs of -*'s* are all phonologically conditioned. The second type of inflectional suffix is {Plural}, which has both phonologically conditioned allomorphs and morphologically conditioned allomorphs as we have observed before. The third type relates to verbal inflection and we have four cases of it. Observe the table below:

Types of verbal inflection

verbal inflection	phonologically conditioned	morphologically conditioned
{3rd person, Sg, Pres}	/iz/ /s/ /z/	Rare (*is*, *has*, *does*, *says*)
{Past}	/id/ /t/ /d/	*took*, *sang*, *broke*, *went*, *cut*, etc.
{Past Participle}	/id/ /t/ /d/	*taken*, *sung*, *broken*, *gone*, *cut*, etc.
{Present Participle}	/iŋ/	(No instance)

The last type of inflectional suffix is that of comparison, i.e. degree suffix attached to adjectives and adverbs: comparative degree suffix -*er* as in *faster* and superlative degree suffix -*est* as in *fastest*.

(B) Resultant category. The function of a derivational suffix is such as to create a new word and, therefore, it may change the category of the entire word to which it attaches. For example, the verb *wash* becomes a new word of a different category, e.g. adjective, after the attachment of -*able*, i.e. *washable*, and the adjective *kind* likewise becomes the noun *kindness* after the suffix -*ness* gets attached to the adjective stem *kind*. But, in other cases, the resultant category remains the same. For example, the adjective *economic* remains the same category when it has the suffix *-al* attached to it, i.e. an adjective *economical*, and the noun *prince* becomes the noun *princess*, though the suffix *-ess* has caused the gender shift from male to female of the person it refers to. The inflectional suffix, on the other hand, does not change the category of the word it attaches to. For example, *book* is a noun just as *books* is, and *walk* is a verb just as *walked* is. No matter what inflectional suffix attaches, the resultant category of the word remains the same.

(C) Meaning. It is occasionally a somewhat notoriously irregular task to calculate the entire meaning of the word that has a derivational suffix attached to it. For example, the suffix *-ion* attaches to a verb and makes a new noun, but the resulting nouns show a variety of idiosyncratic semantic features. Observe the nouns below and their meanings.

(1)   [construct + ion] → *construction*: (a) 'act of constructing'
                                          (b) 'thing that is constructed'
       [destroy + ion] → *destruction*:   (a) 'act of destroying'
                                          (b) *'thing that is destroyed'
       [generate + ion] → *generation*:   (a) 'act of generating'
                                          (b) *'thing that is generated'
                                          (c) 'people with the same, or
                                              similar, backgrounds'
                                          (d) 'a span of 30 years'
       [produce + ion] → *production*:   (a) 'act of producing'
                                          (b) 'thing that is produced'
                                          (c) 'organization that engages
                                              in production, e.g. film
                                              production'
(2)   [complete + ion] → *completion*: "his completion of the task"
                                          means 'He has completed the
                                          task." (Active voice)
       [elect + ion] → *election*: "his election to the post" means 'He
                                     was elected to the post." (Passive
                                     voice)

It is not clear if there is any consistent way to formulate the aberrant types of semantic extension obliged by the attachment of the suffix *-ion*. It seems it is clear that there is nothing of this sort.

Another type of idiosyncrasy can be observed in the case of *-al*. Consider the adjectives below and their meanings.

(3)   [nature + al] → *natural*:   (a) 'of or relating to nature'
       [industry + al] → *industrial*: (a) 'of or relating to industry'
       [category + al] → *categorial*: (a) 'of or relating to category'
       [anecdote + al] → *anecdotal*: (a) 'of or relating to an anecdote'
                                                      (b) 'unreliable, not necessarily true'
       [proverb + al] → *proverbial*: (a) 'of or relating to a proverb'
                                                      (b) 'well known, stereotypical'

The last two adjectives have, in addition to (a) senses, (b) senses as well. This type of (b) senses could hardly be obtained through the regular semantic calculation by which we obtain (a) senses in all of the N-*al* adjectives above. We need one further step to arrive at (b) senses, which fact is sufficient to call the latter senses idiosyncratic.

Next, let us look at the following nouns and their meanings.

(4)   [grow + th] → *growth*: (a) 'process or state of growing'
       [steal + th] → *stealth*: (a) *'process or state of stealing'
                                             (b) 'secrecy'
                                             (c) 'cautious and secret manner'
       [true + th] → *truth*: (a) 'state of being true'
                                         (b) 'fact or belief that is true'
       [weal (well) + th] → *wealth*: (a) *'state of being well'
                                                     (b) *'thing or man that is well'
                                                     (c) 'state of being rich'

The suffix *-th* attaches to a verb or an adjective, and convert them to a noun. As illustrated above, both nouns *stealth* and *wealth* show idiosyncratic senses, i.e. senses (b) and (c) for *stealth* and sense (c) for *wealth*, but they lack the regular ones, i.e. sense (a) for *stealth* and senses (a) and (b) for *wealth*. A total irregularity!

Finally, we observe the idiosyncratic behaviors of the suffix *-able*. The basic semantic property of the suffix *-able* can be summarized as in (5):

(5)   The sentence with an adjective V-*able* has the following paraphrase relation between (a) and (b):

    (a)   This shirt is washable.

    (b)   This shirt can be washed.

But, there are a variety of cases where the paraphrase relation of (5) does not hold. For example, see (6) through (8):

(6)   (a)   *This car is washable.

       (b)   This car can be washed.

(7)   (a)   This book is readable.

       (b)   ?This book can be read.

(8)   (a)   This explanation is questionable.

       (b)   This explanation can be questioned.

The sentence (6a) is odd, because it is something you put on, e.g. clothing, that is washable. Both (7a) and (7b) are syntactically grammatical, but (7a) does not mean (7b), or for that matter, (7b) itself is semantically rather imperfect: (7a) means that the book is enjoyable and (7b) is fine if we add an adjunct phrase to it as in "This book can be read in an hour." Both (8a) and (8b) are grammatical but they can never be interpreted as the paraphrases of each other. In this way, derivational suffixes induce semantic irregularities.

    Contrary to the cases of derivational suffixes as we have seen above, the cases with inflectional suffixes are straightforward. No matter what stem an inflectional suffix attaches to, the entire meaning is invariably regular. For example, *walks* means the same type of meaning composite, i.e. {Walk} and {3rd person, Sg, Pres}, as *takes* does, i.e. the latter means the meaning composite of {Take} and {3rd person, Sg, Pres}. Similar relations hold between a verbal stem and other inflectional suffixes: both *ate* and *went* have the meaning of {Stem} and {Past}, both *broken* and *given* the meaning of {Stem} and {Past participle}, and both *running* and *speaking* the meaning of {Stem} and {Present participle}. And this type of regularity applies to other nominal, adjectival, and adverbial inflections. What is common in these semantic calculations is that the inflected words invariably mean {Stem} coupled with the meaning of an inflectional suffix that is incorporated into the entire word, and, therefore, the meaning of the entire word is transparent and regular.

    (D) Stem. There is no regular rule to decide which stem goes with which derivational suffix. A few examples will suffice to demonstrate this.

Observe the tables below:

What stem goes with -*ness*, -*ity*, and -*th*

Stem	-*ness*	-*ity*	-*th*
kind	kindness	*kindity	*knidth
able	*ableness	ability	*ableth
true	trueness	*tru(e)ity	truth

What stem goes with -*ic*, -*al*, and -*ical*

Stem	-*ic*	-*al*	-*ical*
economy	economic	*economial	economical
category	(*)categoric	categorial	categorical
nature	*naturic	natural	*naturical
ocean	oceanic	*oceanal	*oceanical

Types of stem to which -*able/-ible* attaches

Type of stem	Stem	Word with -*able/-ible* attached
transitive verb	wash	washable
transitive verb	convert	convertible
intransitive verb	laugh (at)	laughable
noun	peace	peaceable
noun	marriage	marriageable
noun	knowledge	knowledgeable
noun	fashion	fashionable
noun	size	sizable
non-existent word	hospit	hospitable
non-existent word	malle	malleable
non-existent word	prob	probable
non-existent word	vis	visible
non-existent word	poss	possible
non-existent word	permiss (< 'permit')	permissible
non-existent word	fease	feasible
non-existent word	fall (< 'fail')	fallible

The first and second tables are self-evident in that they show that there is no general rule to decide which suffix goes with which stem. The third table shows that while in the basic case, -able/-ible attaches to a transitive verb, in other cases, it may also attach to an intransitive verb, a limited group of nouns, and even to non-existent words. Thus, we may rightly say that it is absolutely irregular the way derivational suffixes attach to their host stems.

The inflectional suffixes, on the other hand, attach quite regularly to their stems: verbal inflectional suffixes attach to any verbs, nominal inflectional suffixes to any nouns, and adjectival or adverbial inflectional suffixes to any adjectives or adverbs, though, needless to say, we have to take into account such cases as stative verbs, uncountable nouns, ungradable adjectives and adverbs, and so on.

(E) Order. The derivational suffix comes inside and the inflectional suffix goes outside. For example, see the following examples:

(9)   industry] al] ize] s]
        *industry] al] ize] s] ation]
        industry] al] ize] ation] ist] s]
        *industry] al] ize] ation] ist] s] ic]
        industry] al] ize] ation] ist] ic]
        industry] al] ize] ation] ist] ic] al]
        industry] al] ize] ation] ist] ic] al] ity]
        industry] al] ize] ation] ist] ic] al] ity] es]

As can be seen from above, once an inflectional suffix attaches to a stem, no other derivational suffix will be added.

(F) Class. The derivational suffix attaches to a stem and makes the entire word an open class. In other words, derivational suffixes attach to a stem cumulatively, as we have observed in the previous subsection, i.e. '(E) Order.' The inflectional suffix, on the other hand, attaches just once. In other words, the class to which an inflectional suffix has attached is closed.

(10)   a.   John walks to school every day.
         b.   *John walksed to school yesterday.
         c.   John walked to school yesterday.

The ungrammaticality of (10b) is due to the illegal attachment of an additional inflectional suffix {Past} to the stem that has already one inflectional suffix {3rd person, Singular, Present} attached to it.

(G) Number. As we have observed in the two subsections above i.e. '(E) Order' and '(F) Class,' we can apply multiple derivational suffixes to a stem but, as for inflectional suffixes, we can apply only one in a single derivation of the word.

> **N.B.** Note that such inflectional suffixes as {Plural} and {Genitive} are rather exceptional in that they attach to a noun in this order. For example, expressions like "child*ren's* favorites," "all those boy*s'* playroom," and "the Jones' hometown" are all perfectly fine.

(H) Concord. Concord means a type of dependency among words in a sentence. It is also called Agreement. For example, in sentences like:

(11) a. The prince is coming.
      b. The princess is coming.
(12) a. The boy is coming.
      b. The boys are coming.

The derivational suffix *-ess* has no effect on the form of the verb *be* as shown in (11), but in (12), the inflectional suffix *-s* does affect the form of *be*. Thus, the verb agrees with the plurality of the subject and becomes *are* as shown in (12b). Therefore, the derivational suffix has nothing to do with Concord, but the inflectional suffix has much to do with it. Other cases of Concord relating to inflectional suffixes and their 'concordees' are shown below:

(13) John <u>is</u> eat<u>ing</u> a hamburger.
      John ate <u>two</u> hamburger<u>s</u>.
      John <u>has</u> tak<u>en</u> several courses.
      John <u>was</u> giv<u>en</u> a present.
      John is tall<u>er</u> <u>than Bill</u>. (Cf. *John is tall<u>er</u> <u>in the class</u>.)
      John is the tall<u>est</u> <u>in the class</u>. (Cf. *John is the tall<u>est</u> <u>than Bill</u>.)

In all of these cases above, inflectional suffixes have syntactic relations, or Concord, with elements outside the word they attach to.

So far, we have seen what derivational and inflectional suffixes are, and how they are different from each other. Before concluding this section, let us address the fundamental question: whether all those attributes ascribed to either derivational or inflectional suffixes are randomly allocated to one of these camps, or whether all those attributes naturally follow from a certain basic distinction we have between derivational and inflectional suffixes. The answer is such that there is indeed a basic distinction between derivational and inflectional suffixes and all those attributes are the natural outcome from this distinction. The distinction is: while derivational suffixes create new words, inflectional suffixes are syntactic markers attached to words to signal the syntactic relationships that hold between the words in a sentence. Put another way, derivational suffixes belong to Lexicon and, therefore, their attributes are lexical, or idiosyncratic and irregular, while inflectional suffixes belong to Syntax so that they enjoy syntactic regularity and are free from lexical idiosyncrasies. Readers are invited to examine this distinction and to determine how this distinction derives all these attributes.

> **N.B.** Derivational affixes can further be divided into two classes: Class I and Class II affixes. Class I affixes are, in a sense, more word-central, while Class II affixes are less so. The former are stress-determining, as in *concentr-ate*, *dominat-ion*, and *econom-ic*, while the latter are not, as in *natural-ness*, *effort-less*, and *independent-ly*. The former even attach to a smaller-than-a-word level morpheme (or a bound base), as in *anim-ate*, *domin-ion*, and *publ-ic*, while the latter attach to a full noun, as in the words above with the Class II suffixes.
>
> Class I affixes attach to a stem with a Class I affix already attached to it, as in *Christ-ian-ity*, *prduct-iv-ity*, and *industri-al-iz-ation-ist-ic-al-ity*. Class II affixes attach to a stem with a Class II affix already attached to it, as in *mind-ful-ness*, and *writ-er-hood*. Class II affixes also attach to a stem with a Class I affix already attached to it, as in *express-ive-ness*, and *express-ion-less*. But Class I affixes never attach to a stem with a Class II affix already attached to it, as the ungrammaticalness of **mind-ful-ity*, **brother-hood-ic*, and **warm-th-al* shows. (Note, just in passing, that the word 'ungrammaticalness' has the structure of [[[stem] cal Class I] ness Class II].)

4.4   Types of Word Formation: How New Words Are Formed

There are three major types of creating new words in English: one is to coin entirely new words, the second is to use existing words in an entirely new way, and the last is to apply word formation rules. And each of these major types has a variety of subtypes. In what follows, let us see them in detail.

4.4.1   Coining of New Words
4.4.1.1   Acronym

Acronym is a word coined by picking out the initial letters of the words that make a phrase. Examples are shown in (1):

(1)   Acronyms
      radar < radio detecting and ranging
      laser < light amplification by stimulated emission of radiation
      scuba < self-contained underwater breathing apparatus
      sonar < sound navigation and ranging
      zip (code) < zone improvement plan
      UNESCO < United Nations Educational, Scientific, and Cultural
                 Organization
      UNICEF < United Nations International Children's Emergency
                 Fund
      NATO < North Atlantic Treaty Organization
      ASEAN < Association of South East Asian Nations
      Nabisco < National Biscuit Company
      ESSO < Standard Oil

Acronyms shown above are all pronounced as if they were regular English nouns. But there is another type of words: they are initialisms. Initialisms are words spelled as a string of initial letters of the phrases to be abbreviated, just like acronyms are, but their pronunciation is different from that of acronyms. We pronounce the initial letters separately. Thus, USA, for example, is short for United States of America and pronounced as /júːèséi/, but not as */júːzə/. So these words are sometimes said to constitute another type of acronym. There are a lot more instances of this type, some of which are shown in (2):

(2)   Initialisms
      UK < United Kingdom (of Great Britain and Northern Ireland)
      BBC < British Broadcasting Corporation
      MVP <most valuable player
      VIP < very important person

TV < tele<u>v</u>ision
LED < <u>l</u>ight-<u>e</u>mitting <u>d</u>iode
CD < <u>c</u>ompact <u>d</u>isc
DVD < <u>d</u>igital <u>v</u>ideo<u>d</u>isc (or <u>d</u>igital <u>v</u>ersatile <u>d</u>isc)
VD < <u>v</u>enereal <u>d</u>isease
DOA < <u>d</u>ead <u>o</u>n <u>a</u>rrival
MYOB < <u>m</u>ind <u>y</u>our <u>o</u>wn <u>b</u>usiness
UFO < <u>u</u>nidentified <u>f</u>lying <u>o</u>bject (/jú:fòu/ is also possible)
ASAP < <u>a</u>s <u>s</u>oon <u>a</u>s <u>p</u>ossible (/éisæp/ is also possible)
AOL < <u>a</u>bsent <u>o</u>ver <u>l</u>eave (/éiɔl/ or /éiɔ:l/ is also possible)
AWL < <u>a</u>bsent <u>w</u>ith <u>l</u>eave (/ɔ:l/ is also possible)
AWOL < <u>a</u>bsent <u>w</u>ith<u>o</u>ut <u>l</u>eave (/éiwɔl/ or /éiwɔ:l/ is also possible)

Note that the last five initialisms, or words, may sometimes be pronounced as if they are single words, as shown above.

N.B. Initialisms are also called Alphabetisms.

4.4.1.2   Stump Word / Clipping or Abbreviation

Stump word is a word derived by way of Clipping or Abbreviation. There are four subtypes: (1) one is to retain the initial part of a word, (2) the second to retain the middle part, (3) the third to retain the final part, and (4) the last, somewhat rarely, to retain both the initial and the final part. Examples are:

(1)   ad < <u>ad</u>vertisement
Al < <u>Al</u>bert
Ben < <u>Ben</u>jamin
Bert < <u>Bert</u>ram
Cathy (Kathy) < <u>Cath</u>erine (<u>Kath</u>erine) + -<u>y</u> [diminutive]
cell < cell phone (< cellular phone)
Chris < <u>Chris</u>topher, <u>Chris</u>tabel, <u>Chris</u>tian(a)
deli < <u>deli</u>catessen
Eliza < <u>Eliza</u>beth
exam < <u>exam</u>ination
fan < <u>fan</u>atic
fax < <u>fa</u>c<u>s</u>imile

info < information
gas < gasoline
gym < gymnasium
lab < laboratory
math < mathematics
memo < memorandum
Mike < Michael
Nick < Nicholas
photo < photograph
piano < pianoforte
pop < popular (music)
prof < professor
Tom < Thomas
zoo < zoological garden

(2) flu < influenza
Liz < Elizabeth
fridge < refrigerator

(3) Bert < Albert, Herbert
Beth < Elizabeth
blog < web log
bus < omnibus
phone < telephone
van < caravan

(4) fancy < fantasy
pix < pictures
stats < statistics

4.4.1.3 Portmanteau Word or Blend / Blending

Portmanteau word is a word into which we put many parts that we have picked from some independent words. This process is called Blending, the outcome from which is the portmanteau word, or often called a blend. The typical way to form a portmanteau word is to pick the first half of a word and then to combine it with the second half of another word. Examples are:

brunch < breakfast + lunch
chunnel < channel + tunnel

genome < <u>gene</u> + chromos<u>ome</u>
mook < <u>m</u>agazine + b<u>ook</u>
motel < <u>motor</u> + ho<u>tel</u>
boatel < <u>boat</u> + hot<u>el</u>
smog < <u>smo</u>ke + f<u>og</u>
transistor < <u>trans</u>fer + res<u>istor</u>

N.B. There is a vehicle called *taximeter cabriolet* and we have a couple of new nouns out of this name through the interactions of 'Acronymization,' Clipping, and Blending. First, we have a shortened form *cab* from *cab<u>riolet</u>*, by way of Clipping. Now, *taximeter* and *cab* make *taximeter cab*, or we can say *taximeter cab<u>riolet</u>* is clipped into *taximeter cab*. Next, *tax<u>imeter</u> cab* becomes *taxicab*, with the underlined part suppressed. This process can be analyzed either as clipping the underlined middle part, or as 'acronymizing' the initial parts of the two constituents, i.e. *taxi* and *cab*. The latter process is a type of 'Acronymization' in the sense that initial parts of the constituents are picked up and are made into one. This process of 'Acronymization' seems operative in the formation of *sitcom* from *sit<u>uation</u> com<u>edy</u>*, for example. (So, we could argue that *taxicab* directly came from *tax<u>imeter</u> cab<u>riolet</u>* by way of 'Acronymization.') But we may say that it can also be a process of Blending in the sense that greater portions of the two constituents than initial letters, i.e. two phonological units or (mock-)morphemes, are combined to make a new word *taxicab*. Either way, we have *taxicab*. And finally, there spring out two new words, *taxi* and *cab*, out of this *taxicab*. They are the stump words derived by means of clipping either the first or the second half of *taxicab*. Thus we have the two clipped words, i.e. stump words: *taxi* and *cab*.

The word *email* was coined through a joint process of 'Acronymization,' Clipping and Blending/Compounding: *email* is obtained from *e<u>lectronic</u> mail* by clipping the underlined portion and then blending or compounding the leftovers. Notice that once we have *email*, the traditional postal mail is now sometimes called *snail mail*. This is like the process such that after the appearance of *electric guitar*, we are now obliged to call the traditional guitar *acoustic guitar*.

4.4.1.4   Metanalysis

Metanalysis is the process by which we misconstrue the given structure, 'underive' the derivational stages, and arrive at the 'would be' original structures. To see the point, study the table below:

Table of Metanalysis

Given structure	Misconstrual	New word coined
pease /pi:z/ (sg.)	pea (sg.) + /z/({Pl.})	pea (sg.)
sherris	sherri (sg.) + s ({Pl.})	sherry (sg.)
cheris(e)	cheri (sg.) + /z/ ({Pl.})	cherry (sg.)
a nadder	an adder	adder
a napron	an apron	apron
a numpire	an umpire	umpire
an ewt	a newt	newt
an ekename	a nickname	nickname
mine Ed(ward)	my Ned	Ned
mine Ol(iver)	my Noll	Noll
for then once	for the nonce	nonce
St. Audrey	(/sn/) + /tɔ:dri/	tawdry
hamburger	ham[meat] + burger[buns]	cheeseburger

The singular noun *pea* is the result of misconstruction of *pease* as the combination of {Pea} and {Plural}. Similarly, the singular *sherry* grew out of the misconstruction of *sherris* as {Sherry} and {Pl.}. The singular noun *cherry* likewise has its origin in the ME word *cherise*. The nouns *adder*, *apron*, and *umpire* are the result of misconstruing the original noun's word initial /n/ as the would-be preceding indefinite article's word final /n/. The nouns *newt*, *nickname*, *Ned*, *Noll*, and *nonce* are the result of misconstruing the preceding determiner's word final /n/ as this noun's word initial /n/. The adjective *tawdry* derives from the proper noun *St. Audrey* with the word final /t/ of *St.* ripped away and attached to the following noun word-initially. The word *cheeseburger* is the result of both misconstruction of *hamburger* as a compound of the structure [*ham* ("meat") + *burger* ("buns with patty and/or some other stuff in between")] and replacement of *ham* with *cheese* in this structure. And we sometimes hear new nouns like *fishburger*, *tunaburger*, *chickenburger*, and even *healthy burger* and *rice burger*. In this way, Metanalysis creates new words idiosyncratically and at the same time quite regularly.

4.4.1.5   Backformation

Backformation is a special case of Metanalysis. Generally speaking, we derive a new word by attaching a derivational suffix to a stem. But when we misconstrue the given structure as the result of attaching a derivational suffix to a 'would be' stem, the 'would be' stem comes to be regarded as a new word. This process is called Backformation. Examples abound. See the table below:

Table of Backformation

Given structure	Misconstruction	New word coined
burglar	burgle + -ar /ɚ/	burgle
peddler	peddle + -er	peddle
editor	edit + -or	edit
escalator	escalate + -or	escalate
zipper	zip + -er	zip
typewriter	typewrite + -er	typewrite
babysitter	babysit + -er	babysit
aviation	aviate + -ion	aviate
demarcation	demarcate + -ion	demarcate
television	televise + -ion	televise
contraception	contracept + -ion	contracept
backformation	backform + -ation	backform
window-shopping	window-shop + -ing	window-shop
air-conditioning	air-condition + -ing	air-condition
spoon-fed	spoon-feed + {p.p.}	spoon-feed
taxonomy	taxon + omy	taxon

The verbs *burgle, peddle, edit, escalate, zip, typewrite,* and *babysit* are the result of misconstruction of the respective nouns as the composite of "{verbal stem} + {er/or}." (The word *escalator* is a blend from *escalade* and *elevator*.) The verbs *aviate, demarcate, televise, contracept,* and *backform* are the result of misconstruction of the respective nouns as the composite of "{verbal stem} + {ion/ation}." The verbs *window-shop* and *air-condition* are the result of misconstruction of the respective nouns as the composite of "{verbal stem} + {ing}." The verb *spoon-feed* is the result of misconstruction of the past-participial adjective *spoon-fed* as the composite of "{verbal stem} + {Past participle}." The noun *taxon* is the intentional result of misconstruction of the noun *taxonomy* as the composite of *taxon* + *(n)omy*. The latter process is analogy motivated by the relationship between *etymon* and *etymology*, *etymology* being the word that ultimately goes back to Greek and is a compound composed of *etymon* and *ology*. And the noun *pea*, which is mentioned in the previous section, is also a backformed singular noun by leaving aside the 'would be' inflectional plural suffix *-se* /z/ from *pease*.

4.4.1.6   Loanword / Borrowing

Loanword is a word borrowed from the vocabulary of a foreign language and now is part of the English vocabulary. English has a great number of Loanwords from around the world, and below is only a small part of them.

Table of Loanwords and their origins

Original language	Loanword
French	critique, bourgeois, rouge, silhouette, impasse
Italian	opera, piano, sonata, spaghetti, graffiti
German	hamburger, frankfurter, blitz, biotope, gestalt, festschrift, zinc, Zeppelin
Spanish	paella, salsa
Chinese	kung fu, kung pao (chicken), Taoism, Confucianism
Arabic	alcohol, alkali, sheikh
Japanese	karate, judo, Zen, hibachi, hinoki, sashimi, sushi, tofu, soy, hibakusha
Tahitian	tattoo
Tongan	taboo

In English, there are pairs of words called 'doublets.' Doublets are a pair of words that have the same origin but have arrived at the English vocabulary by taking different routes from each other. In this sense, doublets are a type of loanwords. Below is a short list of doublets:

camera – chamber
catch – chase
channel – canal
fashion – faction
fragile – frail
polite – polish
sure – secure

N.B. It is true that there are many doublets that are loanwords, but there are some that are not. For example, PE *ride* and PE *road* have the same Germanic origin and go ultimately back to OE *rīdan* (PE *ride* < OE *rīdan* ('ride'); PE *road* < OE *rād* ('riding') < OE *rīdan* ('ride')). Thus the pair of PE *ride* and PE *road* are doublets but they themselves are not loanwords. As for the pair of PE *father* and PE *Pope/papal*, while they have the same IE origin, the former is an OE descendant and the latter came from Latin.

In English, we also have 'triplets.' Triplets are the three words that have the same origin but took different routes to reach the English language. Examples are:

cap – cape – chapel
capital – cattle – chattel (N.B. The six words above are etymologically
                                    related in a certain way.)
card – cartel – chart
coy – quiet – quit
shirt – short – skirt

4.4.1.7   Loan Translation or Calque

Loan translation or Calque is to translate a foreign phrase into English in a word-for-word manner with the original syntactic construction of the phrase intact. While Loanwords have exactly the same forms as they have in their respective original languages, Loan translations, i.e. words brought to English through Loan translation, consist of the English words that correspond to the foreign words that constitute the original construction. Examples are found in the table below:

Table of Loan translations

Original language	Word (phrase) to be borrowed	Loan translation
German	Lehnwort	loanword
German	Vorwort	foreword
German	Übermensch	superman
French	secrétaire général	secretary general
French	sans faille	without fail
French	faire une requeste	make a request
French	Il va sans dire que....	It goes without saying that....
Spanish	demarcación	demarcation
Chinese	haojiu, bujian.	Long time, no see.

4.4.1.8   Invention or Root Creation

Invention, or Root creation, means to create an entirely new root on which certain derivational and/or inflectional processes may apply. There are a variety of means to create new roots. Below is a list of only a few of them.

Table of invented roots or words

Invented root or word	Origin or how it was invented or created
abracadabra	magic word
gas	from Greek *khaos* 'chaos'
bowwow	sound symbolism (onomatopoeia)
cuckoo	sound symbolism (onomatopoeia)
twitter	sound symbolism (onomatopoeia)
choo-choo (train)	sound symbolism (onomatopoeia)
zipper	sound symbolism (onomatopoeia)
love ("zero")	folk etymology
kangaroo	folk etymology
braille	Louis Braille

sandwich	John Mongtagu, the Fourth Earl of Sandwich
shrapnel	Henry Shrapnel
diesel	Rudolf Diesel
volt	Alessandro Volta
ampere	André-Marie Ampère
farad	Michael Faraday
joule	James Prescott Joule
newton	Isaac Newton
watt	James Watt
boycott	Charles C. Boycott
derrick	Derrick
maverick	Samuel Augustus Maverick

The word *abracadabra* is a magic word and the word *gas* is based on the Greek word *khaos* 'chaos.' Both are entirely new inventions in the English vocabulary. The words *bowwow, cuckoo, twitter, choo-choo* and *zipper* are instances of onomatopoeia, namely, the result of sound symbolism. The origin of the word *love*, in the sense of "zero" in tennis, can be explained in terms of folk etymology. One theory ascribes its origin to a French word *l'œuf*, which means "the egg," because an egg's shape has a close resemblance to the number "zero." And the French word *l'œuf* sounds like Englsih 'love.' Therefore, *love* means "zero." There is another theory such that the word *love*, meaning "zero or nothing," comes from the saying, "we play for love, but not for money." In this phrase, *love* is equivalent to "zero." The origin of *kangaroo* clearly lies in some of the aboriginal languages in Australia, but it is still unclear what the exact origin is. One says that the noun *kangaroo* just comes from the name of an aboriginal animal in Australia. Another says that it comes from the words uttered by the aborigines when the Westerners asked them what they would call those jumping animals: they said *kangaroo*, which is said to have meant "I don't know" or "I don't understand you" in their native tongue. Either way, *kangaroo* has a folk etymological story. The words *braille, sandwich, shrapnel, diesel, volt, ampere, farad, joule, newton,* and *watt* all come from the proper names of the inventors or scientists of the field. The word *boycott* comes from the name of an Irish land agent. The word *derrick*, a kind of crane to lift heavy objects, comes from a name of a hangman in London. The word *maverick*, meaning "a calf without a mark of a branding iron on it" or "an independent person who refuses to follow the rules of others," comes from the name of a politician who is also an owner of a large herd of cattle in the U.S.

4.4.2   New Use of Existing Words
4.4.2.1   Metaphorical Extension
In general terms, Metaphorical extension is a shift in the form-meaning relationship. There are two types of it: metonymy and synecdoche. Metonymy is a shift of meaning of the given form to a meaning that has a close relationship with the original meaning of the form. Synecdoche is also a shift of meaning that has to do with the reversal of part-whole relation. Some examples are given in the tables below:

Instances of metonymy

Given form	Original meaning	Shifted meaning
cradle	"a baby's bed on rockers"	"birth"
grave	"the ground where the dead are buried"	"death"
crown	"an ornamental headdress worn by a king"	"king" "the highest position"
head	"the topmost part of a body"	"the highest or most important position"
brain	"an organ in the head"	"intelligence" "knowledgeable person"
heart	"an organ of a body"	"the center" "the mental state of a person"
chair	"a piece of furniture for sitting"	"the person in charge of a meeting"
department	"a divided part in a building"	"a division in an institution"

Washington	"where the US government is"	"the US government"
air<u>port</u>	"where ships arrive and leave"	"where airplanes arrive and leave"
space<u>ship</u>	"a vessel on the water"	"a vessel in the space"
mouse	"a rodent"	"a tool for the computer the shape of a mouse"
web	"a spider's construct"	"computers' network"
virus	"cause of animals' diseases"	"cause of computers' corruption"
vaccine	"stuff to cure a disease"	"stuff to restore the lost function of the computers"

Instances of synecdoche

Given form	Original meaning	Shifted meaning
sail	"that part of a ship that catches the wind"	"a ship"
blade	"the cutting part of a sword"	"a sword"
spring	"one of the four seasons"	"one year"
head	"the topmost part of a body"	"a person (when enumerating people)"
creatures	"all the living organisms"	"humans"
universe	"cosmos"	"all the (earthly) world"
the State	"the land, people, and its institution"	"the government"
<u>World</u> Series	"all the global areas"	"the USA and Canada"
to fly to <u>London</u>	"all the area of (Greater) London"	"Heathrow Airport"

Instances of both metonymy and synecdoche above are, it seems, self-evident, but, for a few cases, it may help to understand the words in question better if we give some illustrations. First, we see words regarding metonymy. In the popular phrase "from the cradle to the grave," which means "all through one's life," the meaning of *cradle* is shifted from "a baby's bed on rockers" to "birth," and that of *grave* is likewise shifted from "the ground where the dead are buried" to "death." The word *brain(s)* means "intelligence" when we say "He has no brains," and it means "a knowledgeable person" when we say "He was the brains of the group." Thus, the shifted meanings are all closely related to the original meanings.

Next, we see words regarding synecdoche. The noun *spring* means "year" when used in such a sentence as "This is the third spring ever since I began teaching at Brookfield school." Here in this sentence, *spring* is part of a year and in fact means "year." The noun *head* means "person" when used in such a sentence as "At the restaurant, they paid 20 dollars a head." Here *head* is part of a person and in fact means "a person." Note also the phrase *per capita* "for each person, individually," which is originally a Latin phrase and literally means "by heads." A woman who has won the title "Miss Universe" should, in fact, be the best woman in the world, rather than in the cosmos. Here, the earthly world is part of the cosmos, and the word for the cosmos '*universe*' means the part of it. When we say "John flew to London from New York," John actually arrived at the place called "Heathrow Airport." Here the area of *London* has Heathrow Airport as part of it, and it in fact means "Heathrow Airport." Thus, synecdoche is a type of part-whole reversal in semantic reference.

There is a special kind of metaphorical extension called synesthesia, or synaesthesia, which literally means "feeling two or more senses jointly." This applies to the adjective *cool*, for example. We say "cool weather" meaning that of low temperature. We also say "cool voice" meaning that of sedative, low tone. And we even say "That was cool!" meaning "That was attractive, enjoyable, and a lot of fun!" It is notable that the basic structure of synesthesia, i.e. how the sense-perceptive meanings of an adjective extend, is such that the basic sense one feels is something affected by the concrete objects and then is extended to a more abstract, even emotional, sense. As an illustration of synesthesia with examples, observe the table below:

Synesthesia illustrated

Adjective	←Concrete		[sense organs (receptors)]			Abstract→
	skin	mouth	nose	eyes	ear	brain
cool	*cool* weather	*cool* water		*cool* color	*cool* voice	That's *cool*!
warm	*warm* weather	*warm* coffee		*warm* color	*warm* voice	*warm* welcome
light	a *light* bag	*light* taste		*light* green	*light* music	*light* entertainment
hot	*hot* weather	*hot* and spicy curry	*hot* smell of cordite	*hot* spot	*hot* music	*hot* issue
sweet		*sweet* fruit	*sweet* scent	*sweet* smile	*sweet* music	*sweet* memories
pungent		*pungent* flavor	*pungent* aroma			*pungent* wit
blue				*blue* sky	*blue* note	*blue* Monday
grave					*grave* music	*grave* crisis
social						*social* activities

We can easily observe the general implicational tendency in the table of synesthesia above: once an adjective has a sense-perceptive meaning, it also has other meanings that are more abstract than the original one. Thus, *cool* is a feeling that we perceive through the skin, so it has other meanings that we perceive through the more abstract channels of sense organs (receptors). And on the other end of the scale rests the most sophisticated type of adjective: it is, for example, *social* that has only one meaning. The adjective *social* has the meaning obtained through the most abstract channel, i.e. brain, but has no other meanings of less abstract sense- receptors'.

N.B. The topics in this subsection are about metaphorical extension. But notice that there is a notion, or a term, that happens to be related to the adjective *metaphorical*: it is "metaphor." Metaphor is a technical term in rhetoric that signifies a type of figure of speech where a word for something is used to represent another thing suggesting a kind of similarity between them. For example, "Life is a journey." Here, "life" is likened to "a journey." There is also another technical term in rhetoric: it is "simile." Simile is a figure of speech of another kind where a word for something is used to represent another thing with the aid of such words as *like* or *as*. For example, "Life is like a journey. / Life is sometimes as fierce as a journey in the storm." Here, "life" is likened to "a journey" in the former example, and it is likened to "a journey in the storm" in the latter.

4.4.2.2   Generalization or Broadening

By Generalization, or Broadening, we mean the phenomena where the given form acquires a broader area of semantic coverage than before. This is the case especially when we observe the semantic broadening from a historical point of view. Examples are found in the table below:

Generalization of meaning

Original word and its meaning	PE word and its broadened meaning
OE *brid* "chick (young bird)"	PE *bird* "bird in general"
ME *carrien* "to carry by a cart"	PE *carry* "to carry (by whatever means)"
ME *arrive* "to reach the shore"	PE *arrive* "to reach any destination"

Thus, these words once had specific meanings but now they have general, broadened meanings.

> **N.B.** OE *brid* has undergone the process called Metathesis, which has the effect of having the adjacent two segments, i.e. sounds, interchanged. The segments *r* and *i* in OE *brid* got interchanged, and now we have PE *bird*. Other instances of Metathesis include ModE *clasp* (< ME *clapse*) and ModE *third* (< ME *thridde*).

4.4.2.3   Specialization or Narrowing

By Specialization, or Narrowing, we mean the phenomena where the given form acquires a narrower area of semantic coverage than before. This is the case especially when we observe the semantic narrowing from a historical point of view. Examples are found in the table below:

Specialization of meaning

Original word and its meaning	PE word and its narrowed meaning
OE *mete* "food in general"	PE *meat* "the edible part of an animal's flesh"
OE *dēor* "any quadruped animal"	PE *deer* "that type of quadruped with antlers"
OE *hund* "dog in general"	PE *hound* "hunting dog"
OE *fugol* "bird in general"	PE *fowl* "domesticated bird"
OE *steorfan* "to die"	PE *starve* "to die of hunger"
ME *poyson* (or *puison*) "a drink or potion"	PE *poison* "(a specific type of drink, namely) poison"
ME *garl* (or *gerl*) "child of either sex"	PE *girl* "young woman"

Thus, these words once had broader meanings but now they have specific, narrowed meanings.

4.4.2.4   Reversal

By Reversal, we mean the type of semantic change where the given form acquires the meaning that has got driven to the reverse end of the vector of the original meaning. There are two cases of semantic reversal: Amelioration and Pejoration. See the tables below for examples.

Amelioration of meaning

Original word and its meaning	PE word and its ameliorated meaning
OE *cniht* "boy, servant"	PE *knight* "honorable gentleman"
OE *stigweard* "household keeper"	PE *steward* "head servant, butler"
ME *ministre* "servant"	PE *minister* "head of a government department"
ME *chaunceler* "door keeper, lawcourt secretary"	PE *chancellor* "head of various types of institutions"

Pejoration of meaning

Original word and its meaning	PE word and its pejorated meaning
OE *cnafa* "boy, servant"	PE *knave* "scoundrel, rogue"
ME *wench* "child, young girl"	PE *wench* "prostitute"
ME *vilein* "feudal serf"	PE *villain* "scoundrel, rogue"
ME *undertaker* "one who undertakes a task"	PE *undertaker* "funeral director"
ME *entercours* "dealings between persons"	PE *intercourse* "sexual intercourse"
ModE *queere* "strange"	PE *queer* "homosexual"

Thus, ameliorated words have got their original meanings promoted, and, conversely, pejorated ones have got their original meanings downgraded.

> **N.B.** According to the *Oxford English Dictionary (OED) Online*, an online dictionary by Oxford University Press, the adjective *queer* was once pejorated and still it is, but then it is occasionally ameliorated. *OED Online* says:
>
> (i) Although originally chiefly derogatory (and still widely considered offensive, esp. when used by heterosexual people), from the late 1980s it began to be used as a neutral or positive term (originally of self-reference, by some homosexuals; cf. Queer Nation *n.* and also quot. 1952[2] at queer *n.[2]* 2) in place of *gay* or *homosexual*, without regard to, or in implicit denial of, its negative connotations. In some academic contexts it is the preferred adjective in the study of issues relating to non-traditional ideas of sexuality and gender (cf. *queer theory n.* at Compounds 2). [*OED Online*, s.v. queer, *adj.*1 (Accessed Nov 16, 2022)]
>
> (ii) **3.b.**
> **1990 –**
> Of a person: having a sexual or gender identity that does not correspond to, or that challenges, traditional (esp. heteronormative) ideas of sexuality or gender. Also: of, relating to, or associated with such people or identities; concerned with such people or identities.
> Although the term is recorded earlier in the context of gay rights activism (see e.g. quots. 1970, 1987), this sense emerged alongside **queer theory** *n.* in the early 1990s. Originally used provocatively by LGBT activists such as members of the Queer Nation organization, it

was intended to convey an assertive and radical alternative to conventional notions of sexuality and gender as part of a wider campaign in response to the AIDS crisis. The term may still be considered controversial due to association with pejorative uses of sense 3a.

Queer may be used as an umbrella term similar to *LGBT*, *LGBTQIA*, etc., to include various specific sexual or gender identities. [*OED Online*, s.v. *queer*, ADJECTIVE[1] (Accessed March 24, 2024)]

4.4.3   Word Formation Rules
4.4.3.1   Affixation

We apply a derivational affix to a stem, and we have a new word or a new stem. This process is what we call affixation. As affixes are either prefixes or suffixes, we have two types of derivational affixes: derivational prefixes and derivational suffixes. Examples of prefixation and suffixation abound in the previous sections. We note here the notion of hierarchy in the lexical structure of the word that has got more than one affix attached to it. The basic principle is (1) below:

(1)   Attach one affix at a time.

The principle (1) means that we cannot attach two, or more, affixes to a stem simultaneously. For example, the structure of *enrichment* is (2a) but not (2b):

(2)   a.   [[en [rich]] ment]
     b. *[en [rich] ment]

The structure of *unfriendliness* is likewise (3a) but not (3b), nor (3c):

(3)   a.   [[un [[friend] ly]] ness]
     b. *[[un [friend] ly] ness]
     c. *[un [[[friend] ly] ness]]

Similarly, the structures for *unforgettable* and *unpassivizability* are (4a) and (4b), respectively:

(4)   a.   [un [[forget] able]]
     b.   [[un [[[passive] ize] able]] ity]

Thus, a word with multiple morphemes has a hierarchical lexical structure and this lexical structure has the property of binary-branching.

4.4.3.2   Compounding

Compounding is a process to derive a new word, i.e. a compound, by putting two elements together, e.g. X and Y, and the resultant category is a lexical category Z. Thus, a compound is of the form [X Y$_Z$]. A compound has unique characteristics regarding its syntax, phonology, and semantics.

> **N.B.** By 'lexical category,' we mean such categories as noun, verb, adjective, adverb, and preposition here in the description of morphology. But, later in the description of syntax (Chapter V), specifically in the description about X-bar theory, we tentatively assume that a lexical category is noun, verb, adjective, and no other.

First, let us see syntactic characteristics. In the compound of the form [X Y$_Z$], the right-hand element Y serves as the head of the entire compound. Head determines the category of the entire construction. Thus, [[green $_A$] [house $_N$] $_N$] is a compound noun that means a kind of house that keeps plants growing, and the head of the compound, i.e. the noun *house*, determines the category of the entire compound *greenhouse* such that *greenhouse* is a noun because the head of the compound, i.e. *house*, is a noun. Similarly, *ice cold* is a compound adjective because *cold* is an adjective, *overthrow* is a compound verb because *throw* is a verb, and *into* is a compound preposition because *to* is a preposition.

Another syntactic characteristic is that a compound, no matter how long it is, has a binary branching structure, which is a natural outcome of the basic structure of the compound [X Y$_Z$]. For example, observe the hierarchical structures shown in (1):

(1) a. [[towel] [rack]]
      b. [[towel rack] [designer]]
      c. [[[towel rack] designer] [contest]]
      d. [[[[towel rack] designer] contest] [application form]]

Here, (1a) has a binary branching structure and (1a) itself is a constituent. The latter constituent is the left-hand element of the compound (1b), so (1b) is also binary branching. The new constituent (1b) is the left-hand element of (1c), and (1c) itself is a constituent. We put (1c) and another compound [application form] together to derive a new compound (1d), which is, needless to say, a binary-structured compound.

Next, we see phonological characteristics, specifically those of compound nouns. In the compound noun of the structure [X Y_N], the primary stress falls on the left-hand element X, which fact is in sharp contrast with the phonological facts about the nominal phrasal categories. Here, we tentatively make a notational innovation such that a simple noun is labeled as N, and a nominal phrase that is larger than N but smaller than NP (Noun Phrase) is labeled as N'. (For further details, see Chapter V on Syntax.) Thus, from both the syntactic and the phonological points of view, the differences between the two constructs, i.e. [X Y_N] and [X $Y_{N'}$], are noteworthy. Specifically, the syntactic category of the compound noun [X Y_N], e.g. *greenhouse*, is, needless to say, N (= noun), while that of the phrasal category [X $Y_{N'}$], e.g. *(a) green house*, is N'. The stress pattern of the compound noun is *gréenhòouse*, while that of the phrasal category is *(a) gréen hóuse* or *(a) grèen hóuse*. General phonological tendency is therefore phrased as (2):

(2)   General stress patterns in N and N'
       In nouns, the primary stress goes leftward, while in nominal phrases, it falls on the head noun.

The general guideline (2) applies to many nouns and nominal phrases. Hence, we have such contrasts as [*bláckbòard* $_N$] vs. a [*bláck bóard* $_{N'}$], *the* [*White Hòuse* $_N$] vs. a [*white hóuse* $_{N'}$], [*bláckbìrd* $_N$] vs. a [*bláck bírd* $_{N'}$], [*Bígfòot* $_N$] vs. a [*bíg fóot* $_{N'}$], and [*Lónghòrn* $_N$] vs. a [*lóng hórn* $_{N'}$].

Lastly, we see the semantic characteristics of compound nouns as compared with those of nominal phrases. Compound nouns are essentially semantically irregular, or opaque, while nominal phrases are semantically regular, or transparent. For example, *greenhouse* is not necessarily a green house and, in fact, there are many *white greenhouses*. On the other hand, *(a) green house* should always be green, and therefore *(a) white green house* is ungrammatical or contradictory.

Another characteristic of compound nouns is that there are basically two types of compound centricity: endocentric and exocentric. The former is such that compounds have their own heads, both syntactically and semantically. For example, the head of *greenhouse* is *house*, both syntactically and semantically. Thus, *greenhouse* is an endocentric compound. On the other hand, certain compounds, e.g. *Bigfoot*, do not have a head: *Bigfoot* is by no means a type of foot, but is an ape-like creature with big feet. Thus, *Bigfoot* is an exocentric compound.

Many examples could be adduced to demonstrate these types of semantic opaqueness, or irregularity, of the compound nouns. Thus, when interpreting the compound noun of the form [X Y$_N$], you cannot unambiguously determine the type of semantic relationship that X and Y have, nor can you uniquely specify the type of centricity that the compound assumes. See below for a very small part of examples in the huge body of English compound nouns:

Opaqueness in the compound noun of the form [X Y$_N$]

Compound: [X Y$_N$]	Semantic relationship between X and Y	Type of centricity
White House	The U.S. president's official Y (*house*) that is X (*white*)	Endocentric
greenhouse	Y (*house*) that keeps something X (*green*)	Endocentric
handbag	X (*hand*) grabs and carries Y (*bag*)	Endocentric
handcuff	Y (*cuffs*) secure wrists (near X)	Endocentric
handrail	X (*hand*) holds on to Y (*rail*) that is fixed to the wall	Endocentric
airbag	X (*air*) is in Y (*bag*)	Endocentric
airbus	Y (*bus*) flies in X (*air*)	Endocentric
school bus	Y (*bus*) goes to and from X (*school*)	Endocentric
Bigfoot	A large hairy ape-like creature has X (*big*) Y (*feet*)	Exocentric
bigwig	Important person, formerly wearing a X (*big*) Y (*wig*)	Exocentric
big mouth	Man who *talks* (Y-like) *a lot* (X-like): boaster	Exocentric
Longhorn	A type of cattle have X (*long*) Y (*horns*)	Exocentric
horseshoe	X (*horse*) puts on Y (*shoe*)	Endocentric
alligator shoe(s)	Y (*shoe(s)*) made of X's (*alligator's*) hide	Endocentric
honeybee	Y (*bee*) collects X (*honey*)	Endocentric

honeycomb	Bees make a structure Y (*comb*) to store X (*honey*)	Endocentric
honeymoon	Sweet (X-like) month (Y-like) after marriage	Exocentric
honeytrap	Attractive (X-like) agent conducts a stratagem Y (*trap*)	Endocentric

In addition to the examples in the above table, we have many compounds of other categorial statuses: verbal, adjectival, adverbial, and prepositional compounds. Examples are *overcome*, *seasick*, *outdoors*, and *without*, respectively. And the semantic opaqueness will apply to all of these cases, too.

There is another type of compounds, often called "synthetic compounds," as opposed to those like *greenhouse*, which are called "primary compounds," or sometimes "root compounds." Synthetic compounds have as their heads deverbal nouns, i.e. nouns derived from verbs. Thus, they are of the form either [[X $_N$] [V-*er* $_N$] $_N$] or [[X $_N$] [V-*ing* $_N$] $_N$]. Examples of synthetic compounds are as follows:

(3)   truck driver, air compressor, music lover
(4)   car driving, thesis writing, mountain climbing

There is a noteworthy syntactic characteristic about synthetic compounds: the left-hand element of the compound is necessarily a direct object of the verb from which the right-hand nominal element is derived. Thus, while we have *charity giving*, we never have *orphan giving. This is because *charity* in *charity giving* is a direct object of the verb *give* but *orphan* in *orphan giving an indirect object of the same verb. Note also that compounds like *ice skater* and *handwriting* are, therefore, not synthetic compounds, but rather they are primary (or root) compounds.

> **N.B.** Or it may well be the case that *ice skater* is grammatical because *ice* is the first nominal that comes after the verb *skate*, as in "Mary *skates* on the *ice*." Likewise, *handwriting* is grammatical because of the phrase "Mary always *writes* with her left *hand*."

4.4.3.3   Conversion
Conversion is a process in which an arbitrary structure X is converted

to a new lexical category Y with the internal structure of X intact. In other words, the syntactic category X of the structure in question is relabeled as Y without any change in its internal constituency. This process is roughly formulated as in (1):

(1)   Conversion
[ABC $_X$] ➔ [ABC $_Y$],
where ABC is a non-null arbitrary string of words and/or grammatical formatives, and Y is a lexical category.

N.B. There are certain exceptional cases where the string ABC does not form a constituent: the prenominal *believe-it-or-not* in "believe-it-or-not stories" is a quoted nonconstituent but acts as a single adjective that modifies the noun that follows, and the prenominal *never-before-seen* in "the never-before-seen photograph" is likewise an adjective of the non-constituent origin.

Examples of Conversion are shown in the tables below:

Table of lexical Conversion

Category change	Examples
V ➔ N	report, support, supply, hunt, trust, try, go, take
V ➔ A	go ("Thunderbirds are go!")
A ➔ N	English, Japanese, American, characteristic, final, verbal, nominal, representative
A ➔ V	narrow, warm, cool
N ➔ V	form, box, circle, bat, pin, hint, ink, seat, sentence, host, house, microwave
Adv ➔ A	out, off
P ➔ A	in, on
P ➔ Adv	in, on
N ➔ P	inside, outside
Adv ➔ P	out, off

Table of phrasal Conversion

Category change	Examples
N' → N	black hole, black market, black box, Black Friar, blue Monday, red tape, white paper, New York, Long Island
V' → N	check(-)in, check(-)out, checkup, makeup, pin(-)up, handout
PP → N	afternoon, underground, overnight
PP → A	undercover, in(-)depth, underground, overnight
PP → Adv	underground, overnight
PP → P	onboard

Notice that since Conversion only relabels the topmost syntactic category of the host constituent and does not affect its internal structure, the stress pattern anchored in the structure remains the same. For example, both the verbal and nominal counterparts of *report* have the same stress pattern as in *repórt*, both the phrasal and the nominal counterparts of *black hole* have the same stress pattern as in *bláck hóle*, and so on. This is in sharp contrast with the case of nominal compounds. Observe the stress contrast between the phrase-turned converted nominal *Nèw Yórk* and the nominal compound *Néwark*. The former retains the phrasal stress pattern, while the latter does have the purely nominal stress pattern found characteristically in compound nouns. Other contrasts include *Lòng Ísland* vs. *Lóng Bèach*, *àfternóon* vs. *áftermàth*, *bláck bóx* vs. *bláckbòard*, *bláck márket* vs. *bláckmàil*, *blúe Mónday* vs. *blúe nòte*, *déadwéight* vs. *déadlìne*, and *déad spáce* vs. *déad spòt*. But there are two exceptional cases of converted nominals: one is the case of "V' → N," i.e. *chéck(-)ìn* and others, and the other is the case of "PP → N," i.e. *úndergròund*, *óvernìght* and others. All instances of these two cases are, in fact, simultaneously affected by Conversion and Leftward stress shift rule in nouns (cf. (2) in §4.4.3.2). But there is another possible treatment regarding these two cases. See the following subsection on Nominalization, i.e. §4.4.3.4, for the alternative view.

Since the converted structures are by definition all lexical categories, we expect there should be semantic idiosyncrasy, or opaqueness, in these converted cases, as there is in the compound noun cases, or for that matter, as in the cases of derived nominals with derivational suffixes. And the fact is, it is the case, indeed. Thus, converted nouns can be either endocentric or exocentric. For example, a *black box* is a type of box, so this is an endocentric nominal. However, there are as many converted exocentric nominals. For example, *red tape*, an excessive state of bureaucracy, is exocentric, just as *white paper* is, the latter being a government's official report. Semantic opaqueness may be observed in other converted categories. *Japanese* can be a language, a person, or people, while *American* only means a person and *English* only means a language, though *the English* collectively means people. You can make up almost anything you can, but the meaning of the noun *makeup* is confined to something related to either cosmetics, construction, or some supplementary activities. As another illustration of idiosyncrasy, you can be "*on board* a ship, a train, or an airplane," but you cannot be "**on board* the wood floor," nor can a book be "**on board* the shelf." In this way, the meaning, or the usage, of the converted lexical items is irregular in many ways.

4.4.3.4   Nominalization

In general, Nominalization means to form nouns or nominals from various sources of different structural properties, e.g. by attaching a derivational affix to a stem ("kind*ness*"), attaching a gerundive ending to a verb ("study*ing*"), forming a *for-to* construction ("*For* us *to* study linguistics is fun!"), forming *that* construction ("*That* the earth is round is a self-evident fact nowadays"), and so on. However, in this subsection in the chapter on Morphology, we will confine ourselves to the two types of Nominalization. One is Nominalization by means of stress shift, and the other Nominalization by means of vowel change.

First, Nominalization by means of stress shift. As we have indicated in (2) of §4.4.3.2, nouns generally have their primary stress on the left. This type of stress shift applies to the following cases:

(1)   [compóund ᵥ] → [cómpound ɴ]
       [condúct ᵥ] → [cónduct ɴ]
       [constrúct ᵥ] → [cónstruct ɴ]
       [expórt ᵥ] → [éxport ɴ]
       [impórt ᵥ] → [ímport ɴ]

[prodúce $_V$] → [próduce $_N$]
[projéct $_V$] → [próject $_N$]
[recórd $_V$] → [récord $_N$]
[suspéct $_V$] → [súspect $_N$]
[tormént $_V$] → [tórment $_N$]
[transfórm $_V$] → [tránsform $_N$]
[transpórt $_V$] → [tránsport $_N$]

Note that verbs generally have their stress on the right, which can be seen from the examples in (1). Thus, we have the most general tendency in the stress patterns in nouns and verbs as in (2):

(2)   Stress patterns in N and V: A general tendency
      In nouns, the primary stress goes leftward, while in verbs, it goes rightward.

It goes without saying that (2) is an expression of a gross tendency that is observed in English nouns and verbs, so it is true that many nouns and verbs are consonant with (2) but there are still quite a few of "counter-examples" in the language.

In the previous section, i.e. §4.4.3.3 Conversion, we have noted that there are two exceptional cases of converted nominals: one is the case of "V' → N," i.e. *chéck(-)òut* and others, and the other is the case of "PP → N," i.e. *úndergròund, óvernìght* and others. We have also added that all of these exceptional nominals are, in fact, simultaneously affected by Conversion and Leftward stress shift rule in nouns. However, we may have an alternative view regarding these cases. Thus, a new analysis is such as follows: the origins of such nouns as *chéck(-)òut, chéckùp, mákeùp, pín(-)ùp,* and *hándòut* are "phrasal verbs," and these verbs get nominalized in accordance with (2) above; the nouns *úndergròund* and *óvernìght* are obtained by way of nominalizing the adjectives *ùndergróund* and *òvernìght,* which happen to be the converted adjectives from PP, or by way of directly nominalizing the latter PPs in accordance with the spirit of (2), respectively. This new analysis does not presuppose the simultaneous application of the two rules, Conversion and Leftward stress shift. Rather, since they are independent rules, they need not apply in this order.

Next, Nominalization by means of vowel change. When we make nouns out of verbs, the vowel quality of the secondary stress changes from tense to lax vowel, and this process is accompanied by stress reduction. For example, observe the alteration below:

(3)   [prédicàte v] /prédikèit/ → [prédicate N] /prédikət/

Here, the secondary-stressed tense vowel /èi/ in the verb has become the unstressed lax vowel /ə/ in the noun. This is what we mean when we say Nominalization by means of vowel change. The same type of phonological alteration is found in the following pairs:

Phonological alteration in verb-noun pairs

Secondary-stressed tense vowel /è/ in verbs	Corresponding unstressed lax vowel /ə/ in nouns
[dócumènt v]	[dócument N]
[cómplemènt v]	[cómplement N]
[ímplemènt v]	[ímplement N]
[súpplemènt v]	[súpplement N]

Note that as long as the words in (3) and those in the above table are concerned, it is not the case that verbs have become nouns, but the fact is that nouns have become verbs. The derivational history of these words being aside, there is indeed the very phonological relationship between the verbs and the nouns that we have mentioned above. Thus, we should at least say that vowel change, or alteration, is part of the process of Nominalization.

> **N.B.1** Tense vowel is a type of vowel that is produced with tense muscle movements or positions in the vocal tract. Lax vowel, on the other hand, is another type of vowel that is produced with lax muscle movements or positions in the vocal tract.
>
> **N.B.2** As mentioned above in the text, this type of vowel quality change, i.e. from tense to lax vowel, is accompanied by stress reduction. So, it may well be argued that this is a special case of (2) above, in that the secondary stress in [*prédicàte* v], for example, moves leftward and the verb becomes a noun [*prédicate* N], where the former secondary-stressed segment becomes unstressed, ending up as a lax vowel /ə/.
>
> **N.B.3** Vowel quality change is also observed in such pairs as [*deep* A] vs. [*depth* N], [*long* A] vs. [*length* N], [*strong* A] vs. [*strength* N], [*heal* v] vs. [*health* N], [*breathe* v] vs. [*breath* N], and [*steal* v] vs. [*stealth* N]. But, this

is a different type of vowel change than the one we have discussed above.

4.5   The Boundary between the Lexical and the Syntactic Structure

So far, we have studied the internal structure of English words and, at the same time, how English words are formed. Words are combined to make up a sentence. The study of the latter structure is what we call syntax. The main concern in this section is the comparison and contrast of the two structures: the word-internal, i.e. lexical, structure and the word-external, i.e. phrasal or syntactic, structure. Specifically, as an illustrative example, we take up a compound noun and a nominal phrase. There are three perspectives in terms of which we compare and contrast the two structures: the three perspectives are syntax, phonology, and semantics.

First, as regards syntax, i.e. the way to build up elements to form a constituent, we see a number of differences between the two constructs. Observe the table below:

Syntactic differences between a compound and a phrase

	Compound noun	Nominal phrase
Example	*greenhouse*	*green house*
Maximal category	N (lexical category)	N' (phrasal category)
Internal modification	No (*[*light-green*]*house*)	Yes ([*light-green*] *house*)
Insertion / Separability	No (**green*[*small*]*house*)	Yes (*green small house*)
Substitution by proform	No (**greenone*)	Yes (*green one*)
Ellipsis / Anaphora	No (*to visit *the green and the small house*)	Yes (to visit *the green and the small house*)
Need for the functors	No (*town house*)	Yes (*a house in the town*)

Let us take *greenhouse* and *green house* as examples of a compound noun and a nominal phrase, respectively. The maximal category for the former is a simple noun (N), and that for the latter a phrasal category (N'). This is the clearest syntactic difference between the two constructs. We cannot modify part of a compound (*[*light-green*]*house*), but we can do the same to part of a phrase ([*light-green*] *house*). No insertion is permitted in a compound, nor can a compound be separated (*green[*small*]house*), but that is fine with a phrase (*green small house*). We cannot substitute a head noun in a compound by a proform *one* (*greenone*), but that is fine with a phrase (*green one*). We cannot delete part of a compound even though it has an anaphoric antecedent somewhere in the sentence ("*to visit *the green and the small house*" [in the sense of "to visit the greenhouse and the small house]), but that's fine with a phrase ("to visit *the green and the small house*" [in the sense of "to visit the green house and the small house]). There is no need to use functors, i.e. function words and affixes, to form a compound (*townhouse*), but we do need them to form a phrase (*a house in the town*). The latter point is further illustrated by some other adjectival compounds and their corresponding phrases: the former lack functors but the latter need them. For example, "fat-free" means "free from fat," "user-friendly" "friendly to the users," "law-abiding" "abiding by the law," and "a three-year-old boy" "a boy who is three years old."

Next, as regards phonology, the difference is rightly phrased as in (1) below (cf. (2) of §4.4.3.2):

(1)   General stress patterns in N and N'
      In nouns, the primary stress goes leftward, while in nominal phrases, it falls on the head noun.

Hence, the difference is such that the compound noun is left-stressed as in *gréenhòuse*, while the nominal phrase is head-stressed, i.e. right-stressed in this case, as in *gréen hóuse*, or sometimes *grèen hóuse*.

Thirdly, as regards semantics, the meaning of the entire compound noun is hard to build up from the parts that constitute the very compound, while the meaning of a phrase is straightforward in that it can be calculated entirely from the step-by-step accumulation of the meanings of its parts. In short, the meaning of a compound is irregular and opaque, while that of a phrase is regular and transparent. For example, *a green house* is surely green, while *a greenhouse* is not always green and there are many white *greenhouses*, indeed.

Now that we have compared and contrasted compounds and phrases with *greenhouse* and *green house* as representative constructs, respectively, we conclude that though *greenhouse* and *green house*, for example, consist of the same words and have the same head noun *house*, their behaviors are totally different from each other. The compound noun, or a lexical category, to use more general terms, is full of idiosyncratic information, while the nominal phrase, or a syntactic phrase, can be formed and interpreted by means of a set of regular syntactic and semantic rules. When we speak of the boundary between the lexical and the syntactic structure, what we want to mean is this: it is at the level of 'word' where these two distinct structures meet. Word is the one and only significant level that has Janus-like two faces: the level is open to lexical idiosyncrasies and, at the same time, it starts out with the syntactic regularities.

EXERCISES

1. Imagine a scene where it snowed heavily and the White House is deep in the snow. Suppose that someone pointed at this building and said, "The Snow White House!" Do you find this expression grammatical? Do you think it makes sense? Answer yes or no, and explain why.

2. At the end of §4.3.2, we noted as follows:

    > While derivational suffixes create new words, inflectional suffixes are syntactic markers attached to words to signal the syntactic relationships that hold between the words in a sentence. Put another way, derivational suffixes belong to Lexicon and, therefore, their attributes are lexical, or idiosyncratic and irregular, while inflectional suffixes belong to Syntax so that they enjoy syntactic regularity and are free from lexical idiosyncrasies. Readers are invited to examine this distinction and to determine how this distinction derives all these attributes.

So, examine this distinction and determine how this distinction derives all these attributes.

Chapter V

Syntax

5.1 Domain of the Study of Syntax

Syntax simply means the way to build up elements to form a constituent, but in the overall framework of grammar, syntax is the study of the arrangement of words observed in a sentence. Thus, the basic assumption is such that the largest target structure of syntax is a sentence and the smallest units that make up a sentence are words. Therefore, the domain of the study of syntax is a sentence, and to study syntax means something twofold: one is to explore the intra-sentential dependencies among the constituents in a sentence, and the other to determine the inter-sentential dependences among the related constructions in the language.

> **N.B.** A 'constituent' is, put simply, a block, or a unit. For example, in the expression "Beauty and the Beast," the string [*the Beast*] forms a constituent, but that of [*and the*] does not, since the latter is only a row of fragments and does not constitute one wholeness.

5.2 Phrase Structure and Phrase Structure Rules

5.2.1 Hierarchy or the Phrase Structure

A sentence is not simply a concatenation of words, but it has a hierarchical structure. The hierarchical structure of a sentence is called 'phrase structure,' which specifically represents two types of information. One type is about precedence that holds among words in a sentence such that word *a* precedes word *b*, word *b* precedes word *c*, and so on. The other type of information is about dominance that holds among constituents in the phrase structure such that constituent *x* dominates constituent *y*, constituent *y* dominates constituent *z*, and so on. The latter information can also be phrased as such that word *z* and other words are combined to form a constituent *y*, *y* and other constituents are further combined to form a larger constituent *x*, and so on. Let us take a simple example and see how it is structured.

(1)   The boy ate the hamburger.

The sentence in (1) has five words but it is not a simple concatenation of them all. Some words are so closely related as to form a constituent, but others are totally independent from each other. For example, *the* (an instance of Determiner, abbreviated as Det) and *boy* (an instance of Noun, abbreviated as N) are closely related with each other and they form a 'noun phrase,' abbreviated as NP. On the other hand, *boy* and *ate* (an instance of Verb, abbreviated as V) are not related at all. Rather, *ate* is closely related with the constituent *the hamburger*, another NP formed with *the* and *hamburger*. And *ate* and *the hamburger* make another constituent 'verb phrase,' abbreviated as VP. The 'subject' NP *the boy* and the 'predicate' VP *ate the hamburger*, which comprises the 'main verb' *ate* and the 'direct object' *the hamburger*, form the largest constituent 'sentence,' abbreviated as S. A hierarchy of this sort can be shown as in (2):

(2)   [[[The _Det_] [boy _N_] _NP_] [[ate _V_] [[the _Det_] [hamburger _N_] _NP_] _VP_] _S_]

The precedence relations that hold among words in (2) are self-evident: *the* precedes *boy*, *boy* precedes *ate*, and so on. The dominance relations that hold among constituents in (2) are such that S dominates NP, ('subject NP' *the boy*) and S also dominates VP ('predicate' VP *ate the hamburger*). Thus, we simply say that S dominates NP and VP. Other dominance relations are such that VP dominates V and NP, and NP dominates Det and N.

N.B.1 For convenience' sake, below is a short list of abbreviations.

S < Sentence	Det < Determiner
N < Noun	NP < Noun Phrase
V < Verb	VP < Verb Phrase
A < Adjective	AP < Adjective Phrase
Adv < Adverb	AdvP < Adverbial Phrase
P < Preposition	PP < Prepositional Phrase

N.B.2 Some additional terms, either for technical use or for expository purposes, should be introduced here. A constituent is marked by its syntactic category. For example, [*the boy*] is marked or labeled as NP like [[*the* Det] [*boy* N] NP] as in (2). The marker of the constituent, e.g. NP, is called a 'node' in the phrase marker. The node S in (2) dominates all nodes in this S, but S 'directly dominates' only NP and VP. Similarly, VP in (2) dominates all nodes in this VP, but it directly dominates only V and NP. The node directly dominated by a 'mother node,' or simply a 'mother,' is called its 'daughter node,' or simply its 'daughter.' The nodes directly dominated by their 'mother' are called 'sister nodes,' or simply 'sisters.'

5.2.2   Constituency

It is not a trivial task to answer the question of how a sentence is structured: it is a rather difficult task to explore the kind of phrase structure that the sentence has. Phrase structure is not an a priori entity. We need evidence to determine the structure of a sentence, or its constituency. For example, we propose that the sentence (1) surely has the phrase structure (2), and this is because we have many pieces of syntactic evidence to support this structure.

(1)   The boy ate the hamburger.
(2)   [[[The Det] [boy N] NP] [[ate v] [[the Det] [hamburger N] NP] VP] s]

When we deform a sentence to create a related construction to it, we arrange (i.e. move, delete, or substitute) phrasal categories in the sentence. And the hidden assumption here is the very basic assumption (3):

(3)   Basic assumption on Movement, Deletion and Substitution
      We can move, delete, or substitute only a phrasal constituent.

There are a number of constructions that are thus derived from (1), i.e. by way of arranging phrasal constituents in the structure of (2).

(4)   a.   Passive: <u>The hamburger</u> was eaten by <u>the boy</u>.
      b.   Cleft: It is <u>the boy</u> that ate the hamburger.
      c.   Cleft: It is <u>the hamburger</u> that the boy ate.
      d.   Pseudo-Cleft: What the boy ate is <u>the hamburger</u>.
      e.   Pseudo-Cleft: What the boy did was <u>(to) eat the hamburger</u>.
      f.   VP Deletion: They say that the boy won't eat the hamburger, but I'm sure he will [Δ]. (Δ = 'eat the hamburger')
      g.   VP Preposing: They say that the boy won't eat the hamburger, but <u>eat the hamburger</u> he will [Δ]. (Δ = 'eat the hamburger')
      h.   Pronominalization: <u>He</u> ate <u>it</u>. ('He' = 'the boy'; 'it' = 'the hamburger')
      i.   Extraposition: It is clear <u>that the boy ate the hamburger</u>. ('it' = 'that the boy ate the hamburger')

The constructions or processes named Passive, Cleft, Pseudo-Cleft, VP Deletion, VP Preposing, Pronominalization, and Extraposition all involve movement, deletion, or substitution of a phrasal constituent: the affected constituents are the underlined portions in the examples of (4). Therefore, we conclude that the syntactic arrangements in (4) are all in line with the constituency shown in (2) and the correct phrase structure for (1) is, therefore, the one in (2).

> **N.B.** Some terminological notes are in order here. Passive sentence has its active counterpart just as (4a) has (1). Cleft sentence has the basic structure: "It is [Focus] that [Presupposition]." A constituent to be focused in a sentence should be put in the [Focus] position, and the rest of the sentence is placed after *that*, which part means a presupposition. Pseudo-cleft sentence has the basic structure: "What [Presupposition] is [Focus]." In Pseudo-cleft sentence, the constituent to be focused should be put in the [Focus] position, i.e. after the verb *be*, and the rest is placed in the *What*-relative clause, which functions as a presupposition. VP Deletion deletes a VP, and VP Preposing preposes a VP. Pronominalization pronominalizes into a pronoun a variety of syntactic phrasal category. Extraposition moves a sentential constituent to the end of a sentence and leaves an expletive *it* in its original position.

5.2.3   Phrase Structure Rules

Now, it is clear that we have the phrase structure (2) for the sentence (1):

(1)   The boy ate the hamburger.

(2)   [[[The $_{Det}$] [boy $_N$] $_{NP}$] [[ate $_V$] [[the $_{Det}$] [hamburger $_N$] $_{NP}$] $_{VP}$] $_S$]

We assume next that we have, as part of the grammatical devices, the following Phrase Structure Rules, abbreviated as PSRs, to derive the structure (2).

(3)   S → NP VP
        VP → V NP
        NP → Det N

Let us illustrate how PSRs are interpreted. The PSR "S → NP VP," for example, is read as "S arrow NP (and) VP," "S expands as NP (and) VP," or "S is rewritten as NP (and) VP," and it means that "S directly dominates NP and VP." Thus, the PSRs in (3) jointly make up the phrase structure of (2). In order to derive sentences of other sorts shown in (4), we need some more PSRs as in (5).

(4)   a.   The boy slept.
        b.   The boy slept on the sofa.
        c.   John drank coffee.
        d.   John [[ate] [the bananas on the table]].
        e.   John [[ate] [the bananas] [in the dining room]].

(5)   VP → V (cf. (4a))
        VP → V PP (cf. (4b))
        VP → V NP PP (cf. (4e))
        NP → N (cf. (4c, d, e))
        NP → Det N PP (cf. (4d))
        PP → P NP (cf. (4d, e))

The facts in (1) and (4) mean that VP stands with or without a direct object; VP stands with or without a prepositional phrase, which is abbreviated as PP; NP stands with or without a Determiner; NP stands with or without a PP. The optional existence of direct objects, PPs, and Det is expressed by collapsing the rules in (3) and (5) through the use of parentheses, a convention for rule abbreviation such that items in parentheses are optional. Thus, the PSRs should be those in (6):

(6)   S → NP VP
      VP → V (NP) (PP)
      NP → (Det) N (PP)

Needless to say, as we go further to analyze more complicated constructions, we will need to have our PSRs elaborated somewhat further. But, as it stands, (6) covers a great number of cases, so at least for the expository purposes, the set of PSRs like (6) suffices.

> **N.B.** According to our regular terminological practice, "VP → V (NP) (PP)," for example, is in fact not a PSR, but rather it is a 'phrase structure rule schema.' A phrase structure rule schema is an abbreviated formula of multiple PSRs. But, simply for the purposes of exposition, we will not employ the term 'phrase structure rule schema' in the text. It is important to note, however, that this type of abbreviatory convention may constitute part of our 'knowledge of language' in that the one rule schema is shorter than two (or more) rules and, thus, is easier to learn, i.e. easier to store in the brain; the convention makes it possible to state the natural consequence that the PSRs "VP → V," "VP → V NP," "VP → V PP," and "VP → V NP PP," for example, are related by the rule schema "VP → V (NP) (PP)," but otherwise, they would be claimed to be independent and have nothing in common at all among them as would "S → NP VP" and "VP → V NP."

5.2.4   Structural Ambiguity

When an expression has more than one meaning, we say it is ambiguous. For example, sentences in (1) are all ambiguous in the sense that they mean either of the two corresponding construals, i.e. possible constructional interpretations, in (2).

(1)   a.   The boy saw the girl on the sofa.
      b.   The boy watched the girl with a telescope.
      c.   The boy beat the dog before the man.
(2)   a'.   The boy [saw [the girl on the sofa]].
      a".   The boy [saw [the girl] [on the sofa]].
      b'.   The boy [watched [the girl with a telescope]].
      b".   The boy [watched [the girl] [with a telescope]].
      c'.   The boy [beat [the dog before the man]].

c". The boy [beat [the dog] [before the man]]

The sentence (2a') means that the boy saw the girl who was on the sofa, while (2a") means that the boy, who was on the sofa, saw the girl. The sentence (2b') means that the boy watched the girl who had a telescope, while (2b") means that the boy watched the girl, using a telescope. The sentence (2c') means that the boy beat the dog and the dog was right in front of the man, while (2c") means that the boy beat the dog and this incident took place in front of the audience among which the man was. This type of ambiguity is due to the difference between the two types of phrase structures made possible by the legitimate applications of PSRs. Thus, we call this type of ambiguity phrase-structural ambiguity. For other types of ambiguity, see Chapter VI on Semantics.

N.B. It may happen that (2c) means either that the boy beat the dog before he beat the man, or that the boy beat the dog before the man beat the dog. If so, these interpretations have to do with the reduction of "before he beat the man" into "before the man," and also with that of "before the man beat the dog" into "before the man." In this case, in addition to phrase-structural ambiguity, we see some elliptical processes involved.

5.2.5 Recursiveness

We have not only simple sentences but other types of sentences where more than one sentence is involved in a larger sentence. For example, see below:

(1) Coordination
   a. Mike is a singer.
   b. [Mike is a singer], and [Eliza is an actress].
   c. [Mike is a singer], [Eliza is an actress], and [George is a director].
(2) Subordination or Embedding of 'argument'
   a. John is a genius.
   b. Bill thinks [that John is a genius].
   c. Mary believes [that Bill thinks [that John is a genius]].
(3) Subordination or Embedding of 'adjunct'
   a. John ate up a large hamburger [because he was so hungry].
   b. John believes [the theory [that humans have evolved from

apes] NP].

c. John believes [the theory [that those Darwinians put forth decades ago] NP].

Coordination, as we observe it in (1), is a process where we put together two (or more) constituents by means of a coordinate conjunction, or a coordinator for short, e.g. *and, but,* and *or.* Subordination or Embedding, as we observe it in (2) and (3), is a process where we make a constituent one part of a larger constituent by means of a subordinate conjunction, or a subordinator for short, e.g. *that, if, when,* and so on. Thus, in (2), the sentence "John is a genius" becomes part of a larger sentence, i.e. matrix sentence, as in "Bill thinks that John is a genius." In this case, we call "John is a genius" an embedded sentence, and the process is what we call 'embedding.' Note here that the embedded element is an obligatory item for the matrix to be a grammatical construction: in the case of (2), this embedded obligatory item is an object of the matrix verb. Technically, the type of obligatory element required by a verb is called an 'argument' of the verb. On the other hand, there is a constituent called 'adjunct,' which is an optional element adjoined to a host construction. Adverbial clauses like that in (3a) and noun-modifying clauses like those in (3b, c) (appositive clause and relative clause, respectively) are all optional and constitute part of the entire sentence. Since this type of clause is adjoined to a host construction and becomes part of the matrix clause, the adjunct clause clearly shares the defining features of embedding with the argument clause that we observed in (2): they function as part of the whole.

Notice that coordination and embedding are also possible in NP structures. NP coordination is possible as shown in (4). NP embedding is possible, via PP construction, as shown in (5).

(4)   [[John NP] and [Mary NP] NP] are a couple.

(5)   John is sitting in [NP the chair [PP under [NP the tree [PP by [NP the house]]]]]

In order to accommodate the facts in (1)–(5), we need the following PSRs, modifying those proposed in §5.2.3.

(6)   S' → Comp S
      S' → S' *and* S'
      S → NP VP (S')

VP → V (NP) (PP) (S')
NP → NP *and* NP
NP → (Det) N (PP) (S')
PP → P NP

A few words are in order here regarding the rule "S' → Comp S." Now, S' is the initial symbol that starts the rewriting of PSRs. Comp, short for Complementizer, is a syntactic position where either a subordinate conjunction fills in (as in (7a)), or a WH phrase (e.g. *what, when, whether*, etc.) fills in (as in (7b, c)), or otherwise nothing fills in (as in (7d)).

(7) a. I think [$_{S'}$ [$_{Comp}$ that] [$_S$ John is a genius]]
     b. I don't know [$_{S'}$ [$_{Comp}$ whether] [$_S$ John is a genius]]
     c. [$_{S'}$ [$_{Comp}$ what] [$_S$ is John ___]]?
     d. [$_{S'}$ [$_{Comp}$] [$_S$ John is a genius indeed]]

Note that although Comp is an indispensable syntactic position, we won't refer to it where it won't affect the line of syntactic argumentations.

Now, going back to (6), one of the most important properties of the PSRs in (6) is the possibility that the symbols S and NP reappear on the right of the arrow, and that they can do so for indefinite times. When a certain category appears in the phrase structure more than once (e.g. 'verb' in (2b, c) and PP in (5)), there is a recursive symbol S or NP along the line in the phrase structure that connects the very same categories in question. This property is called 'Recursiveness' of the PSRs, or we say that the set of PSRs in (6) are 'recursive.' This very property guarantees that we have no limit on the length of a sentence: the would-be longest sentence will become longer if S or NP is to be coordinated to or embedded in it. This very property also guarantees that we have an infinite number of sentences in the language: if all sentences in the language are numbered 1 through x, for example, we still have another sentence numbered $(x+1)$ that is longer than, and thus different from, the sentence numbered x. This means that there is no limit on the number of the sentences in the language. Recursiveness, therefore, constitutes part of our linguistic creativity.

5.3   X-bar Theory

5.3.1   Motivations for X-bar Theory

A grammar that has Phrase Structure Rules (PSRs) as very important and indispensable part of it is called a Phrase Structure Grammar (PSG). We say that a grammar 'generates' all and only grammatical sentences in the given language. We accordingly say that a PSG shown in (1) below generates all and only grammatical sentences that are relevant to the present discussion, e.g. those declarative sentences given in the previous section, i.e. §5.2.

(1)   (= §5.2.5 (6))
   S' → Comp S
   S' → S' *and* S'
   S → NP VP (S')
   VP → V (NP) (PP) (S')
   NP → NP *and* NP
   NP → (Det) N (PP) (S')
   PP → P NP

However, if we look at the PSRs in (1) from a theoretical point of view, i.e. from a viewpoint about a theory of grammar, things are not so easy as we hope them to be. There is indeed much room for improvement. But what? Let us see in the following sections what it is and how X-bar Theory accommodates the problems that arise. X-bar Theory is a theory concerned about the universal features of various types of PSGs. Among those theoretical notions X-bar Theory assumes, there are two major types:

(2)   Two major notions assumed in X-bar Theory
   a.   Category variable: X is a category variable that represents any one of the lexical categories.
   b.   Bar notation: phrasal categories are of the highest bar-level, and lexical categories the lowest bar-level; when a category of a certain type directly dominates another category of the same type, the bar-level of the latter is one-degree smaller than that of the former.

There are two universal features, or hypotheses, relating to PSGs that we propose are contingent on these assumptions: one is about uniformity in the system of bar-notation and the other about cross-categorial generalizations in the syntax and semantics of phrases, both of which will be explained below.

Before leaving this subsection, we want to make it clear that X-bar Theory is not a kind of PSG, but that it is a theory about PSG. In other words, X-bar Theory determines the possible types of PSG. Just as a PSG of English, for example, is a theory about all phrase structures at 'Deep Structure' in English, so X-bar Theory is a theory about all PSGs of human languages.

5.3.2   Uniformity in Bar-notation: Uniform Bar-levels

Observe the sentence and the NP below:

(1)   a.   [$_S$ The enemy destroyed the city in the 15th century $_S$]
      b.   [$_{NP}$ the enemy's destruction of the city in the 15th century $_{NP}$]

We reasonably assume that the phrase structures for (1a–b) are (2a–b), respectively:

(2)   a.   [$_S$ [The enemy $_{NP}$] [[destroyed $_V$][the city $_{NP}$] $_{VP}$] in the 15th century $_{VP'}$] $_S$]
      b.   [$_{NP}$ [the enemy $_{NP}$]'s [[destruction $_N$][of [the city $_{NP}$] $_{PP}$] $_{N'}$] in the 15th century $_{N''}$] $_{NP}$]

Though the structures above are different from each other, they have common features. In (2a), the verb *destroy* has a direct object *the city* attached to it, and they form a VP. This VP has an adverbial phrase *in the 15th century* attached to it, and they form a VP'. This VP' has a subject NP *the enemy* attached to it, and they form a sentence S. In (2b), on the other hand, the noun *destruction* has a semantic direct object *the city* attached to it, though the preposition *of* links the two items because but for the preposition, the noun cannot be followed by an object. In other words, the noun *destruction* semantically requires a direct object and syntactically does a PP with a direct object in it. And the noun and the PP form an N'. This N' has a modifying phrase *in the 15th century*, and they form an N". This N" has a semantic subject *the enemy* attached to it, and they form a NP.

We see systematicity, or common features, underlying the structures of (2): the smallest bare category, either V or N, grows larger successively, and it ends up as a maximal category, either S or NP. Suppose we make a notational innovation such that if a category becomes one-degree larger, it will be assigned an additional prime marker. Thus, in the case of (2a), V (*destroy*) becomes V' (= VP), this V' becomes V" (= VP'), and this V" becomes V'" (= S). Similarly, in the case of (2b), N (*destruction*) becomes N', this N' becomes N", and this N" becomes N'" (= NP). Notice that these structures are phrase structures, so they can be generated by a set of PSRs like below:

(3)   a.   V'" → NP V"
             V" → V' PP
             V' → V NP
       b.   N'" → NP N"
             N" → N' PP
             N' → N PP

Now, we can observe a striking uniformity among the bar-levels. In short, the maximal bar-level is three, and the level gradually comes down to zero. Thus, the maximal category of three primes, i.e. the triple-prime category, consists of a subject and the double-prime category, the double-prime category consists of the single-prime category and a modifier, and the single-prime category consists of the zero-prime (bare) category and a direct object. Note that in the case of "N' → N PP," this PP becomes [P NP], the latter NP being the semantic direct object of the zero-prime N. This is the uniformity of bar-levels among categories that is claimed to be observed universally. And this notion can be formulated only through the system of bar-notation we have employed.

> **N.B.** We have used a prime notation in the text to indicate the level of the phrase. Originally, however, it was the bar that was used on top of the category symbol to indicate the phrasal level: no bar means the zero-prime, one bar the single-prime, double-bar the double-prime, and so on. Because of this ontological history, the system has since been called X-bar theory. Sometimes, the numeral has also been employed as a superscript level marker. For example, V^0, or V with no numeral, means the zero-prime V, V^1 the one-prime V', V^2 the double-prime V", and so on. It happens that we may occasionally use one notation after another during the same discourse. But, the prime notation, the bar notation, and the numerical notation are all notational variants, so they are equivalent.

5.3.3   Cross-categorial Generalizations

Observe the sentence and the NP below:

(1) a. [$_V$''' [The enemy $_{NP}$] [[destroyed $_V$][the city $_{NP}$] $_V$'] in the 15th
century $_V$''] $_V$''']

  b. [$_N$''' [the enemy $_{NP}$]'s [[destruction $_N$][of [the city $_{NP}$] $_{PP}$] $_N$'] in
the 15th century $_N$''] $_N$''']

From the syntactic categorial perspective, the verb *destroy* and the noun
destruction are different items from each other, or put simply, they are
totally different words. But they are quite similar in that they both have the
same 'subject NP' *the enemy*, the same modifier phrase *in the 15th century*,
and the same 'object NP' *the city*. More specifically, 'subject NP' *the
enemy* is directly dominated by either V''' or N''', a modifier phrase *in the
15th century* is directly dominated by either V'' or N'', and 'object NP' *the
city* is directly dominated by either V' or N', though in the latter case, later
in the course of derivation, the preposition *of* pops up and acts as a case
marker for the following NP that would otherwise end up as caseless. Thus,
the two structures in (1) have the same "meaning," and this very meaning
can be expressed either in the form of V''' (= S) as in (1a) or in the form of
N''' (= NP) as in (1b). However, we have no way to formulate this
similarity or sameness observed in (1), because it is the PSG proposed in
the previous subsection that is the only tool responsible for the generation
of such expressions with the same propositional meaning. The PSG as it
stands has no function to relate the verb and the noun.

Now, we introduce such notions as Constant and Variable into the
PSG notation. See below:

(2) Constant: a specific syntactic category, e.g. N, V, and A
Variable: any one of the syntactic categories from among N, V,
and A

We exploit these notions and are able to reformulate the PSRs in question
as in (3), where X is a variable representing N, V, or A.

(3) X''' → NP X''
X'' → X' PP
X' → X NP

N.B.1 In (2), we have stipulated that the category variable X can be N, V,

or A, but some would say that it may range over Adv and P in addition to
N, V, and A. But note that we are here concerned with the structural
similarities among the phrases projected from the 'major' or 'basic'
lexical categories of N, V, and A. This is simply because X-bar syntactic
treatment of other categories, i.e. Adv and P, requires a certain amount of
empirical observations and theoretical assumptions, and this would,
therefore, go way out of the bound of the current subsection. Thus, we
confine ourselves only to N, V, and A, which we call lexical categories.

N.B.2 In (3), we have focused on the degrading of the bar-levels only on
the part of the variable X, and, therefore, have reserved the intuitively
familiar terms for other categories, i.e. NP and PP, instead of employing
bar-notation such as N''' and P'''.

The PSRs in (3) are revealing in that if we say X is 'projected' to the
structure at a higher bar-level, and eventually up to the structure at the
triple-bar level, we can easily see that the PSRs in (3) alone prescribe that
all lexical categories N, V, and A have the same structures at each of the
higher levels up to the highest. This is a type of syntactic, or con-
figurational, generalization. There is another type of ultimately semantic
generalization such that NP directly dominated by X''' is a subject and can
be interpreted as Agent when the main verb is an actional-volitional verb,
and so on. These generalizations are valid no matter what lexical category
X assumes. Hence, we say these are cross-categorial generalizations.

The PSRs in (3) can be viewed as the target of further abstraction.
Thus, the general X-bar schema that emerges from those PSRs is (4) and
we can define the notion 'head' in terms of this schema, as in (5).

(4)   General X-bar schema
       $X^n \rightarrow \ldots X^{n-1} \ldots$, where $1 \leq n \leq 3$ (X = N, V, or A)
(5)   Head of X^n is either X^{n-1} or X^0.

The notion 'head' in (5) essentially requires that every phrase should have
a head in it. This requirement is quite significant. For example, such PSRs
as in (6) are in principle ruled out because the string on the right of the
arrow lacks a head, and in fact there is no such structures in the language
that are the result of the application of these rules.

(6)   *VP $\rightarrow$ Det N
       *NP $\rightarrow$ V AP

If we assume that children are born with this kind of 'knowledge' about the head of a phrase and start acquiring the language spoken in the community in which they are raised, they would not have to worry about making a guess at the impossible PSRs as in (6). They would rather concentrate only on the possible PSRs, instead, as in (7):

(7)   VP → V AP
       NP → Det N

That way, X-bar theory paves the way quite successfully for the children to acquire language. In this respect, we reasonably take X-bar theory to be part of our general knowledge of grammar. In linguistics, the latter knowledge is known as Universal Grammar, or also as General Linguistic Theory. In order to explain the successful language acquisition by infants and children in quite a short period, linguists assume that all humans are already equipped with a certain language faculty at their birth that guarantees and enables the quick and rich language acquisition as it is observed.

Up until here, we have only examined the cross-categorial generalizations over V and N. Let us now take up cross-categorial instances that range over N, V, and A.

(8)   a.   John ignored the fact that the earth is round.
       b.   John's ignorance of the fact that the earth is round surprised everyone.
       c.   John is ignorant of the fact that the earth is round.

The crucial point is that no matter what category the predicate "IGNORE" assumes, X-bar theory, or the general schema of (4), predicts the same skeletal structures for the phrases projected from the verb *ignore*, the noun *ignorance*, and the adjective *ignorant*. Details aside, these structures have in common the following properties: it is the subject *John* directly dominated by X''' that does not know something and it is the direct object *the fact that the earth is round* dominated by X' that is what *John* doesn't know.

X-bar theory also makes it possible for us to give a principled description of form-meaning relationships in phrases. Here, let us take NP as an example. The syntactico-semantic correlations in NPs are systematically represented in terms of bar levels. Below is the gist of this, i.e. the semantics of bar levels.

(9) The semantics of bar levels in NP

$[_{N'''}$ SPEC $[_{N''}$ MOD $[_{N'}$ $[_N$ N $_N]$ ARG $_{N'}]$ MOD $_{N''}]$ $_{N'''}]$

(SPEC: Specifier, MOD: Modifier, ARG: Argument)

Thus, the argument, or the direct object, of N^0 is directly dominated by N'
and is adjacent to N^0, though later in the derivation, this argument NP gets
accompanied by a preposition to form a PP; the modifier, a daughter of N",
modifies N'; the specifier, a daughter of N''', which is a type of determiner
that is realized as an article, a demonstrative, or a genitive, modifies N".
Some examples are shown below:

(10) a. $[_{N'''}$ the enemy's $[_{N''}$ $[_{N'}$ $[_N$ destruction $_N]$ of the city $_{N'}]$ in the
          15th century $_{N''}]$ $_{N'''}]$ (= (1b))

      b. $[_{N'''}$ John's $[_{N''}$ $[_{N'}$ $[_N$ ignorance $_N]$ of the fact that the earth is
          round $_{N'}]$ through lack of education $_{N''}]$ $_{N'''}]$ (= Subject NP of
          (8b) with *through lack of education* added)

      c. $[_{N'''}$ the $[_{N''}$ proper $[_{N'}$ $[_N$ treatment $_N]$ of social inequalities $_{N'}]$
          $_{N''}]$ $_{N'''}]$

      d. $[_{N'''}$ that $[_{N''}$ handsome $[_{N'}$ $[_N$ student $_N]$ of physics $_{N'}]$ with
          long hair $_{N''}]$ $_{N'''}]$

      e. $[_{N'''}$ the $[_{N''}$ $[_{N'}$ $[_N$ king $_N]$ of England $_{N'}]$ from France $_{N''}]$ $_{N'''}]$

We understand that nouns like *destruction, ignorance,* and *treatment* all
have an object NP as an argument because these nouns are semantically
predicates. But what about the nouns *student* and *king*? The answer is: a
student is one who studies something, so the noun *student* semantically
requires an argument specifying a certain area of discipline and syntactically has an optional object NP; a king is one who reigns over his country,
so the noun *king* semantically requires an argument specifying the name of
the country over which he reigns and syntactically has an optional object
NP. Next, modifiers modify N' and, therefore, stand before or after N', as
exemplified in (10). Semantically speaking, modifiers contribute to the
establishment of truth values. Observe the following:

(11) a. That handsome student of physics with long hair came out of
          the room.

      b. That handsome student of physics with short hair came out of
          the room.

      c. That handsome student of physics with long hair, who you just introduced to me yesterday, came out of the room.

d. That handsome student of physics with short hair, who you just introduced to me yesterday, came out of the room.

e. That handsome driver of the city bus with long hair came out of the room.

Imagine a situation where a handsome student of physics with long hair came out of the room but no other man did so. In this case, the proposition (11a) is true but the proposition (11b) is not, i.e. false. And the proposition (11c) is also true but the proposition (11d) is false. This means that the N' modifiers determine the truth value of the proposition (in other words, whether the proposition is true or false), but that modifiers like nonrestrictive relative clauses do not. Needless to say, elements lower than N' also determine the truth value, as is clearly indicated by the falsehood of (11e) if it is uttered in the same situation as before.

Before concluding, let us touch upon the syntactic property of the pronoun *one*. In contrast to the pronoun *it* (or *he*, or *she*), which replaces the entire N''', *one* of the following usage replaces part of N''', i.e. N'. Observe the sentences below:

(12) a. The king of England from France was jolly, but the one from Germany was obnoxious.

b. *The king of England from France was jolly, but the one of Scotland from Germany was obnoxious.

The sentence (12a) is grammatical because *one* in the second conjunct is the replacement of the N' structure [$_{N'}$ [$_N$ king $_N$] of England $_{N'}$] in the first conjunct, but the example (12b) is ungrammatical. This is because in (12b), *one* is only referring back to the structure [$_N$ king $_N$], which is prohibited because *one* should be an N' proform. If *one* in (12b) is intended to mean the N' structure [$_{N'}$ [$_N$ king $_N$] of England $_{N'}$], then the subject of the second conjunct would become "*the king of England of Scotland from Germany," which is clearly wrong. Thus, the pronoun *one* of this usage is sometimes called N' pronoun *one*.

N.B.1 In this section, we introduced the X-bar syntactic notion of "head." Now it will be clear that this means that structures guaranteed by X-bar theory are all endocentric structures. We assumed here that S is V''', which means we assumed S is an endocentric structure and its head is V.

There is a group of linguists, however, who assume that the head of S is INFL, a category of inflectional Tense and Agreement, or C, a category dominating such complementizers as *that*. Thus, S is IP, a maximal bar-level of I, or CP, a maximal bar-level of C, in their terms. In the text above, we have shown a rather basic and classical interpretation of the phrase S such that S = V'''. There is also another group of linguists who assume that S is not an endocentric structure, but that it is an exocentric structure. As for the centricity status of S, it is a highly theoretical type of controversy.

N.B.2 In Chapter IV, we have labeled the simple noun as N, and we also have tentatively labeled a nominal phrase as N'. As examples for the structure N', we referred to such phrases as *a* [*gréen hóuse* $_{N'}$] and *a* [*bláck bóard* $_{N'}$]. But, strictly speaking, this was a kind of simplification for the sake of expository purposes, since the correct category type for the above phrases should be N" rather than N'. Thus, their respective structures are *a* [*gréen hóuse* $_{N''}$] and *a* [*bláck bóard* $_{N''}$].

5.4 Transformations

We have so far assumed that Phrase Structure Grammar (PSG) generates grammatical sentences and that X-bar theory prescribes the possible types of Phrase Structure Rules (PSRs). In this section, we will go a step further to introduce a new type of rules that are necessary to have a linguistically significant generalization in the description of the language. They are transformational rules, or transformations, for short. Motivations for transformations will be accounted for shortly.

Observe, first of all, the sentence below:

(1)   John admires Mary.

In order to generate (1), we apply PSRs and have a skeletal structure like (2), which lacks a terminal string, or, put simply, a skeletal phrase structure without lexical items and some grammatical formatives. The grammatical formatives that may appear in the phrase structure are perfective *have*, progressive *be*, and passive *be*, among others.

(2)   [$_S$ [$_{NP}$ [$_N$ ____ $_N$] $_{NP}$] [$_{VP}$ [$_V$ ____ $_V$] [$_{NP}$ [$_N$ ____ $_N$] $_{NP}$] $_{VP}$] $_S$]

We then insert into the slots the lexical items that are appropriate to the structure, which process we call "lexical insertion." But what counts as being "appropriate"? The lexical item *John*, for example, is an instance of the category Noun, so it is appropriate for it to be inserted into the position [$_N$ ___ $_N$]. Likewise, *Mary* can also be inserted into another [$_N$ ___ $_N$] position. At this stage, we have (3):

(3)　[$_S$ [$_{NP}$ [$_N$ <u>John</u> $_N$] $_{NP}$] [$_{VP}$ [$_V$ ___ $_V$] [$_{NP}$ [$_N$ <u>Mary</u> $_N$] $_{NP}$] $_{VP}$] $_S$]

Next, when we insert verbs, we have to take note of the syntactic environment into which they are inserted. The lexical item *admire* is of the category verb, and it is a transitive verb, which requires an object NP adjacent to it, and in fact, technically, the verb and the object NP should be sisters. Thus, the phrase structure (3) is eligible for the insertion of the verb *admire*, and the result of this process is (4):

(4)　[$_S$ [$_{NP}$ [$_N$ <u>John</u> $_N$] $_{NP}$] [$_{VP}$ [$_V$ <u>admires</u> $_V$] [$_{NP}$ [$_N$ <u>Mary</u> $_N$] $_{NP}$] $_{VP}$] $_S$]

This is fine.

Now, observe the passive counterpart of (1), i.e. (5) below:

(5)　Mary is admired by John.

In generating (5), we arrive at a point where we have yet to insert a verb, i.e. the structure (6) below. Note that passive *be* should already be present at this stage.

(6)　[$_S$ [$_{NP}$ [$_N$ <u>Mary</u> $_N$] $_{NP}$] [$_{VP'}$ be [$_{VP}$ [$_V$ ___ $_V$] [$_{PP}$ [$_P$ <u>by</u>] [$_{NP}$ [$_N$ <u>John</u> $_N$] $_{NP}$] $_{PP}$] $_{VP}$] $_{VP'}$] $_S$]

Here we face a serious problem: the lexical item *admire* is a transitive verb, but the slot in (6) is not appropriate for *admire* to be inserted into because there is no object NP (sister NP) that should follow the transitive *admire*. Therefore, we would have to conclude that we cannot generate (5), or that (5) is ungrammatical because the derivation of it has involved a violation of the proper process of lexical insertion. Anyhow, this conclusion is seriously contrary to the fact that (5) is 100% grammatical and no less.

In order to overcome this type of difficulty, we propose there should be rules like transformations. Transformations are a type of rules that have a function to transform one phrase structure into another. Thus, we have "Passive Transformation," or simply "Passive," a somewhat simplified version of which is shown in (7). Though (7) is somewhat simplified because no auxiliary verb appears in SD, the simplification is meant to be due to the expository purposes.

   (7)   Passive Transformation
        SD: X, NP_1, V, NP_2, Y
        SC: 1, 2, 3, 4, 5 → 1, 4, be +3*en*, by + 2, 5

Let us see how Passive Transformation (7) applies. Note that X and Y in (7) are string variables, which represent any string of category symbols, including the case of no category symbol involved. The symbols NP_1, V, and NP_2, on the other hand, are called constants. Structural Description, abbreviated as SD, dictates how the terminal string of the phrase structure, i.e. that of (4) in this case, be categorized. Thus, in the phrase structure (4), *John* is of the category NP, *admire* is of the category V, *Mary* is of the category NP, and no string corresponds to X or Y. Therefore, the phrase structure (4) satisfies the SD of (7). This means that we can affect the Structural Change, abbreviated as SC, of (7) to the phrase structure (4). The numbers in SC each correspond to the first category in SD, i.e. X, the second category in SD, i.e. NP, the third category in SD, i.e. V, and so on. The SC enforced is such that the terminal string be reordered so as to be categorized as, in effect, X, NP_2, be + V*en*, by + NP_1, Y, where V*en* means the past participle of V. With this change of the terminal string enforced and subsequently the appropriate phrase structure reconstruction completed, we have the derived phrase structure (8), the very phrase structure of the passive sentence (5).

   (8)   [s [NP [N <u>Mary</u> N] NP] [VP' is [VP [V <u>admired</u> V] [PP [P <u>by</u>] [NP [N <u>John</u> N] NP] PP] VP] VP'] s]

This process, we call "transformation," or "mapping," the effect of which is such that the phrase marker (4) in the form of a phrase structure is transformed to the phrase marker (8) in the form of a phrase structure.

    Now that we have a new type of rules, of which Passive is one, we no longer face the kind of problem we would face if we decided to derive passives only by means of PSRs. There are in fact a number of transformations that we propose have the effect of converting one construction to another. Details aside, below is a short list of transformations and their related constructions:

(9)   *to*-Dative Movement
    a. John gave a ring to Mary.
    b. Jon gave Mary a ring.

(10)   *for*-Dative Movement
    a. John bought a ring for Mary.
    b. John bought Mary a ring.

(11)   Particle Movement
    a. John looked up the word in the dictionary.
    b. John looked the word up in the dictionary.

(12)   Subject-Aux Inversion (SAI)
    a. John will visit the museum next week.
    b. Will John visit the museum next week?

N.B. Aux means any one of the auxiliary verbs, which include (a) modal auxiliary verbs like *will*, *can*, and *may*, (b) auxiliary *do*, (c) perfective *have*, progressive *be*, passive *be*, and (d) main verb *be* (especially when it is inverted by SAI and when it carries a negative particle *not*).

(13)   WH Movement
    a. John saw Mary [Who].
    b. Who did John see?

(14)   Topicalization
    a. I really like a bacon cheeseburger.
    b. A bacon cheeseburger, I really like.

(15)   Left Dislocation
    a. I really like a bacon cheeseburger.
    b. A bacon cheeseburger, I really like it.

(16)   Right Dislocation
    a. I really like a bacon cheeseburger.
    b. I really like it, a bacon cheeseburger.

Let us briefly see what kind of structural changes these transformations induce. First, the transformation "*to*-Dative Movement" places the Dative NP into the position immediately after the verb and takes the preposition *to* away. There is another Dative rule "*for*-Dative Movement," which also places the Dative NP into the position immediately after the verb and takes the preposition *for* away. "Particle Movement" places the particle into the position immediately after the object NP. "Subject-Aux Inversion" places Aux right in front of Subject. It is responsible for not only such interrogative sentences as (12b) and (13b), but it is also responsible for the sentences like (17a, b), but not for the embedded interrogatives like (18a, b) below:

(17) a. Never have I dreamed of such a miracle in my life.
      b. Had John ever followed my advice, he could have passed the exam.
(18) a. I wonder if John will visit the museum next week.
      b. I don't know who John saw.

"WH Movement" simply moves the WH word to the front of the clause in which it was situated, as in (18b), or the rule is in tandem with "Subject-Aux Inversion" to derive an interrogative like (13b). "Topicalization" moves the NP that we want to bring into focus to the sentence initial position. Thus, (14b) means "It is a bacon cheeseburger that I really like." "Left Dislocation," on the other hand, moves the NP that we take as topic to the sentence initial position and leaves a pronoun in the site from which the dislocated NP moved. In this construction, the fronted NP is a topic and the clause that follows is a comment on it. Thus, (15b) means "Speaking of a bacon cheeseburger, I really like it." "Right Dislocation" is responsible for the sentence like (16b), in which the right-dislocated NP gives additional information about the pronoun *it*. In this construction, the postposed NP supplies information that is missing in the preceding clause. Thus, (16b) roughly means "I really like it. Oh, if you don't know what I mean by *it*, I'll tell you it's a bacon cheeseburger."

5.5   Constraints

So far, we have conceived of syntax, a component of grammar, as comprising PSRs, Lexicon, and Transformations. The roles and functions of these subcomponents in syntax are summarized as below:

(1) Syntax
     a. PSRs: Rewriting rules that define phrase structures that lack lexical items
     b. Lexicon: A set of lexical items and their lexical information, from which lexical items are picked up and inserted into the phrase structures defined by PSRs

   c. Transformations: A new level of rules that transform one phrase marker in the form of phrase structure to another phrase marker in the form of phrase structure

Now, we apply due procedures of the rules in (1), and we generate grammatical sentences such as those in (2):

(2) a. John saw Mary yesterday.
     b. Who did John see yesterday?

The process of generating (2a) is straightforward. In order to generate (2b), first, we replace *Mary* with *who* in (2a), next, this *who* is WH-moved to the sentence initial position, and finally Subject-Aux Inversion applies. This process gives the grammatical sentence (2b).

5.5.1 Coordinate Structure Constraint

Now, observe the following:

(1) a. John saw Mary and Sue yesterday.
     b. *Who did John see ___ and Sue yesterday? [Underline marks the site from which *who* moved.]

In (1a), after having *Mary* replaced by *who*, we apply WH Movement to this phrase structure. This should be a legitimate process of rule application, but the result is an unfortunate grammaticality, (1b) being ungrammatical. Now we face a problem.

In order to overcome the type of difficulty observed in (1), we now introduce a new category of system, which we will call Constraint. Constraint is a system such that its function is to constrain the application of rules in such a way as to prohibit the improper application of rules and allow only the proper one. Thus, as a first example of this type of system, we have Coordinate Structure Constraint.

(2) Coordinate Structure Constraint
     No rule can move only one conjunct out of the coordinate structure.

Thus, Coordinate Structure Constraint prohibits the movement of [$_{NP}$ *who*] out of the structure [$_{NP}$ [$_{NP}$ *who*] *and* [$_{NP}$ *Sue*]], because it is only one conjunct of the entire coordinate structure that is displaced from the coordinate structure. Thus, (1b) is ungrammatical.

> **N.B.** The meaning that is purported to be conveyed by (1b) should not be expressed in a single interrogative. How is it, then, that we can express this meaning? It is simply to say that in two sentences, for example, "John saw someone and Sue yesterday. Who was it?"

With the constraint (2) being effective to the entire rule applications, we can generate all and only grammatical sentences without any modification to PSRs or Transformations.

5.5.2   Complex NP Constraint

Next, observe the following:

(1) a.   John believes that Bill kissed Mary yesterday.
      b.   Who does John believe that Bill kissed ___ yesterday?
(2) a.   John believes the claim that Bill kissed Mary yesterday.
      b. *Who does John believe the claim that Bill kissed ___ yesterday?

In (1a), after having *Mary* replaced by *who*, we apply WH Movement to this phrase structure. This is a legitimate process of rule application, and the result is fine, (1b) being grammatical. In (2a), however, after having *Mary* replaced by *who*, we apply WH Movement to this phrase structure. This should be a legitimate process of rule application, but the result is the unfortunate grammaticality, (2b) being ungrammatical. Now, we face a problem.

In order to overcome the type of difficulty observed in (2), we now introduce Complex NP Constraint. Below are the characterizations of Complex NP and Complex NP Constraint:

(3)   Complex NP
      Complex NP is such an NP that dominates both a lexical head noun and S.
(4)   Complex NP Constraint
      No rule can move an item dominated by S that is dominated by the Complex NP out of this Complex NP.

Thus, Complex NP Constraint prohibits the movement of [$_{NP}$ *who*] out of the structure [$_{NP}$ [$_{NP}$ *the claim*] [$_S$ *that Bill kissed who yesterday*]], because it is an item dominated by S that is dominated by the Complex NP.

> **N.B.** The meaning that is purported to be conveyed by (2b) should not be expressed in a single interrogative. How is it, then, that we can express this meaning? It is simply to say that in two sentences, for example, "John believes the claim that Bill kissed someone yesterday. Who was it?"

With this constraint being effective to the entire rule applications, we can generate all and only grammatical sentences without any modification to PSRs or Transformations.

Note also that Complex NP Constraint is at work when (5b) is ruled out.

(5) a. John interviewed the athlete who won the gold medal.
     b. *Which medal did John interview the athlete who won ___ ?

This is because in (5b), *Which medal* is moved out of the relative clause attached to an antecedent, i.e. out of the structure [NP [NP *the athlete*] [S *who won* [NP *which medal*]]], which is clearly another case of the structure dictated in (4). Thus, WH Movement should be applicable to (5a), but it in fact cannot apply because of the violation of Complex NP Constraint.

5.6   Case Studies in Syntax

In this section, we will illustrate a number of case studies of syntactic manipulations applied to the English language, and in so doing, we will show what it is like to do syntactic analyses.

5.6.1   Sequential Application of Transformations

In §5.4, we have introduced several of the Transformations that have so far been proposed in the literature. There, each of the Transformations is responsible for the construction that is derived. Here in this subsection, we will demonstrate that there are cases where only through the interaction of Transformations can we arrive at the desired result, "desired" in the sense that it is both empirically correct and theoretically sound, i.e. requiring no more rules than needed.

Observe the following:

(1) a. John gave a book to Mary.
     b. A book was given to Mary.
     c. *Mary was given a book to.
(2) a. John gave Mary a book.
     b. Mary was given a book.
     c. A book was given Mary.

This array of facts in (1) and (2) are expected, or explained, if we have
to-Dative Movement and Passive Transformation and we assume that they
apply in this order. Thus, details aside regarding the exact shape of the
phrase structure, we apply Passive Transformation (3) to (1a), and derive
(1b) but not (1c) because SD of (3) is not satisfied if we were to derive (1c)
from (1a). We apply *to*-Dative Movement (4) to (1a) and derive (2a).

(3) Passive Transformation (= §5.4 (7))
     SD: X, NP_1, V, NP_2, Y
     SC: 1, 2, 3, 4, 5 → 1, 4, be +3*en*, by + 2, 5
(4) *to*-Dative Movement
     SD: X, V, NP_1, *to*, NP_2, Y
     SC: 1, 2, 3, 4, 5, 6 → 1, 2 + 5, 3, Ø, Ø, 6

The derived structure of (2a) is worth mentioning. The SC of (4) dictates
that the 5th term be adjoined to the 2nd term, which means that the
category that dominates the derived sequence of [2 + 5] is the same as the
one that dominates the original term of [2], i.e. V in this case. Thus, (2a)
roughly has the following phrase structure:

(2) a'. [s [NP John NP] [VP [V [V gave V] [NP Mary NP] V] [NP a book NP]
          VP] s]

There are two important points to be noted: one is that [NP *Mary* NP] is
adjacent to the verb [V *gave* V], and the other is that [NP *a book* NP] is
adjacent to the verb [V [V *gave* V] [NP *Mary* NP] V]. The former is responsible for the grammatical passive sentence (2b), and the latter for the
grammatical passive sentence (2c). This analysis regarding the facts (1)
and (2) proves that *to*-Dative Movement and Passive Transformation
should optionally apply in this order to derive grammatical sentences and
to exclude the ungrammatical derivations.
   Now, observe the following:

(5) a. John bought a book for Mary.
     b. A book was bought for Mary.
     c. *Mary was bought a book for.
(6) a. John bought Mary a book.
     b. *Mary was bought a book.
     c. *A book was bought Mary.

We have *for*-Dative Movement as in (7) to relate (5a) to (6a).

(7) *for*-Dative Movement
     SD: X, V, NP$_1$, *for*, NP$_2$, Y
     SC: 1, 2, 3, 4, 5, 6 → 1, 2 + 5, 3, Ø, Ø, 6

In order to accommodate the facts in (5) and (6), we decide that Passive Transformation and *for*-Dative Movement should optionally apply in this order. Thus, once we skip Passive Transformation and go on to apply *for*-Dative Movement to (5a), we obtain (6a), but we no longer have access to Passive Transformation. Therefore, we could never derive passive counterparts from (6a). Hence the ungrammaticality in (6b, c).

Next, observe the following:

(8) a. John fixed up a hamburger for Mary.
     b. John fixed a hamburger up for Mary.

In order to relate (8a) to (8b), we have Particle Movement as in (9), where Prt is short for Particle.

(9) Particle Movement
     SD: X, V, Prt, NP, Y
     SC: 1, 2, 3, 4, 5 → 1, 2, Ø, 4 + 3, 5

N.B. The derived structure of Particle Movement has as part of the entire phrase structure the VP structure of the form [$_{VP}$ [$_V$ *fixed* $_V$] [$_{NP}$ *a hamburger* $_{NP}$] [$_{Prt}$ *up* $_{Prt}$] $_{VP}$]. The makeup of the latter VP structure is based upon the regular VP structure with an optional adverb such as the one like "to throw the ball (away)."

Now, we have another set of grammatical sentences in (10) below:

(10) a. John fixed up a hamburger for Mary. (= (8a))
      b. John fixed up Mary a hamburger.
      c. John fixed Mary up a hamburger.

In order to accommodate the facts in (8) and (10), we decide that *for*-Dative Movement and Particle Movement should optionally apply in this order. Thus, since we can choose not to apply *for*-Dative Movement to (8a), we go on to apply Particle Movement and derive (8b). Next, we turn to (10a). Applying *for*-Dative Movement to (10a), we obtain (10b). To (10b) we apply Particle Movement and derive (10c). The grammatical sentence (10c) is significant in several respects. First, no phrase structure grammatical analysis seems to be a feasible way to derive (10c), or for that matter (8b). That is to say, the verb-particle combination [*fix up*] of the single transitive verb status is broken apart in (8b) and (10c), which fact, the discrete dependency, could not be accounted for solely in terms of phrase structure rules. Secondly, if the two rules were ordered the other way around, we could not expect the grammatical (10c). This fact endorses the correctness of this ordering of these rules. Thirdly, the surface word order is intriguing if we compare (8b) and (10c), but it is not surprising if we assume the sequential application of the two transformations. That is to say, the fact that in (8b) we have the sequence "fixed a hamburger up" while in (10c) we have "fixed Mary up" does not force us to be confused as to what *John* fixed up and for whom *John* did something, even though Accusative NP *a hamburger* and Dative NP *Mary* fall in one and the same syntactic position between *fix* and *up*. Assuming the analysis with transformations applied in a specified order, we naturally arrive at the desired result.

> **N.B.** In general terms, Accusative Case is the case that Direct Object of the verb assumes, and Dative Case the case that Indirect Object of the verb assumes. See (i). The NP with Dative Case is sometimes paraphrasable as a prepositional object as in (ii).
> (i)   John gave Mary a book. / John bought Mary a book.
> (ii) John gave a book to Mary. / John bought a book for Mary.

Transformational analyses illustrated so far of the facts presented in this subsection, therefore, provide correct predictions about the empirical observations, and at the same time do away with improbable theoretical complication of each of the rules defined as they are, simply by postulating transformations in the specified order.

> **N.B.** The sentences derived by *to*-Dative Movement and *for*-Dative Movement are called double object construction (DOC). Passive Transformation may or may not apply to DOC and the results are shown in (2)

and (6). We are assuming that grammaticality judgments shown in these examples are the canonical patterns as far as DOC and Passive Transformation are concerned. But we need to note some variable factors regarding the grammatical behaviors of this construction.

In what follows, NP_1 means the subject of DOC, NP_2 the Dative object of DOC, and NP_3 the Accusative object of DOC in "NP_1 give/buy NP_2 NP_3."

   (i) In (2c), as the sentence "A book was given Mary" shows, the syntactic pattern 'NP_3 be given NP_2' is perfectly grammatical, but NP_2 appears, more often than not, in the form of pronoun (e.g., *me*, *him*, etc.) rather than in the form of full NP (e.g., *John, the boy, the gentleman from Tokyo*, etc.).

   (ii) In contrast to (2c), the syntactic pattern of (6c) exemplified in "*A book was bought Mary" is invariably ungrammatical: the syntactic pattern '*NP_3 be bought NP_2' is necessarily ruled out irrespective of the form NP_2 carries, i.e. whether a pronoun or a full NP.

   (iii) The syntactic pattern of (6b) exemplified in "*Mary was bought a book" is canonically ill-formed, but the pattern 'NP_2 be bought NP_3' sometimes surfaces as being acceptable, or being extended as grammatical. (As for the notions 'grammaticality' and 'acceptability,' see §7.2 "Grammaticality and Acceptability" in Chapter VII Pragmatics.) Below are some examples:

     (a) He was bought a few drinks by workmates…. (BNC Online) (Accessed June 21, 2023)

     (b) She was bought a guitar, which she learnt to play while supine. (WordbanksOnline) (Accessed June 21, 2023)

The reason the pattern 'NP_2 be bought NP_3' comes to be accepted is that the pattern has a close semantic similarity with the pattern 'NP_2 be given NP_3' in that in both cases NP_2 is a recipient of Theme NP_3. (Theme is a semantic term for something that moves along in the scene.) In this case, we say that the pattern 'NP_2 be bought NP_3' is derivatively obtained (or extended) on the model of the pattern 'NP_2 be given NP_3.'

5.6.2   Syntactic Regularities over Meaning

In general, syntactic constructions have associated with them certain semantic properties that include, for example, Agent, Patient, Activity, State, and the like. For example, the active sentence (1a) has (1b) as its passive counterpart.

(1)   a.   The dog chased the cat.

   b.   The cat was chased by the dog.

In the active sentence (1a), subject NP *the dog* is the Agent of the Activity *chase*, and this physical activity is directed toward the Patient *the cat*. In the passive sentence (1b), on the other hand, the Patient assumes the subject position and the Agent is dislocated down into the object position in the *by*-phrase. Next, we have a construction called "Existential *there* construction" like the one in (2a), and there is good reason to believe that this construction has much to do with "Locative Adverb Preposing construction" in (3a, b), where both Locative Adverb Preposing and Subject-Verb Inversion have applied. But, since "Existential *there* construction" has already established its own syntactic status in the grammar of English, *there* in "Existential *there* construction" is simply a grammatical marker and therefore no longer functions as a locative adverb. This is evidenced by the existence of the adverb *here*, which would have to be contradictory if *there* were also a locative adverb in (2b). Compare the ungrammatical (3c, d), where the preposed adverb and the sentence final *here* are semantically mutually exclusive of each other. Therefore, "Existential *there* construction" as in (2) and "Locative Adverb Preposing construction" as in (3) are distinct constructions from each other, at least by now: *there* in "Existential *there* construction" is simply a grammatical marker, while a locative adverb in "Locative Adverb Preposing construction" is simply an adverb. Thus, *there* in "Existential *there* construction" is a function word and does not in the least refer to some kind of entity.

   (2)   a.   There is a unicorn in the yard.
          b.   There is also a tricorn here.
   (3)   a.   There lies a giant panda.
          b.   Around the corner stands a mysterious mansion.
          c.   *There lies a giant panda here.
          d.   *Around the corner stands a mysterious mansion here.

Now, observe the following:

   (4)   a.   We believe that there is a unicorn in the yard.
          b.   We believe there to be a unicorn in the yard.
          c.   There is believed to be a unicorn in the yard.

In the object position where the verb *believe* has an embedded finite (or tensed) clause in (4a), there is an embedded infinitival clause in (4b). Applying Passive transformation to (4b), we obtain (4c). This is a regular process of syntactic rule application. But there is a remarkable point here, regarding the syntax-semantics relationship. Semantically speaking, passive subject should be a Patient as we saw in the case of (1b), but the one in (4c) is not a Patient, let alone a concrete physical entity. It is merely a grammatical marker and it happens to fall in the very position reserved for the 'Patient'! In addition, notice that the verb "is" in the collocation of "There is ..." in (4c) is not the 'existential *be*,' but rather it is a 'passive *be*.' The 'existential *be*' appears down in the embedded clause as an infinitival form "to be." Recall the fact that the verb "is" in the collocation of "There is ..." in (2a, b) is rightly the 'existential *be*.' Observing all these properties that (4c) has, we claim that it happens that as the result of due processes of syntactic rule applications, the semantic properties on which certain syntactic manipulations are based may sometimes be overridden. This is one of the types of cases where syntactic regularities extend over meaning.

Let us cite another case. Observe the following:

(5)   a.   John fixed up a hamburger for Mary. (=§5.6.1 (8a))
      b.   John fixed a hamburger up for Mary. (=§5.6.1 (8b))
      c.   John fixed up Mary a hamburger. (=§5.6.1 (10b))
      d.   John fixed Mary up a hamburger. (=§5.6.1 (10c))

The verb-particle combination *fix up* is followed by an Accusative Object as in (5a), and the particle may jump over this Accusative Object to form the sentence (5b). This is the effect of Particle Movement. But once *for*-Dative Movement has applied as in (5c), Particle Movement subsequently applies and it is now Dative Object that the particle jumps over, as shown in (5d). Recall the fact that the NP in the structure "V NP Prt" is Patient (or Theme) as it is with the case of the structure [$_{VP}$ [$_V$ *throw*] [$_{NP}$ *the ball*] [$_{Adv}$ *away*]]. However, in the case of (5d), the NP over which Prt jumps to derive the structure "V NP Prt" is not Patient (or Theme) but it is Benefactive, the semantic case that receives some kind of benefit. Thus, again we claim that as the result of due process of syntactic rule applications, the semantic properties on which certain syntactic manipulations are based may sometimes be overridden as in the case of (5d). This is another type of case where syntactic regularities automatically extend so far as to go beyond meaning on which certain syntactic manipulations are originally based.

5.6.3   Transformational Ambiguity and Disambiguation

There is a certain number of sentences that are said to be ambiguous due to the application of transformations. Observe below:

(1)   Flying planes can be dangerous.

Details aside, there are two syntactic sources for (1): one is essentially the structure that has the meaning "If you fly airplanes, then that act can be dangerous," and the other is the structure with the meaning "Planes that are flying can be dangerous." In the former reading, the head of the subject NP is *flying*, which is a gerund: gerund is a verb-turned nominal in the form of V*ing*. In the latter reading, the head of the subject NP is *planes* modified by the present participle *flying*: present participle is a type of verbal inflection in the form of V*ing*. The two distinct structures are proposed to end up as the sentences with one and the same surface word order as in (1) through the applications of relevant transformations.

Observe another case in (2) below:

(2)   The chicken is ready to eat.

The sentence (2) is ambiguous: one interpretation is such that the chicken is ready and it will eat something, and the other is such that the food stuff, e.g. roast chicken, is ready and we will eat it. In this case, too, we assume that relevant transformations have applied to the distinct structures to derive one and the same surface form (2).

Thirdly, the sentence (3) below is ambiguous.

(3)   The door was closed.

One reading is such that the door was closed by someone, and the other is such that the door was in the state of being closed for a while. The former is a passive counterpart of an active sentence with actional meaning, while the latter is a stative description of what the door was.

While there is a type of phenomena where transformations induce ambiguity as in the cases of (1) through (3), we have cases where transformations help disambiguate the potential ambiguities. Let us call this process 'transformational disambiguation.' Observe below:

(4) a. John kicked the bucket.
     b. The bucket was kicked by John.

The active sentence (4a) is ambiguous between literal and idiomatic readings, the idiomatic reading being "John died." But once Passive transformation applies, it helps disambiguate (4a), and (4b) has the literal reading only. Similarly, there is a transformation that we propose is called "*so is* Subject" Construction Formation, whose effect is to interchange the subject and *so* over *be*. This transformation serves to disambiguate the possible ambiguities.

(5) a. This curry is hot, and so is this Sichuan dish.
     b. This curry is hot, and so is this coffee.
(6) a. The chicken is ready to eat, and so is the puppy.
     b. The chicken is ready to eat, and so is the salad.

In (5a), *this curry* can only be interpreted as being spicy, while in (5b), it can only be of high temperature. In (6a), *the chicken* can only be interpreted as the one that is about to eat something, while in (6b), it can only be interpreted as the food stuff that we eat.

Thus, we have a body of facts about transformational ambiguity and transformational disambiguation, and it is because we have such means as transformations that these facts can be properly analyzed in a natural and least artificial way.

5.6.4 Grammatical Naturalization

There is a syntactic process we would like to term Grammatical Naturalization, a typical set of examples of which are shown below:

(1) a. John drank a quick cup of coffee.
     b. John drank a cup of coffee quickly.

If you simply look at only the sequence *a quick cup* in (1a), you would be puzzled because you are forced to try to interpret the phrase and imagine something like "the cup that is quick." The reality is, however, the sentence (1a) is not strange at all, or rather, it is perfectly grammatical. The adjective *quick* of (1a) is, in fact, originally an adverb that modifies the VP "to drink a cup of coffee," as is clearly shown in (1b).

This type of syntactic process is motivated by the pair of sentences in

(2):

   (2) a. John is a frequent visitor to the museum.

         b. John visits the museum frequently.

Here, the adjective *frequent* of (2a) is semantically related to the adverb *frequently* of (2b), and this adjective *frequent* prenominally modifies the noun *visitor*. The adverb-adjective alteration phenomena of this type can be rephrased in more general terms such that an adverb-turned adjective may prenominally modify the noun that is both moving and highlighted in the entire situational framework into which the activity of (2) is encoded. This is the phenomena we call Grammatical Naturalization. In semantics, something that moves along a certain path is called Theme. Thus, in (2), the noun *visitor* is Theme, and the adverb-turned adjective *frequent* prenominally modifies the Theme noun *visitor*. Similarly, in (1), the noun *cup* is Theme, and the adverb-turned adjective *quick* prenominally modifies the Theme noun *cup*. Observe another case of Grammatical Naturalization in (3) below:

   (3) a. An occasional sailor strolled by.

         b. A sailor strolled by occasionally.

Here again, the adverb-turned adjective *occasional* prenominally modifies the Theme noun *sailor*.

     Based on the observation thus far, we will be justified in saying that there is a syntactic process Grammatical Naturalization such that a VP-adverbial may be turned into an adjective and this adjective falls in the prenominal position of the noun that serves as Theme in the entire semantic representation of the sentence. Now, we will see below the application of this syntactic Grammatical Naturalization to one of the most recalcitrant idioms. The idiom "to kick the bucket" is an informal phrase that means "to die," and this phrase is a syntactic hard nut that rejects almost all syntactic processes. Ungrammatical examples below are intended to mean idiomatic readings only, which means of course they are grammatical under the literal readings.

   (4) a. John kicked the bucket.

         b. *John kicked a/his/this/that bucket.

         c. *John kicked the wooden bucket.

         d. *John kicked the bucket that he bought yesterday.

    e. *The bucket was kicked by John.
    f. *It was the bucket that John kicked.
    g. *The bucket, John kicked.
    h. *The bucket, John kicked it.

In the examples (4b–h), the idiom is resistant to such syntactic manipulations as paradigmatic alterations of determiners, modification by an adjective, relativization, passivization, Cleft sentence formation, Topicalization,
and Left Dislocation, respectively. But surprisingly, Grammatical Naturalization is a unique syntactic process that does apply to this idiom. See
below:

    (5) a. John kicked the proverbial bucket.
          b. John kicked the bucket in the stereotypical (=proverbial)
              way.

The adverbial *in the stereotypical (=proverbial) way* in (5b) is now turned
into an adjective *proverbial* and this adjective modifies the noun that
follows, as shown in (5a). Although modification by an adjective is
prohibited in the idiom "to kick the bucket" as shown in (4c), Grammatical
Naturalization nevertheless applies and derives the grammatical (5a). In
this sense, Grammatical Naturalization is so unique that it deserves mention.

    Grammatical Naturalization is unique in the sense that even when
many of the syntactic processes are inapplicable to a certain construction,
Grammatical Naturalization still applies to this very construction, as we
have seen in (4) and (5). On the other hand, there is a case such that where
many of the syntactic processes are applicable, Grammatical Naturalization
is inapplicable. Observe the following:

    (6) a. John served a cup of coffee.
          b. John served several cups of coffee.
          c. John served a paper cup of coffee.
          d. John served a cup of coffee that Mary brewed.
          e. A cup of coffee was served by John.
          f. It was a cup of coffee that John served.
          g. A cup of coffee, John served.
          h. A cup of coffee, John served it.
    (7) a. *John served a quick cup of coffee.

b.   John served a cup of coffee quickly.

Now, it is certainly clear that various syntactic manipulations are applicable to (6a) so that we have various types of sentences (6b–h) derived from (6a). But Grammatical Naturalization alone does not apply, as shown in (7). That way, Grammatical Naturalization is a unique syntactic process.

N.B.1 "Paradigmatic alterations of determiners" simply means putting any one of the articles, demonstratives, and possessives into the position before the noun. Cleft sentence is such a construction that has the form like "it is [FOCUS] that [PRESUPPOSITION]." We pick a phrase out of a sentence and put it into the FOCUS position: this phrase receives focus. Next, we put the rest of the sentence into the PRESUPPOSITION position and this part semantically represents the presupposed information.

N.B.2 Grammatical Naturalization is so called because a foreign item gets guised so as to be formally settled, i.e., naturalized, in the new domestic area where there is no semantic kith or kin around the newcomer. For example, in (1), *quickly* gets guised as *quick* so as to be formally settled in the NP where there is no semantic relationship between *quick* and the following noun *cup*. This is naturalization in the case of grammar. Hence, Grammatical Naturalization. See Nakazawa (2003) for the detail.

N.B.3 Grammatical Naturalization is a special case of what has traditionally been called "Transferred Epithet." Transferred Epithet is the case where prenominal adjectives are semantically related to various sorts of syntactic origins and the nouns modified by these adjectives are not necessarily confined to those of the category Theme. A couple of examples will suffice to show the difference between Grammatical Naturalization and Transferred Epithet. In the examples of Transferred Epithet below, a-sentences have their 'Epithet' transferred from b-sentences.

(i)   a.   John is a <u>rural</u> policeman.
      b.   John is a policeman in charge of the rural area.
(ii) a.   Since that <u>victorious</u> day, peace had reigned in Pac-World. (WordbanksOnline) (Accessed July 6, 2023)
      b.   Since the day the enemy was defeated, peace had reigned in Pac-World.

N.B.4 To be sure, the sentence (i) is another case that demonstrates that syntactic regularities have surpassed the meaning on which Grammatical Naturalization was originally motivated.

(i)   John kicked the proverbial bucket. (= (5a))
(ii) a.   John is a frequent visitor to the museum. (= (2a))

    b. John drank a quick cup of coffee. (= (1a))

    c. An occasional sailor strolled by. (= (3a))

That is, (ii) is the original case on which Grammatical Naturalization is based, and the nouns modified by the grammatically naturalized adjectives are the nouns that refer to concrete objects with the semantic role of Theme. But, their counterpart noun in (i) is *bucket*, which is by no means a referential object in the idiomatic reading of the sentence, nor is it Theme. But in the proverbial sense, *the bucket* is truly a fictional Theme. Therefore, the fact that we have Grammatical Naturalization in idioms means that we have another case for the syntactic regularities that may extend over meaning.

5.7   Some Universals in Syntax

Arguments about linguistic universals should go in a careful and elaborate manner because universals are either confirmed or falsified only on the basis of the grammatical descriptions of all natural languages. In other words, mere empirical facts about certain languages are not sufficient in themselves for linguists to argue for or against certain universals: we need regularities about these empirical facts in order to probe into the linguistic universals, which are essentially the regularities about "regularities about the empirical facts." In what follows, we see a number of abstract syntactic features that we believe we may rightly propose to be universals.

N.B. X-bar Theory is one kind of Universals that could be argued for as a system of principles that govern the behaviors of Phrase Structure Rules of all human languages.

5.7.1   Structural Constituency

As a first category of linguistic universals, we propose that grammar should rely on structural constituency. In other words, grammatical manipulations should be applicable only onto constituents. This type of universal allows for a number of realizations. Among these possibilities, we will see two of them below.

It seems there are at least two types of universals as far as the structural constituency is concerned. One is about categorial generalization, and the other is about formal properties of rule application.

5.7.1.1   Categorial Generalization

Now, we look into categorial generalization. The crudest form of this generalization is such that word is the minimum form of constituent in a sentence. In languages where words do not form any larger constituent, there should not be phrases, by definition, and we have two possibilities of this type: one is such that a single word constitutes a sentence and the other is such that there is dependency among words in a sentence without recourse to phrases. As for the latter notion of dependency, see §5.7.2.

> **N.B.** In fact, it is not a given fact that every language has a unit, or notion, called "word." The definition of 'word' largely relies on the analysis we regard as something we take to be practically sound or reasonably flaw-less. The bottom-line universal might then be such that every language has a means to express ideas. In some languages, ideas may be encapsulated into a word, and in others they may be not. Here, however, we are begging the question and assuming that all languages have a syntactic constituent "word."

In languages where words may form larger constituents, i.e. phrases, syntactic manipulations are applicable only onto these constituents. In this case, we may have the following three generalizations, among others. They are about (A) Branching, (B) Substitution, and (C) Movement. They are related to the form of the syntactic structures.

First, we note a categorial generalization about branching that can be phrased as below:

(A)   Branching
      Only a constituent has a branching structure.

Examples of this categorial generalization are illustrated in (1):

(1)   That only a constituent has a branching structure means that it is the case that a certain string of categories form a constituent. For example, the string of [V NP] forms a VP, that of [Det N] an NP, that of [NP VP] an S, and so on. In other words, Phrase Structure Rules (PSRs) rewrite a single category symbol into a string of grammatical entities, but they do not rewrite two, or more, category symbols at a time into a string of some entities. In this way, we have a hierarchical phrase structure for a sentence.

Next, we have a categorial generalization such that a constituent be substituted for another constituent, as shown below:

(B) Substitution
     If an item *a* of the category X is in the structure S, then another item *b* of the category X is in the structure S.

Examples of this categorial generalization are abundant. A few of them are illustrated in (2):

(2) If an item *book* of the category Noun is in the structure "this [$_N$ book]," then another item *movie* of the category Noun is in this structure. Hence, we have "this [$_N$ movie]". Informally speaking, if we have "This [$_N$ book] is good," then we have "This [$_N$ movie] is good," "This [$_N$ picture] is good," and so on. We also say that if we have "[$_{NP}$ The boy] is from Tokyo," then we have "[$_{NP}$ The tall boy] is from Tokyo," "[$_{NP}$ The boy with a pen in his hand] is from Tokyo," "[$_{NP}$ The boy who won the prize] is from Tokyo," "[$_{NP}$ He] is from Tokyo," and so on.

Thirdly, we have a categorial generalization such that only a constituent be moved, as shown below:

(C) Movement
     Only constituents move.

Examples of this categorial generalization are illustrated in (3):

(3) When we have a passive sentence derived from an active one, we move such constituents as Subject NP and Object NP. For example, the passive sentence "The tall girl was kissed by John" is obtained from the active "John kissed the tall girl" by moving the constituents "John" and "the tall girl." But movement of a nonconstituent is prohibited, as the ungrammaticality of "*The tall was kissed [$_{NP}$ __ girl] by John," "*The girl was kissed [$_{NP}$ _ tall _] by John," and "*Tall girl was kissed [$_{NP}$ the __] by John" shows.

N.B. Note that in the last example of (3), [tall girl] may be a constituent of the type N", but the result is ungrammatical. So, technically speaking, the universal should be: only constituents of the maximum bar-level move.

In general terms, the universal of (A) Branching says that grammar has Phrase Structure Rules (PSRs), the universal of (B) Substitution says that constituents of the same syntactic category assume the same function in the given structure, as, for example, in the case of lexical insertion, and also in the case of the structures with the same syntactic labels, and the universal of (C) Movement says that rules like transformations (or, to be precise, constants in SD) can only refer to constituents.

5.7.1.2 Formal Properties of Rule Application

In addition to the universals above, we may have two universals regarding formal properties of rule application. In languages where the grammar has Phrase Structure Rules (PSRs) and where embedding is a recognized process, we may be justified in saying that PSRs are recursive. But from one perspective, it might be that the universal of "Recursiveness" below is a special case of the universal on (A) Branching above. But from another perspective, we can say that this universal guarantees that PSRs be applied for indefinite times. In this sense, "Recursiveness" may be regarded as a universal on how to apply rules.

(D)   Recursiveness
      A certain type of constituent reappears in the host structure.

Applications of this formal universal are illustrated in (4):

(4)   The category S is recursive in the structure like "I think [s that John believes [s that Mary expected [s that Adam would win]]]. The category NP is recursive in the structure like "Mary was standing by [NP the old oak tree in front of [NP the house near [NP the railroad station]]]."

Next, in languages where the grammar has PSGs, we may have another universal on the application of rules, as shown below:

(E)   Superiority
      If there is more than one target constituent for a constant in a rule to operate on, it is the "highest" constituent among them that gets the effect of the rule.

One instantiation of this universal is Coordinate Structure Constraint, which we discussed in §5.5.1.

(5)   Coordinate Structure Constraint
      No rule can move only one conjunct out of the coordinate structure.

Coordinate Structure Constraint essentially says that out of the coordinate structure, you should pick out the largest constituent, i.e. the coordinate structure itself, rather than each one of the conjuncts. Observe the following examples:

(6)   a.   John and Mary will win the race.
      b.   Will John and Mary win the race?
      c.   *John and will Mary win the race?
(7)   a.   John admired Aaron and Beth.
      b.   Who did John admire?
      c.   *Who did John admire and Beth?
      d.   *Who did John admire Aaron and?

N.B. The universal on superiority is otherwise called "A-over-A principle." The exact nature of the latter is varying depending on the definition of it, but it essentially means that you pick the higher category A that is situated over, i.e. dominates, the lower category A.

In general terms, the universal of (D) Recursiveness says that PSRs are recursive and that of (E) Superiority says that rules like transformations observe the specific manner of application when there is more than one target constituent.

N.B. We may say that languages that have phrase structures must have a certain version of X-bar theory. As far as this observation is tenable, X-bar theory assumes a universal character of this restricted sense.

5.7.2   Dependency among Constituents

Assuming that a sentence consists of multiple words, we naturally claim that there is dependency that holds among these words. And across languages, there are ways to represent the types of dependency among words. The crudest form of dependency is "free dependency," as it were. It means any possible semantic relationship that holds among constituents in a phrase or a sentence. Observe below:

(1)   [N applesauce] [N apple tree] [N Christmas tree] [N Christmas

song] [N love song] [N birdsong]
(2) a. a good knife
     b. a good firewall
     c. a young policeman
     d. a local policeman
(3) a. Dancing in the hall for an hour, Mary got exhausted.
     b. Dancing in the hall for an hour, Mary kept on singing her favorite songs.
(4) a. The CEO of the company, John Smith wanted to meet the famous economist.
     b. The CEO of the company, John Smith wanted to meet (him).

In (1), we have words of the form [N X Y] and the semantic relationship between X and Y can be anything that is conceivable. In (2a), *a good knife* is a knife which should be sharp, while *a good firewall* is something which may be thick and sturdy. In (2c), *a young policeman* is young, while *a local policeman* should never be local but is stationed in a local area. Thus, an adjective semantically modifies the following noun the way any reasonable semantic interpretation is tenable. In (3), if we want to paraphrase (3a) and (3b), the conjunction to be employed in (3a) is not the same as that of (3b). Likewise, in (4), the semantic relationship that holds between *The CEO of the company* and the following matrix sentence in (4a) is not the same as that of (4b). These are the examples of what we regard as the cases of "free dependency."

When there is dependency other than free dependency among constituents, we have several possibilities. One way to represent dependency is word order. In English, for example, word order determines Subject and Object, among others, and accordingly their respective semantic roles, as shown below:

(5) Word order
     "John kissed Mary"
     [Subject '*John*'-Agent, Main verb '*kiss*'-Action, Object '*Mary*'-Patient]
     "Mary kissed John"
     [Subject '*Mary*'-Agent, Main verb '*kiss*'-Action, Object '*John*'-Patient]

Here, word order determines who is Agent, and who is Patient when the main verb is an actional verb. There are also other means than word order to represent dependency: they are word-internal and word-external means. The former is called inflection, which represents the type of dependency of concord or agreement. The latter employs ad-positions, which include prepositions and postpositions.

(6)   Word-internal means: Inflection
      a.   "Declension" of nouns: "I admire her" vs. "*Her admires I"
      b.   "Conjugation" of verbs: I/You/We/They walk; He walks; I/You/He/We/They walked; I am; You/We/They are; He is; I/He was; You/They/We were.

The word-internal marking of dependency is called inflection, which comprises declension and conjugation. The former typically marks the Case that a noun assumes, e.g. Nominative, Accusative, and so on. English examples are given in (6a). The latter typically marks the combined form of tense, person, and number (and possibly gender) that a verb assumes, e.g. Present/Past, 1st/2nd/3rd person, and singular/plural (and possibly male/female/neuter). English examples are given in (6b).

(7)   Word-external means: Ad-position
      a.   Preposition: "on the desk" [Locative], "from London to New York" [Source-Goal]
      b.   Postposition: "tukue-de/ni"   [Locative],   "rondon-kara nyuuyooku-made" [Source-Goal]

In (7a), one of the word-external means, i.e. preposition, is employed, and in (7b), the other means, i.e. postposition, is employed. The former is of the English examples, and the latter of the Japanese counterparts.

In short, languages employ certain formal means to represent dependency among words in a sentence.

N.B. There are a group of languages called polysynthetic languages, where a single word can mean the content (or proposition) that a full sentence in other languages usually means. In this case, too, there is dependency among the morphemes in a word.

5.7.3   Island: An Insulated "Domain"
It is true that we have various types of dependency among words in a

sentence, but it is still the case that there is a "domain" in a sentence such that one constituent inside the domain and another outside the same domain cannot be interrelated with each other. This kind of insulated domain, we call Island. Thus, we have the universal as in (1):

(1)   Island
      There is a kind of domain called Island such that no rule can relate an element inside this domain with another outside.

Since the notion of Island in (1) is a universal characterization, the grammar of each language has a language particular definition of the domain of Island. One interpretation of (1) is Complex NP Constraint, which we discussed in §5.5.2.

(2)   Complex NP Constraint
      No rule can move an item dominated by S that is dominated by the Complex NP out of this Complex NP.

Complex NP Constraint is dearly needed when we analyze the following array of English examples:

(3)   a.   Bill kissed Mary yesterday.
      b.   Who did Bill kiss yesterday?
(4)   a.   John believes [that Bill kissed Mary yesterday].
      b.   Who does John believe [that Bill kissed yesterday]?
(5)   a.   John believes [the claim that Bill kissed Mary yesterday].
      b. *Who does John believe [the claim that Bill kissed yesterday]?

There is no island in (3a), so we can relate the WH phrase *who*, which is a substitute for *Mary*, with the sentence initial position: this means that we can move *who* from the object position of the verb *kiss* to the sentence initial position. The result is a grammatical sentence (3b). In (4a), the bracketed part is not an island, and we derive (4b) without any violation. But in (5a), because the bracketed part is clearly an island, we cannot derive (5b). Hence it is ungrammatical.

It seems quite reasonable to say that the ungrammaticality of (7b) below is due to another interpretation of (1), i.e. (6):

(6)   Adverbial Island Constraint
      No rule can move an item out of an adverbial clause.
(7)   a.   John ate the hamburger [when Mary was watching TV].
      b.   *What did John eat the hamburger [when Mary was watch-
           ing]?

In (7a), because the bracketed part is an adverbial clause, we cannot move the WH phrase *what* out of this island and put it in the sentence initial position. Hence (7b) is ungrammatical.

> **N.B.** Generally, you cannot extract an item out of an 'adjunct' as in (7b) above, while you can out of an "argument" as in (4b) above. An adjunct is an optional phrase, and an argument is an obligatory one.

An idiomatic expression of the most "frozen" type, e.g. *kick the bucket*, can be said to be an island in the sense that no syntactic rule applies to it. Observe the examples in (8) (= (4) in §5.6.4), where each of the examples are intended to have an idiomatic reading:

(8)   a.   John kicked the bucket.
      b.   *John kicked a/his/this/that bucket.
      c.   *John kicked the wooden bucket.
      d.   *John kicked the bucket that he bought yesterday.
      e.   *The bucket was kicked by John.
      f.   *It was the bucket that John kicked.
      g.   *The bucket, John kicked.
      h.   *The bucket, John kicked it.

A word itself seems to constitute an island when any syntactic and/or semantic operation cannot relate an element inside it with another that stands outside. For example, you cannot have *light* internally modify *green* in "*a *light* [N *green*house N]." Cf. §4.5.

> **N.B.** In this entire section, i.e. from the subsection of §5.7.1 through that of §5.7.3, we have observed an array of possible syntactic universals. This is in a sense a bird's-eye view of universals. There is, however, another perspective to view all these universals. It is a dynamic view which supposes a set of core basic conceptions that will eventually develop into a full set of linguistic properties. For this view, see grammatical dynamism at the end of §5.8.

5.8   Theories of Syntax: Some Approaches

So far, we have assumed that syntax mainly consists of PSRs, Lexicon, and Transformations, and that the representations formed in syntax include Deep Structure and Surface Structure, among others. Deep Structure is the phrase structure that is the result of applying PSRs and lexical insertion. Surface Structure is the phrase structure that is the result of all possible applications of Transformations.

There are, however, a variety of linguistic theories proposed so far in the literature that claim different types of grammatical architecture than the one we have presented in this chapter. To cite a simple case or two, one theory claims no transformations, or another claims no PSRs. The model that we have introduced here above is one of the modest, and indeed 'classical,' ones that, the author believes, readers of this introductory course book will find easy to follow in order to understand the overall picture of the structure of English. There are, however, not a few linguistic theorists who go still farther to explore the fields that might have escaped our sight and to propose new theoretical apparatuses that would accommo-date the broader area of linguistic (and, occasionally, psychological) facts. Though the present book is an introductory course book to the structure of English and not the one to theoretical linguistics, we will touch upon a couple of theoretical issues in this section.

Generally speaking, linguistic theories can be divided into two groups according to the goals they set. One is such that the advocates of this group of theories, either explicitly or implicitly, aim to explain why and how language acquisition is successfully achieved. The other is such that the advocates of this group of theories simply aim to describe the language and its grammar as precisely as possible. In the former group, one of the representatives is generative grammar, one of the leading linguists of which is Noam Chomsky. In the latter, one of the representatives is a version of formal semantics, or Montague grammar, so called because of the pioneering works by Richard Montague. But, in between the two camps, we see various types of theories abound, so it is hard to draw a clear demarcation line to tell which one belongs to the former and which one otherwise.

Linguistic theories can be classified form another perspective. Theo-ries differ as to what type of notions they take as the most primitive or important in constructing particular grammars. One theory would say that formal properties of syntactic productivity is the essential part of the grammar and that, therefore, form is important. Another would say that semantic creativity is the origin of grammatical productivity and that, therefore, meaning is important. Still another would say that function is the most important notion that rules the various types of grammatical behaviors. A fourth party would say that the very technical notion of "construction" plays a fundamental role in grammatical descriptions. Yet there is another theory that would say that grammar is merely part of cognition so that grammatical behaviors are reflexes of cognitive abilities and that, therefore, grammar be constructed on the basis of cognitive notions. All in all, there are theories and theories, and we leave the whole variety of technical discussions to the kind of books that deal with grammatical theories or theoretical linguistics.

> **N.B.** One example of a guidebook to a variety of grammatical theories is Heine and Narrog (eds.) (2010, 2015^2). This is a one-volume collection that gives us an occasion to understand the diverse ways in which contemporary theories try to construct grammars to analyze various types of linguistic facts.

There is a third point of view that distinguishes one group of theories from another. It is the point of view that is related to how language acquisition is conceived of in constructing a grammar. Virtually all linguistic theories we mentioned above form one group where language acquisition is assumed to be made possible instantaneously and the result is the grammar itself. The other group, however, assumes that grammar is the outcome of the step-by-step process of language acquisition. Though the two groups might appear to be alike, the fundamental difference between the two leads to a significant difference. Take for example the following sentences and see how we analyze them.

(1) a. The airport is far from the city.
    b. John is far from innocent.
    c. John's explanation far from exhausts the possibilities.

The structures for (1a–c) are roughly those of (2a–c) below, respectively.

(2) a. [$_S$ [$_{NP}$ the airport] [$_{VP}$ is [$_{AP}$ [$_A$ far] [$_{PP}$ [$_P$ from] [$_{NP}$ the city]]]]]
    b. [$_S$ [$_{NP}$ John] [$_{VP}$ is [$_{AP}$ [$_A$ far] [$_{PP}$ [$_P$ from] [$_A$ innocent]]]]]

    c. [$_S$ [$_{NP}$ John's explanation] [$_{VP}$ [$_?$ far from] [$_V$ exhausts] [$_{NP}$ the possibilities]]]

The first stage of acquisition is such that children acquire the AP structure [$_{AP}$ [$_A$ far] [$_{PP}$ [$_P$ from] [$_{NP}$ the city]] in (2a), which is the basic structure, and the NP [$_{NP}$ the city] designates the source point from which the subject [$_{NP}$ the airport] is displaced for a certain amount of distance, i.e. "far." In (2b), at the next stage, this AP structure is somewhat extended to have the quality "innocent" as the source point from which John's legal liability is displaced. Note here that the sequence *far from* virtually has the adverbial sense of *hardly*, which is shown by the structure of (3):

    (3)   [$_S$ [$_{NP}$ John] [$_{VP}$ is [$_{AP}$ [$_{Adv}$ hardly] [$_A$ innocent]]]]

Once the sequence *far from* acquires the negative adverbial function, we enter the third stage such that this adverb [$_{Adv}$ *far from*] modifies verb or verb phrase as in (4):

    (4)   [$_S$ [$_{NP}$ John's explanation] [$_{VP}$ [$_{Adv}$ far from] [$_V$ exhausts] [$_{NP}$ the possibilities]]]

It seems quite natural to suppose that only through the step-by-step process of acquisition of this sequence *far from*, can we arrive at the negative adverbial use of [$_{Adv}$ *far from*], and that any instantaneous model of language acquisition has no non-ad-hoc way of explaining the adverbial use of it. This is a nontrivial difference between the two groups of theories, one group representing an instantaneous acquisition model and the other a dynamic, i.e. step-by-step, acquisition model. Needless to say, the latter should be more highly evaluated than the former from a descriptive point of view about the native speakers' intuitions, as well as from an explanatory point of view about language acquisition.

    N.B. The perspective that advocates that language acquisition is made possible through a step-by-step process and that the grammar is the result of, and reflects the features of, this process is called a dynamic theory of grammar. Dynamic approach to language acquisition, or the thesis about grammatical dynamism, is advocated by Masaru Kajita. For more about this approach, see Kajita (1997). See also Nakazawa (2018, 2021) for a revised format of this model.

EXERCISES

1. Analyze the sentences below, or in other words, describe the step-by-step processes, i.e. from deep to surface structure, through which the sentences are derived.
   (i) They sent him out all the documents.
   (ii) The English Department, why don't you check it out?

   Hint 1: Consider for example the sentences below:
   (a) They sent out all the documents to him.
   (b) You don't check out the English Department.

   Hint 2: When the object of a verb-particle combination is a pronoun, the sequence '*V Prt Pro' is not allowed, but instead we have 'V Pro Prt' as a grammatical sequence: Particle Movement is obligatory when the object is a pronoun, and it is optional otherwise (i.e. when the object is a full NP).

2. There is a so-called "Accusative with infinitive" construction, the surface word order of which is "NP-V-NP$_{ACC}$-Infinitive...." We have three types of verbs used in this construction, as in (i)–(iii):
   (i) John wants Mary to examine Bill.
   (ii) John believes Mary to have examined Bill.
   (iii) John forced Mary to examine Bill.
   Study the phrase structure of each of these sentences, and find out the structural differences among them. Propose a transformation if you think you need one. If you need help, consult a reference book that you may have beside you and find a transformation or phenomenon called "Raising."

   Hint 1: If the embedded clauses in (i)–(iii) are passivized, do you think the entire sentences have the same meanings as those with the original ones? That is, does each of (i)'–(iii)' have the same meaning as the original sentence?
   (i)' John wants Bill to be examined by Mary.
   (ii)' John believes Bill to have been examined by Mary.
   (iii)' John forced Bill to be examined by Mary.

Hint 2: If the sequences of words of the deep structures of each of (i)–(iii) are supposedly those like below, what do you think would happen? We assume that all instances of *John* in these examples refer to the same person.

(i)"   "John wants John to examine Bill."

(ii)"   "John believes John to have examined Bill."

(iii)"   "John forced John to examine Bill."

Possibilities are: the second instance of *John* becomes null (i.e. deleted), a pronoun (i.e. *him*), a reflexive form (i.e. *himself*), or else.

Chapter VI

Semantics

6.1 Domain of the Study of Semantics

Semantics is the study of meaning. But one may wonder: The meaning of what are linguists and grammarians studying? The answer may have some possibilities: the meaning of a word, a phrase, or a sentence. But, we will confine the domain of the study of semantics only to the meaning of a sentence, where the meanings of words and phrases are anyway actually involved.

> **N.B.** Pragmatics is another discipline that studies "meaning." But, technically speaking, pragmatics studies the intended or conveyed "meaning" (sometimes called "intention," "implicature," or otherwise) of an utterance on the basis of the interaction of the three parties involved: they are sentence, setting, and participants, i.e. the meaning of a sentence (which is, supposedly, a grammatical counterpart of an utterance), the environment in which an utterance takes place, and the speaker-hearer, respectively. For example, if a fragile lady says to a massive guy, "This trunk is so heavy," the addressee will take the utterance to mean that he should carry it. Semantics gives the meaning of a sentence, and pragmatics calculates the "intention" on the part of the lady when she says that sentence on this very occasion. See Chapter VII for the detail.

6.2   What Is Meaning?

In this section, we are concerned with the types of definitions of meaning. After showing several characteristics associated with these approaches to meaning and pointing out the specific inadequacies related to each of the approaches, we will show a tentative solution in our own way at the end of this section.

When you are on the street and asked what meaning is, it may appear to be a trivial matter to answer such a question. This is because we believe we exactly know what meaning is and, therefore, we are quite successful in communicating with each other in everyday conversation. But once we are determined to inquire into meaning, we realize that meaning is so elusive that no one has ever succeeded in defining the meaning of meaning properly. In what follows is a short appraisal of the linguists' efforts to answer the question "What is meaning?"

6.2.1   Dictionary Meaning or Paraphrase

First, when asked, for example, what *bachelor* means, you might answer like (1):

(1)   *Bachelor* means an unmarried young man.

This is what most dictionaries do when they define words. Thus, "unmarried young man" is a definition in a dictionary, or it is a 'dictionary meaning,' so to speak. In this case, we say that "unmarried young man" is simply a paraphrase of *bachelor*. This type of defining the meaning of *bachelor* is shown in (2), which is in line with the practice of componential analysis, where component features build up to form the entire meaning of a constituent, i.e. a word.

(2)   *bachelor*: [unmarried, young, man]

It is true that componential analysis covers a variety of word meaning cases, but it fails to accommodate such cases as *democracy* and *love*. The noun *democracy* can be defined, or paraphrased, as (3a), but this definition cannot be decomposed into components such that the simple sum of these components could end up as the meaning of *democracy*, as is shown by the inappropriateness in (3b):

(3)   a.   *democracy*: "a type of government where people's voices are highly respected"
      b.   *democracy*: *[government, people's voices, highly respected]

Thus, a simple decomposition is not all we want for the definition of meaning. Furthermore, definition by means of paraphrase sometimes faces a serious problem.

(4)   a.   *love*: "a profoundly tender, passionate affection for another person" (*RHD²*)
      b.   *affection*: "fond attachment, devotion, or love" (*RHD²*)

N.B. See also the definitions of *affection* and *fond* in *COD*[12].
   (i)   *affection*: "a feeling of fondness or liking"
   (ii)   *fond*: "having an affection or liking for"
   (iii) *love:* "an intense feeling of deep affection"
         Readers are advised to consult other dictionaries, e.g. *Webster*[3], for the definitions of these words.

The definitions in (4a, b) are the typical cases we would commonly find in the dictionaries of everyday use. As we can see, it is hard to tell the difference between *love* and *affection*. Similarly, we have pairs of nouns such as *freedom* and *liberty*, *chance* and *opportunity*, and *manner* and *way*. And we have pairs of verbs such as *admire* and *respect*, *evaluate* and *appreciate*, *stroll* and *loiter*, and *affect* and *effect*. The members in each of these pairs certainly share part of their meanings, but they are clearly distinct and therefore should be distinguished from each other. But the problem is how we could do that. No matter how tactful the respective paraphrases should be for the two words in a pair, it seems that these paraphrases always leave room for further elaboration, which means that the respective meanings will have endless elaboration. Furthermore, there are cases where we are not able to tell the difference, e.g. that between *mother* and *Mom*, solely in terms of paraphrase. The difference of meaning between *mother* and *Mom* does not reside in paraphrase but in certain emotional factors attached to these words when they are put into actual use. Thus, paraphrase is not something from which we can expect a total answer to the question of "What is meaning?"

6.2.2   Reference or Referent

Next, as an answer to the question "What is meaning?" posed above, some would say that it lies in the referential system. In the referential system, there are two important notions, 'reference' and 'referent.'

(5)   a.   reference: "act of referring"
      b.   referent: "something referred to"

Simply put in this framework, the meaning of the word, say, *John* should be its reference, i.e. the act of referring to the man "John" himself, or the meaning of *John* should be its referent, i.e. the entity "John" itself. Similarly, the meaning of the expression *the morning star* and that of *the evening star* are one and the same planet Venus if we take the meaning of an expression to be its referent, while, if we take the meaning of an expression to be its reference, their respective meanings reside in their respective act of referring: *the morning star* is the one you can see in the morning, and *the evening star* the one you can see in the evening. It is true that this type of approach to meaning is very helpful in cases of concrete nouns, but when it comes to abstract nouns, it is hard to shape the clear ideas of their meanings. For example, consider the cases of *love* and *affection* cited above. It would remain unclear how we should formally and explicitly define and differentiate the meanings of *John's love* and *John's affection* in the referential system, i.e. in terms of the notions of reference and/or referent. Furthermore, if we confine ourselves to the referential system, it seems difficult to define and differentiate the meanings of such 'intercategorial twins' as the adjective *clear* and the adverb *clearly*, and the verb *destroy* and the noun *destruction*. Do they have the same meaning, or not? It seems plausible to say that they have the very same 'meaning' but do differ only in the syntactic category they assume. If this observation is correct, the referential approach to meaning is not the best one among those we can conceive of.

6.2.3   Connotation or Denotation

Thirdly, meaning is often identified as connotation or denotation. These two terms are ambiguously used, or used to mean different things, as shown below:

(6)   a.   connotation: abstract description of an object

   b. denotation: an object described by connotation
(7) a. connotation: augmented meaning implied by the literal
          meaning
   b. denotation: the literal meaning itself

In the terminology of (6), the connotation of the word *bachelor*, for example, is "unmarried young man," and the denotation of the same word is the man *John*, if *John* is a bachelor. In the terminology of (7), the connotation of the word *Mom*, for example, is the child's affinity and dependency towards the woman he or she calls *mother*, and the denotation of the same word is the child's mother's motherhood. Things are fine up to this point. However, assuming either of the two terminologies (6) and (7), we still have certain problems. For example, what will come about if we are to obtain the meaning of the expressions below?

(8) a. the Fifth Amendment to the US Constitution
   b. a unicorn

The nominal expression (8a), *the Fifth Amendment to the US Constitution*, says something about an abstract entity, and, therefore, by definition, fails to pick out a denotation in the sense of (6b). And it seems reasonable to say that (8a) also fails to have a connotation in the sense of (7a). The nominal expression (8b), *a unicorn*, on the other hand, says something about an imaginary entity, and, therefore, by definition, fails to pick out a denotation in the sense of (6b). But one would say that in the imaginary world he or she wishes to have, *a unicorn* surely has a denotation in the sense of (6b). In this case, however, the connotation of *a unicorn* in the sense of (7a) seems to be endlessly diverse. Similarly, it seems reasonable to say that *the Fifth Amendment to the US Constitution* of (8a) also fails to have a connotation of (7a), or at least that (8a) fails to define a unique connotation of (7a) that everyone would agree upon. Thus, it is rather fair to say that we should expect no consistent approach to meaning in the connotation-denotation framework.

6.2.4 Truth Condition

   The fourth approach to meaning is such that meaning is identified with truth condition. Truth condition is a logical notion as explained in (9):

(9) Truth condition: A condition where a given sentence (or proposi-

tion) proves to be true

For example, imagine a situation where John ate only one hamburger and only John ate a hamburger. In this situation, the sentence in (10a) is true and other sentences (10b–e) are all false.

(10) a. John ate a hamburger.
      b. John ate a cheeseburger.
      c. John ate two hamburgers.
      d. John didn't eat a hamburger.
      e. Bill ate a hamburger.

In this case, the meaning of the sentence (10a) should be identified with this very situation mentioned above, or, to be more precise, with the condition to be satisfied by this situation. And this condition we call truth condition, i.e. a condition for (10a) to be true. Truth condition is well at work when we consider sentences like those below:

(11) a. Everyone in this classroom speaks at least two languages.
      b. At least two languages are spoken by everyone in this classroom.

It is often the case that an active sentence and its passive counterpart have the same 'meaning,' but the active and passive pair of (11) will show a slightly different behavior. The meaning of (11a) is not the same as that of (11b). For example, let us assume that there are three students named Adam, Ben, and Cathy in this classroom. Of the possible interpretations of (11a) and (11b), those that are directly related to the issue here are (12a) and (12b), respectively.

(12) a. Adam speaks English and Japanese, Ben French and Chinese, and Cathy German and Korean.
      b. Adam speaks English and Japanese, Ben English and Japanese, and Cathy English and Japanese.

Clearly, the 'meanings' of (12a) and (12b) are different from each other, and this difference lies in the fact that the situations in (12a) and (12b) are different from each other. In this case, we say that (12a) and (12b) have different truth conditions from each other. Similarly, we may cite another pair of sentences for the cause of truth conditional meaning.

(13) a. That the enemy destroyed the city is unlikely.
      b. The enemy's destruction of the city is unlikely.

It may be the case that both (13a) and (13b) have the same truth condition, i.e. the same meaning: both are comments on the past event. But it may also be the case that (13a) is a comment about the past event, while (13b) says something about the event that will take place in the future. The latter interpretations are endorsed by the grammaticality difference of the following examples:

(14) a. *That the enemy destroyed the city is likely to happen.
      b. The enemy's destruction of the city is likely to happen.

As far as the grammaticality judgments shown in (14) are tenable, the two sentences in (14) do not have the same meaning. And this difference of meaning is indeed truth conditional. Thus, in this case, too, truth condition deserves to be identified as meaning. So far, so good.

Now, consider the sentences below:

(15) a. Mary is unmarried.
      b. Mary is a spinster.
(16) a. (As a reply to "What did John do?")
          John kicked the ball.
      b. (As a reply to "What happened to the ball?")
          The ball was kicked by John.

From the truth conditional viewpoint, both sentences (15a) and (15b) should have the same meaning, and so should both of (16a) and (16b). But, at least to some speakers of English, (15b) has a somewhat derogatory connotation that is absent in (15a). Thus (15a) does not have the same meaning as (15b). In (16a) *John* is old information and the entire sentence is predicated of him, while in (16b) *the ball* is old information and the entire sentence is predicated of this ball. Thus, from the viewpoint of information structure, (16a) does not have the same meaning as (16b).

Observe, furthermore, the sentences below:

(17) a. Open the window!
      b. Will you open the window?
      c. Would you be kind enough to open the window?
      d. I would be very happy if you could open the window.

All of the sentences in (17) are understood as expressions of order or request, but their 'literal meanings' differ from each other. (17a) is an imperative sentence and thus literally means an order; (17b, c) are yes-no interrogatives and thus literally mean a question; (17d) is a declarative sentence and thus literally means a statement of, in this case, the speaker's state of mind. Furthermore, though the sentences in (17) all express the speaker's order or request, there is a cline, or gradience, of politeness along which all of these sentences are arranged: (17a) is the most direct and (17d) the most polite. Thus, although in a truth conditional approach the sentences in (17) might be said to have the same meaning, they are, in fact, taken to convey different meanings from each other. Truth condition, therefore, is not all that is required of meaning.

> **N.B.** It is commonly assumed that only declarative sentences can be true or false. In other words, sentences embodying order or request cannot be true or false. But if we assume that relating a sentence to the setting in which the very sentence can best be appropriately produced is one type of approaches to meaning, then we could well consider the meaning of the sentences with order or request to be the setting in which those sentences can best be produced, even though they may never be true or false. That way, the sentences in (17) can be viewed in a somewhat truth conditional approach.

6.2.5   Meaning is a Multidimensional Composite

Thus far, we have examined some of the typical approaches to meaning and have shown that they have both their own excellent features and inadequacies at a time. All of these considered, we may conclude that meaning is not a monolithic entity but a multidimensional composite. In our everyday discourse, one or more than one aspect of meaning may be brought into focus and will get highlighted. Thus, it may happen that a specific aspect of meaning is important and significant in one occasion but not in another. We therefore arrive at an answer to the question "What is meaning?" as in (18):

(18)   Assuming that Language is a realistic entity, a sentence has two footings in the real world, or, in linguistic terms, a sentence mediates between the two empirical entities: form (i.e. sound) and meaning. From this vantage point of grammatical architec-

ture, the answer to "What is meaning?" is very simple and rudimentary: meaning is form's counterpart in the real world via a sentence structure.

If the view expressed in (18) is on the right track, the study of semantics is a continuous, and indeed endless, endeavor, accompanied by syntax, to look into the whole variety of factors we perceive as constituting the real world.

6.3   Types of Meaning Properties and Relations

There are a variety of meaning properties and relations that hold among words, phrases, and sentences. In other words, these properties are dimensions that make up (part of) the entity 'meaning.' In what follows, we will see a number of such properties with illustrations.

6.3.1   Meaningfulness

When an expression succeeds in obtaining a semantic interpretation, it is meaningful. For example, the noun *bachelor* has a couple of meanings, and when *bachelor* means an "unmarried young man," *a handsome bachelor* is a meaningful phrase, but **a female bachelor* is not, or it is meaningless. The oddity of **a female bachelor* can be accounted for by the inappropriate combination of the features [female] and [man], as illustrated in (1):

(1)   The NP **a female bachelor* means "a [female] [unmarried young man]," where the feature [female] modifies the feature [man] and this modification is contradictory because [man] implies [male], which should never be [female]. Hence, **a female bachelor* does not make sense and, therefore, is meaningless.

The NP *a handsome bachelor*, on the other hand, does not have such a contradiction and it is, therefore, meaningful. Note that in cases where *a female bachelor* makes sense, *bachelor* means a "person who graduated from a university and holds an academic degree" but not an "unmarried young man."

6.3.2   Anomaly / Contradiction / Meaninglessness

When an expression fails in the semantic interpretation, it is anomalous, contradictory, or meaningless. *A female bachelor*, for example, where *bachelor* means an "unmarried young man," is anomalous, contradictory, or meaningless since it makes no sense, because the adjective *female* and the semantic feature [male] in the semantic component [man] of *bachelor* surely prevent the interpretive amalgamation from yielding the well-formed semantic interpretation: one cannot be both [female] and [male] at once. Similarly, the example below is no way meaningful in that no two adjacent words in (1) are semantically well-formed:

    (1)   Colorless green ideas sleep furiously.

Thus (1) is semantically anomalous, but still, it is important to note that (1) is syntactically sound from the categorial phrase-structural viewpoint.

6.3.3   Synonymy

When more than one form has the same meaning, we say that forms that share the same meaning are synonymous. The following two sentences are synonymous.

    (1)   a.   John is a bachelor.
            b.   John is an unmarried young man.
    (2)   a.   The glass is half full.
            b.   The glass is half empty.
    (3)   a.   John admires Mary.
            b.   Mary is admired by John.
    (4)   a.   John fixed up the hamburger.
            b.   John fixed the hamburger up.

According to the hows and whys of the synonymy, i.e. how and why the given forms are synonymous, the above pairs of examples are classified into several major groups: (1) is the type of lexical synonymy, where a lexical item and its paraphrase are synonymous; (2) is the type of lexical-interpretive synonymy, where the lexical meanings of *full*, *empty*, and *half* contribute to the semantic interpretation of the two sentences; and both (3) and (4) are the type of transformational synonymy, where transformations are at work to derive the synonymous sentences.

6.3.4 Antonymy

Antonymous expressions are in semantic opposition with respect to each other. There are four types of antonymy, among others. The first is the affirmative vs. negative antonymy, as shown in (1):

(1) Opposition in terms of negation
    a. "The man is married." vs. "The man is not married (= single)."
    b. "John ate lunch." vs. "John didn't eat lunch."
    c. "John is happy." vs. "John is unhappy (= not happy)."

The second is the opposition on the scale where two items in question are placed on the opposite ends. Examples in (2a, b) show opposition on a vertical scale, those in (2c) do so on a horizontal scale, and those in (2d) do so on a width scale.

(2) Opposition in terms of relational scale
    a. "The man is tall." vs. "The man is short."
    b. "The bug flies high." vs. "The bug flies low."
    c. "The bridge is long." vs. "The bridge is short."
    d. "The river is wide." vs "The river is narrow."

The third type of opposition will be termed 'converse relation' in that an event that is described from one viewpoint could also be described from another converse viewpoint, as shown in (3):

(3) Converse relation
    a. "I give you the book." vs. "You take the book from me"
    b. "John sent the book to Mary." vs. "Mary received the book from John."
    c. "John sold the book to Mary." vs. "Mary bought the book from John.
    d. "John admires Mary." vs. "Mary is admired by John."

In (3a–c), the converse relation is based on the three pairs of verbs: *give-take*, *send-receive*, and *sell-buy*. Depending on the verb one sentence chooses as a main verb, such grammatical roles as subject, direct object, and prepositional object assume the appropriate semantic roles from among those the verb requires, e.g. source, goal, and theme. Sentences with *give*, *send*, and *sell* depict each of the events from the source's viewpoint, whereas those with *take, receive,* and *buy* do so from the goal's viewpoint. In (3d), the converse relation is realized by the active and the passive voices: the former sees the event from the agent's viewpoint and the latter does so from the patient's.

> **N.B.** The semantic role called 'theme' means an entity that moves from the position called 'source' to the position called 'goal' in the situation described by the sentence. When a verb depicts an action, the doer is an agent and the target of the action is a patient.

The fourth type of opposition could be termed 'opposite process relation' in the sense that the original state that has been transformed into a resultant state could be restored by the opposite process of the action that has derived that resultant state. Examples below will tell what this relation is like:

(4)   Opposite process relation
  a.   "John opened the door." vs. "John closed the door."
  b.   "John locked the door." vs. "John unlocked the door."
  c.   "John went to the park." vs. "John came back from the park."

6.3.5   Ambiguity

When one form has more than one meaning, we say that it is ambiguous. The following sentences are all ambiguous.

(1)   John went to the bank. (lexical ambiguity)
  a.   "John went to the bank [elevated land along a river]."
  b.   "John went to the bank [financial institution]."
(2)   John watched the girl with a telescope. (phrase-structural ambiguity)
  a.   "[s [NP John] [VP' [VP [V watched] [NP the girl with a telescope]]]]."
  b.   "[s [NP John] [VP' [VP [V watched] [NP the girl]] [PP with a telescope]]]."
(3)   John saw the fool on the hill. (phrase-structural ambiguity)
  a.   "[s [NP John] [VP' [VP [V saw] [NP the fool on the hill]]]]."
  b.   "[s [NP John] [VP' [VP [V saw] [NP the fool]] [PP on the hill]]]
(4)   John saw her duck/swallow/dress. (phrase-structural ambiguity)
  a.   "[s [NP John] [VP [V saw] [NP her duck/swallow/dress]]]."

b.   "[s [NP John] [VP [V saw] [NP her] [V duck/swallow/dress]]]."
(5)   She will make him a good wife. (phrase-structural ambiguity)
    a.   "She will [V make] [Object him] [Objective Complement a good wife]." (semantically anomalous)
    b.   "She will [V make] [Dative of Interest him] [Subjective Complement a good wife]." (= "She will become a good wife for him.")
(6)   Flying planes can be dangerous. (transformational ambiguity)
    a.   "Flying planes [= Planes that are flying] can be dangerous." (*flying* = participle)
    b.   "Flying planes [= To fly planes] can be dangerous." (*flying* = gerund)
(7)   The chicken is ready to eat. (transformational ambiguity)
    a.   "The chicken is ready to eat something."
    b.   "The chicken is ready for us to eat."

According to the hows and whys of the ambiguity, i.e. how and why the given forms are ambiguous, the examples above are classified into several major groups: (1) is the type of lexical ambiguity, (2)–(5) the type of structural ambiguity to be attributed to different applications of phrase structure rules, and (6)–(7) the type of transformational ambiguity. The possible interpretations follow each of the ambiguous sentences (1) through (7).

N.B. Ambiguity is explained also in §5.2.4 and §5.6.3.

6.3.6   Vagueness

A vague expression has a certain area of unspecified meaning. The semantic property called vagueness should not be confused with the semantic property called ambiguity. Ambiguity and vagueness are clearly distinct notions. An ambiguous expression has more than one distinct meaning as we saw in §6.3.5 above, while a vague expression has only one meaning but leaves part of the meaning unspecified.

As for the examples of vagueness, we may cite *brother* and *sister*. Observe the sentence (1):

(1)   John has a brother.

In (1), the noun *brother* has clearly one distinct meaning, but the noun

lacks the specification with respect to the age: it is unclear whether the
brother is older or younger than *John*. This point highlights the contrast
that we have between English *brother* and Japanese counterparts. English
brother corresponds to two Japanese nouns, *ani* and *otouto*. *Ani* means
"older brother," and *otouto* "younger brother." Thus, the English noun
brother is vague with respect the relative age, while the Japanese nouns *ani*
and *otouto* are clearly not. This type of linguistic difference also applies to
the female counterparts of brotherhood, i.e. the kinship terms of sisterhood.
The English noun *sister* is vague with respect the relative age, while the
Japanese nouns *ane* ("older sister") and *imouto* ("younger sister") are
clearly not.

As for another example, let us take the verb *kick*. Observe the
sentence (2):

(2)   John kicked the ball.

In (2), it is unclear which leg, right or left, he chose to activate the motion
of kicking. Notice that the sentence (2) is not ambiguous, but it is vague
with respect to the leg that he hit the ball with. If it were ambiguous, it
would have to have two distinct meanings: the kicking by the right leg or
the kicking by the left leg. But in the case of kicking, it is clearly not the
case that (2) has distinct two meanings.

Similarly, in the sentence (3) below:

(3)   John met Mary last week.

It is unclear on which day, Monday, Tuesday, or else, John met Mary.

6.3.7   Fuzziness

When it is unclear whether an expression has a certain well-defined
distinct semantic feature, the expression is fuzzy with respect to this
semantic feature. For example, how can the semantic notion of *bird-*
likeness be applied to such animals as a canary, a chick, an ostrich, a
penguin, a bat, and a dragon? In other words, the point is whether it is
appropriate to say that "a canary is a bird," "a chick is a bird," "an ostrich
is a bird," "a penguin is a bird," "a bat is a bird," or "a dragon is a bird."
We are certainly sure that "a canary is a bird," but a little bit less so in the
case of *a chick*: we are much less sure whether "an ostrich is a bird," and
even less so in the case of *a penguin*: even though a bat flies, we are

somewhat reluctant to say that "a bat is a bird," and we are fully sure that "a dragon is NOT a bird." Thus the expression *a chick* is mildly fuzzy as to the notion *bird*-likeness, and forms like *an ostrich* and *a penguin* are fuzzier than *a chick* is as to this notion. The expression *a bat* is not so fuzzy with respect to *bird*-likeness because we know it is shaped like but is not a bird and it is in fact a mammal. The expression *a dragon* is not fuzzy at all with respect *bird*-likeness.

Let us take up another example. What is it that defines *cup, bowl, dish, plate*, and *saucer*? What is it that defines *cup, glass*, and *mug*? It may happen that when a certain object contains coffee in it, it may be called a *cup*, but the same object may be called a *mug* with beer in it. When a certain object contains grilled fish and vegetables in it, it may be called a *dish*, but the same object may be called a *bowl* with salad in it. Fuzziness is the notion attributed to these objects when they are called in one case either *cup* or *mug*, or in the other either *dish* or *bowl*.

Fuzziness is often mapped onto a scale called 'gradience' or 'cline.' For example, English nouns for dining utensils mentioned above find their place on the conceptual gradience scale that extends from "less flat" to "more flat." It is true that these nouns represent distinct notions but it is yet hard to draw demarcation lines to explicitly divide these notions. See the gradience below:

(1)   A conceptual gradience of dining 'containers'

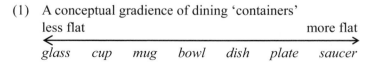

Suppose, for example, that a certain object is said to be more like *cup* with coffee in it, and that the same object is said to be more like *mug* with beer in it. Then we say that this object rests in the fuzzy area on the gradience scale between *cup* and *mug*. Fuzziness is characterized as a continuous transition on a scale from a 'more like' attribute point to a 'less like' attribute point. Therefore fuzzy properties should never be discrete independent properties, but rather they constitute one continuous 'more-or-less' gradience.

Another case for fuzziness is found in the names of items for sitting: *stool, chair*, and *sofa*. A stool does not have a back or arms with it, but a chair does. So what do you call an item that resembles a stool but has a short back with it? A stool or a chair? Actually, this item is fuzzy with respect to the indeterminacy between *stool* and *chair*. A sofa is a long upholstered seat with a back and arms for a number of people to sit in. So what do you call an item that is an upholstered seat for only one or two people? A chair or a sofa? Actually, this item is fuzzy, too, with respect to the indeterminacy between *chair* and *sofa*.

It is sometimes argued that there is indeed a fuzzy area in syntax. Certain syntactic structures are said to form a syntactic fuzziness gradience. For example, we have a number of syntactic noun phrases (NPs) with different internal structures as shown in the brackets in (2):

(2)   a.   [John] surprised everyone.
      b.   [The enemy's destruction of the city] surprised everyone.
      c.   [The enemy's destroying the city] surprised everyone.
      d.   [That the enemy destroyed the city] surprised everyone.

But, applying passive transformation to all of the sentences in (2), we have different results of grammaticality.

(3)   a.   Everyone was surprised by [John].
      b.   Everyone was surprised by [the enemy's destruction of the city].
      c.   OK/?Everyone was surprised by [the enemy's destroying the city].
      d.   *Everyone was surprised by [that the enemy destroyed the city].

On the other hand, application of extraposition transformation to the same sentences in (2) will show another array of grammatical consequences.

(4)   a. *It surprised everyone [John].
      b. *It surprised everyone [the enemy's destruction of the city].
      c. *It surprised everyone [the enemy's destroying the city].
      d. It surprised everyone [that the enemy destroyed the city].

A short glimpse of the facts above is enough to show that NPs of different internal structures behave differently with respect to the type of rules they get involved in. Thus, NPs of pure noun-like type are in good terms with the passive construction, while NPs with a sentential structure are fit for the extraposition construction. This is nothing but a gradient phenomenon in the category of NP.

> **N.B.** Note that the sentence of (4a) "*It surprised everyone [John]" is bad,
> but a similar sentence like "He*i* surprised everyone, [John*i*]" is perfectly
> grammatical, where *He*i and *John*i are coreferential NPs. This is because
> the latter is a right-dislocated construction and not an extraposed one.
> Similarly, (4b, c) are OK if interpreted as the results of the rule of Right
> Dislocation, with a comma intonation between *everyone* and the follow-
> ing constituent.

6.3.8   Redundancy

When a certain semantic feature appears more than once in a phrase
or a sentence, that expression is redundant with respect to that very feature.
The following sentences embody redundancy.

> (1)   a.   John is an unmarried bachelor. [*bachelor* = "unmarried
>   young man"]
>   b.   That bachelor is unmarried.

> **N.B.** The sentence (1b) is called an analytic sentence, where the truth of
> the sentence is guaranteed automatically by way of an appropriate logical,
> semantic, or syntactic analysis. In this case, since *bachelor* is [unmarried
> young man], *that bachelor* is always "unmarried." Therefore, (1b) is
> always true. On the other hand, the sentence (i) below is called a synthetic
> sentence, whose truth value ('true' or 'false') is determined only after we
> know whether *John* is married or not.
> (i)   John is unmarried.
>   The synthetic sentence needs to be referred to the real world and to
> obtain the relevant information in order to decide its truth value, while the
> analytic sentence does not.

6.3.9   Overlap

There is a semantic overlap among the following words: *man, boy,
king, prince, bachelor, father, son, brother, ox, bull*, and *cock*. The
semantic feature [male] is shared by all of these words. Likewise, the
feature [absolute value], or [−gradable], is shared by the adjectives like
true, perfect, dead, alive, alone, favorite, honest, red, black, and *white*.
These adjectives have neither comparatives nor superlatives. The feature
[relative value], or [+gradable], is shared by the adjectives like *tall, high,
long, short, wise, slow, fast, warm, cold, rich*, and *poor*. These adjectives

have both comparatives and superlatives. Such verbs as *say*, *speak*, *talk*, *utter*, *pronounce*, *voice*, *murmur*, *shout*, and *whisper* are all characterized by the semantic feature [verbs of speaking].

6.3.10   Hyponymy

Hyponymy is the state of relation such that if a certain name of an entity is an instance of another name of that entity, then the former is the hyponym, or subordinate word, of the latter, which is called a hypernym, or superordinate word. In general, we have such a hierarchical relation that "a hyponym is a type of a hypernym." For example, *Robin, canary, nightingale, dove, crow,* and *penguin* are all hyponyms of *bird*: *bird* is the hyponym of *animal. Animal* is superordinate with respect to *beast, ape, bird, fish, snake* and others. See below for a sample list of hypernyms and hyponyms:

(1)   Hyponymy: A sample hierarchy of concepts

animal									
beast		ape		bird				fish	snake
lion	...	chimp	...	robin	canary	dove	...	salmon	...	cobra	...

Another instance of hyponymy is: *drink* is the hypernym with respect to such hyponyms as *beverage* and *wine*; *beverage* is the hypernym with respect to such hyponyms as *tea, coffee,* and *cola; wine* is the hypernym with respect to such hyponyms as *champagne, claret,* and *hock.*

6.3.11   Family Resemblance

Family resemblance is a notion that encompasses a group of somewhat similar items. In other words, items that share family resemblance with each other are regarded as members of a certain category, but it is at the same time highly difficult to define the characteristic feature of that category itself. The category is like a family: family members resemble each other but it is hard to find out the defining feature of that family. Take, for example, the word *game*. There are a number of games in the world, such as chess, card games, casino games, physical games that include football, baseball, basketball and even Olympic Games. Other types of games with a prenominal modifier are war game, banking game, power game, pool game, bingo game, domino game, hunting game, sex game, computer game, and video game. It does not seem to be the case that any single semantic feature that defines the entire class of these 'games' could be found. Generally speaking, members of the class of a certain family resemblance cannot be defined in terms of necessary and sufficient conditions.

Furniture is another word that represents the notion of family resemblance. The word comprises a whole variety of objects with different sizes, colors, materials, uses, functions, locations to put them in, and so on. Items of *furniture* include *table, desk, bureau, chair, sofa, couch, bed, cot, curtain, cupboard, cabinet, chest, mirror* and others. It seems implausible to argue for one and only feature, or a limited number of features, that could define the category and exclude the others. For example, a definition with combined features like "a wooden product used by people in the room" would accommodate a number of items above, but it definitely fails to include items made from steel, cloth, or glass; furthermore it would make a false inclusion of wooden bowls, knives, forks, pencils, and hangers.

> **N.B.** Related to family resemblance is a prototype theory of meaning, which distinguishes the typical exemplars of a category from the peripheral ones. For example, as instances of a category *bird*, such types of bird as *canary, robin, nightingale, dove,* and *crow* are central, prototypical exemplars, but, on the other hand, birds like *penguin, ostrich,* and *emu* are regarded as peripheral.

6.3.12   Entailment

Entailment is a logical notion that holds between two sentences, or, in logical terms, two propositions. Entailment is defined as follows:

(1)   Entailment
      A sentence S_1 entails a sentence S_2 if the truth of S_1 guarantees the truth of S_2 and the falsity of S_2 guarantees the falsity of S_1.

Here are some examples:

(2) S_1: This car is red.
      S_2: This car has a color. [=It is not the case that this car is black or white.]
(3) S_1: John managed to win the race.

S_2: John won the race.

(4) S_1: John proved to be innocent.
      S_2: John was innocent.

(5) S_1: This needle is too short.
      S_2: This needle is not long enough.

In the examples of (2) through (5), S_1 entails S_2.

6.3.13   Presupposition

The notion presupposition is ambiguously used in linguistics. One use of presupposition is such that presupposition is a logical notion that holds between two sentences, or, in logical terms, two propositions. Presupposition is defined as follows:

(1)   Presupposition
      A sentence S_1 presupposes a sentence S_2 if the falsity of S_2 causes S_1 not to have a truth value (i.e. neither true nor false). And it is very important to note that if S_1 presupposes S_2, then $\sim S_1$ also presupposes S_2. [Read $\sim S_1$ as "not S_1."] That is, both S_1 and $\sim S_1$ have the same semantic presupposition S_2.

N.B. A slightly different characterization of presupposition is such that S_1 presupposes S_2 if S_1 entails S_2 and $\sim S_1$ entails S_2. But this characterization is not equivalent to the one just given.

Below are some examples:

(2) S_1: John regretted/didn't regret that he had his car stolen.
      S_2: John had his car stolen.

(3) S_1: The king of France is/isn't bald.
      S_2: There is a king of France.

In the examples of (2) and (3), S_1 presupposes S_2. But a few words are in order here about the examples in (3). The sentence (3-S_2) is in fact false, but in the possible world where France has a king and he is bald, the sentence "The king of France is bald" is true and the sentence "The king of France isn't bald" is false. And it is in the world in which there exists a king in France that we can say that (3-S_1) presupposes (3-S_2).

There is a group of predicates that are called factive predicates, some of which are given below:

(4) Factive predicates: *regret, realize, forget, remember, know, discover, find out, learn, notice, be odd, be strange, be surprising*

They have the characteristic such that the sentences whose matrix predicates are factive predicates presuppose their complement sentences. One example of this type of predicates is shown in (2), i.e. *regret*, but for others, readers can easily confirm each of the cases.

The other use of presupposition is such that presupposition is something we see from the viewpoint of information structure. As shown in (5) below, we regard a sentence as a package of information, and it consists of two main parts: presupposition and assertion.

(5) The propositional content of a sentence viewed from the perspective of information structure:
[s PRESUPPOSITION + ASSERTION]

It is notable that these two parts have structural counterparts in such constructions as Cleft sentence and Pseudo-cleft sentence. Below are some examples:

(6) John ate the hamburger.
   a. It is John that ate the hamburger.
   b. It is the hamburger that John ate.
   c. What John ate was the hamburger.
   d. What John did was eat the hamburger.

Cleft sentence has the basic structure: "It is [Focus] that [Presupposition]." A constituent to be focused in a sentence should be put in the [Focus] position, and the rest of the sentence is placed after *that*, which part semantically represents the presupposed information. For example, (6a) roughly says that someone ate the hamburger [presupposition] and the man who did it was John [assertion]. Pseudo-cleft sentence has the basic structure: "What [Presupposition] is [Focus]." In Pseudo-cleft sentence, the constituent to be focused should be put in the [Focus] position, i.e. after the verb *be*, and the rest is placed in the *What*-relative clause, which functions as a presupposition. For example, (6d) roughly says that John did something [presupposition] and the action he did was to eat the hamburger [assertion].

6.4   Semantic Interpretation of a Sentence

Semantic interpretation of a sentence is achieved through the process that is characterized as "from the bottom up to the top." Constituents in a sentence are hierarchically structured so that the lower elements are combined to form a larger structure and this process finally arrives at the top node S.

(1)   [s [NP [Det The] [N boy]] [VP [V kicked] [NP [Det the] [N ball]]]]

In interpreting the entire sentence of (1), we first of all know that the verb *kick* is an action verb and that subject NP means the agent, and object NP means the patient, of this action. Next, [Det the] and [N ball] are combined to form [NP the ball] and it means "the semantically definite ball." Furthermore, [V kicked] and this NP are combined to form [VP kicked the ball] and it means "[NP the ball] is the patient of the kicking action." Finally, after identifying the meaning of [NP the boy] as "the semantically definite boy," this NP and [VP kicked the ball] are combined to form the entire sentence and this sentence means "[NP the boy] acted as agent and exercised his kicking action onto the patient [NP the ball]." This is the general idea of semantic interpretation of a sentence, and we say that the sentence has a compositional meaning.

But what happens if a sentence has an idiomatic expression as in the following?

(2)   John kicked the bucket.

In this case, (2) is ambiguous: [VP kick the bucket] has either a literal meaning or an idiomatic one. When (2) has a literal meaning, i.e. a compositional meaning, the semantic interpretation process is just like the one shown above. On the other hand, when (2) has an idiomatic meaning, we start with the equation like (3) below, which specification is part of the entries of Lexicon in the grammar of English.

(3)   Idiom rule:
       [VP kick the bucket] = "die"

Now, the VP [VP kicked the bucket] means "died," and since subject NP of the verb "die" means the experiencer of this process, the entire sentence means "the man designated by the proper noun *John* experienced the process of dying."

6.5   Semantics of "Deep Structure"

Deep Structure is one of the theoretical levels in syntax and it is claimed to be an input to semantics, where semantic interpretation is achieved. Such semantic notions as thematic relations or semantic roles (e.g. agent, patient, etc.) are determined at the level of Deep Structure. For example, in sentences like "John kissed Mary" and "Mary was kissed by John," the agenthood of *John* and the patienthood of *Mary* is determined at the level of Deep Structure.

There are other types of semantic notions that are peculiar to Deep Structure. Such types of semantic interpretation as Part-Whole relation and Exhaustiveness vs. Nonexhaustiveness of the activity are determined at the level of Deep Structure. For example, the NP standing as the direct object (or subject, cf. (4)) at Deep Structure receives the Whole or the Exhaustive interpretation, while the NP in the adjunct position at Deep Structure receives the Partitive or Nonexhaustive interpretation. To see this, let us observe (1a, b) below. In (1a), John sprayed paint, presumably all the paint he had, onto a part of the entire wall. In (1b), on the other hand, John sprayed the entire wall using presumably part of the paint he had.

(1)   a.   John sprayed paint on the wall.
      b.   John sprayed the wall with paint.

The same type of semantic interpretation applies to the pairs of (2a–b), (3a–b), and (4a–b). The Whole or Exhaustive interpretation applies to the direct objects in the cases of (2) and (3), and this interpretation goes to the subjects of the sentences in the pair of (4). On the other hand, those adjunct NPs in the prepositional complement in (2) through (4) happen to have the Partitive or Nonexhaustive interpretation.

(2)   a.   John loaded hay onto the wagon.
      b.   John loaded the wagon with hay.
(3)   a.   John wiped the handkerchief across his forehead.
      b.   John wiped his eyes with the handkerchief.
(4)   a.   Bees are swarming over the garden.
      b.   The garden is swarming with bees.

6.6 Semantics of "Surface Structure"

Surface Structure is one of the theoretical levels in syntax and it is claimed to be an input to phonology, where phonetic representation is determined. In other words, Surface Structure has been up to now claimed to have no contribution to the meaning of the entire sentence. But things are not so straightforward. Sentences with quantifiers (e.g. numerals, *many*, *few*, *all*, *some*, *every*, and negative *no/not*) are susceptible to the change of scope interpretations if the order of the quantifiers is changed at the Surface Structure level. Observe the pairs of (1a–b), (2a–b), and (3a–b):

(1) a. Everybody in this classroom speaks at least two languages.
   b. At least two languages are spoken by everybody in this classroom.
(2) a. Many men read few books.
   b. Few books are read by many men.
(3) a. The police didn't arrest many of the demonstrators.
   b. Many of the demonstrators weren't arrested by the police.

It is often the case that an active sentence and its passive counterpart have the same 'meaning,' but the active and passive pairs in (1) through (3) will show a slightly different behavior. In each of the pairs, the meaning of (a) sentence is not the same as that of (b) sentence. For example, in (1), let us assume that there are three students named Daniel, Eliza, and Fred in this classroom. Of the possible interpretations of (1a) and (1b), those that are directly related to the issue here are (4a) and (4b), respectively.

(4) a. Daniel speaks English and Japanese, Eliza French and Chinese, and Fred German and Korean.
   b. Daniel speaks English and Japanese, Eliza English and Japanese, and Fred English and Japanese.

Clearly, the 'meanings' of (4a) and (4b) are different from each other, and this difference lies in the fact that the surface order of the quantifiers, i.e. *every* (in *everybody*) and *two* (in *at least two languages*), has been reversed when passive transformation has applied. This means that Surface Structure determines part of the semantic interpretation of a sentence. Similarly, in (2), of the possible interpretations of (2a) and (2b), those that are directly related to the issue here are (5a) and (5b), respectively.

(5) a. There are many men who read only one or two books. [E.g. George read only *Huck Finn*, Harry only *Harry Potter*, Ian only *Gone with the Wind*, and so on.]

   b. There is only one or two books that many men read. [E.g. George read only *Huck Finn*, Harry only *Huck Finn*, Ian only *Huck Finn*, and so on.]

It is clear that the meanings of (5a) and (5b) differ, and it is the surface order of *many* and *few* in (2) that is responsible for this difference. Likewise, the relevant interpretations for (3a) and (3b) should be (6a) and (6b), respectively.

(6) a. It is not the case that the police arrested many people. [The police arrested only Jack and Ken.]

   b. There are many people who were not arrested by the police. [It may be true that the police arrested a number of demonstrators, but the police didn't arrest Larry, Mike, Nick, and many others.]

In this case, too, Surface Structure contributes to the semantic interpretation of a sentence.

N.B. When (1a), for example, has an interpretation like that of (4a), we say that the quantifier *every* has a wider scope than the quantifier *two*. The unmarked principle of scope interpretation is such that with regard to the surface word order in which more than one quantifier appears, the quantifier that comes first has a wider scope than the second one, and so on. There are, however, many special cases where this unmarked principle does not hold: in the sentence "All that glitters is not gold," for example, we may have the interpretation such that *not* has a wider scope than *all*, as well as the one where *all* is wider than *not*.

There is another type of phenomena where Surface Structure has much to do with semantic interpretation. Observe below:

(7) a. [Mary admires John$_i$ and loves John$_i$]
   b. Mary admires John$_i$ and loves him$_i$. (John$_i$ = him$_i$)
   c. *Mary admires him$_i$ and loves John$_i$.
   d. Mary admires him$_i$ and loves John$_j$. (him$_i$ ≠ John$_j$)

(8) a. [John$_i$'s daughter kissed John$_i$]

b. John$_i$'s daughter kissed him$_i$ (John$_i$ = him$_i$,)

c. *He$_i$ was kissed by John$_i$'s daughter.

d. John$_i$ was kissed by his$_i$ daughter. (John$_i$ = his$_i$)

e. He$_i$ was kissed by John$_j$'s daughter. (He$_i$ ≠ his$_j$)

Assume that (7a) and (8a) are terminal strings of certain sentences at the level of Deep Structure, or put simply, they each represent a coreferential relation between the two instances of *John* with the same subscript i. Assume further that sentences (7b–d) and (8b–e) are "Surface" strings of their respective structures. Now it should be clear that when one of the two coreferential NPs gets pronominalized (i.e. becomes a pronoun), it is sur-face word order that endorses the coreferential reading of a sentence with two NPs of the same subscript. Here again, Surface Structure contributes to the semantic interpretation of a sentence.

6.7   Word Meaning and Syntax

It is true that syntax enjoys syntactic regularities but it so happens that semantics does regulate, or does have much to do with, certain syntactic behaviors. This section illustrates this type of phenomena.

6.7.1   The Semantics and Syntax of *street* and *avenue*

There are such thoroughfare nouns in English as *street* and *avenue*. Syntactically, they are simply of the same category 'noun,' but from a semantic point of view they are not the same. And it is this semantic difference between them that regulates their respective syntactic behaviors. Let us see in detail how they differ.

As part of their meanings, the nouns *street* and *avenue* have such semantic features as in (1a) and (1b), respectively.

(1) a. *street*: [two-dimensional], [nearby area], [around Ego].

  b. *avenue*: [one-dimensional], [to the far end from here], [away from Ego]

Plainly, *street* means an area of everyday activities which shape part of your life, whereas *avenue* means a linear path leading to a goal, which is the place you have probably never been to, or you have presumably little knowledge of. The connotations of these thoroughfare nouns are reasonably explained if we look into their etymologies, i.e. their historical origins. See their abridged histories below:

(2)   a.   street < OE stræt < LL (via) strata "paved/covered (way)"
      b.   avenue "broad thoroughfare" 19c. < avenue 17c. < F avenue
            (fem. p.p.) ← avenir < L advenire ← ad+venire

Briefly, the noun *street* originates from Late Latin phrase *via strata*, which literally means "paved/covered way." The latter becomes OE *stræt*, the direct ancestor of PE *street*, with the left-hand element *via* (="way") clipped away. Thus, *street* originally means "paved or covered," which leads to the two-dimensional, small areal implication of the word. On the other hand, the noun *avenue* originates from Latin verb *advenire*, which literally means "to/toward+come." The latter becomes French feminine past participle *avenue*, which is now turned into the English noun *avenue*. Thus, *avenue* originally means "to arrive or approach," which leads to such an implication of the word as the one-dimensional route to the far goal.

It is notable that it is the shades of meaning discussed above about the two nouns that determine their syntactic behaviors. Observe the examples below:

(3)   a.   the man in/on the street
      b.   *the man in/on the avenue
(4)   a.   street fashion, street children
      b.   *avenue fashion, *avenue children
(5)   a.   an avenue to success/happiness
      b.   *a street to success/happiness
(6)   a.   a road/way from poverty to success/happiness
      b.   *a street from poverty to success/happiness

Regarding the examples in (3), when we mean the ordinary man leading his average daily life, we call the person "the man in/on the street," but not "*the man in/on the avenue," simply because *street* means the area of everyday activities. Likewise, in (4), the fashion and the children we see every day around us are the "street fashion" and the "street children," but not the "*avenue fashion" or the "*avenue children," respectively. On the other hand, when we have a goal far away from here, the path that leads to the destination we call, for example, "an avenue to success/happiness/ prosperity," but not "*a street to success/happiness/prosperity." There are other nouns in (6) that have the similar collocational behaviors, i.e. *road* and *way*. The latter two nouns do have the one-dimensional source-goal implication, while the noun *street* does not. Examples in (3) through (6) are the facts about the collocation of each of the nouns, and this is evidently due to their semantic properties. In this sense, we are justified to say that semantics may sometimes regulate syntactic behaviors.

N.B. The semantics of *street* and *avenue* has some interesting conse-quences when they are the head nouns in the thoroughfare names such as *Main Street* and *Park Avenue*. For example, the most salient difference between *Main Street* and *Park Avenue* is such that the former is left-hand stressed and the latter right-hand stressed. Details aside, there is good reason to believe that the former is a compound noun, while the latter a phrase-turned noun via a process called conversion. See Nakazawa (2010) for the detail.

6.7.2   Target of Negation: What *not* Negates

Generally speaking, the negative particle *not* negates every syntactic category, as shown by some of the typical examples in (1):

(1) a. It is not (the case) that the sun goes around the earth.
     b. John didn't eat the hamburger: he only drank beer.
     c. John ate the hamburger, but not the cheeseburger.
     d. John isn't in the classroom, he's in the gym.
     e. John wasn't lazy: he was only reluctant.

In (1a) through (1e), the particle *not* negates such syntactic categories as S, VP, NP, PP, and A (or AP), respectively. This is clearly the case where *not* negates the constituent that follows it. But there are cases where *not* negates the nonadjacent constituents. Observe the contrast in the pairs of (2) and (3), where the respective readings in brackets are surely implied.

(2) a. That one standing there isn't a boy. [That one is a girl.]
     b. That one standing there isn't a handsome boy. [That one is a boy.]
(3) a. John isn't the guy who studies linguistics. [John doesn't study linguistics.]
     b. John isn't the only guy who studies linguistics. [John studies linguistics.]

While in (2a) the negative particle *not* negates the following NP "a boy," the particle negates only the nonadjacent adjective *handsome* in (2b). Now, in (3a), it is not that the particle *not* negates the following entire NP "the guy who..." but that it does negate a part of it, i.e. the VP "studies linguistics." Furthermore, in (3b), the particle negates the word *only*, which is also only a part of the predicative NP. Thus, it might appear from a syntactic viewpoint that there should be no systematic principle that governs the interpretation about the target of the negative particle *not*. From a semantic viewpoint, however, the principle is straightforward, and it could be phrased as in (4):

> (4) Target of the negative particle *not*
>   The negative particle *not* negates the semantically most salient element that is placed additionally on the basic reading of a phrase or a sentence.

For example, in (2a), what is at issue is whether the one is a boy or not, and the particle *not* negates the most salient element "a boy." But in (2b), we know that the one is a boy and, in addition to that, what is at stake is whether he is handsome or not. In this case, the particle negates this semantically most salient element *handsome*, which is an added feature to the person in question. Other examples above are all accommodated in the same fashion. Thus, most plainly and informally put, (4) can be para-phrased as (5):

> (5) Target of the negative particle *not* (informally stated)
>   The negative particle *not* negates something that pops up in your sight.

6.7.3 The Semantics and Syntax of Reflexives, Reciprocals, and Pronouns

Reflexives are the NPs that have such suffixes as *-self* or *-selves* attached to them, like *myself, ourselves, yourself, yourselves, himself, themselves* and so on. Reciprocals are the NPs of the form *each other* or *one another*. Reflexives and reciprocals refer back to certain NPs that are called antecedents. The basic assumption about the use of reflexives and reciprocals is shown in (1), where the clause mates are meant to be the NPs that are constituents of the same single sentence, e.g. subject and object of the same single sentence.

(1)   The well-formedness condition of reflexives and reciprocals
The reflexive and its antecedent must be clause mates, and so
must be the reciprocal and its antecedent.

Observe for instance the sentences below, where NPs with the same sub-
scripts are coreferential, i.e. referring to the same entity. Note that a pair of
brackets indicate the extent of a sentence.

(2)   a.   [John$_i$ shaved himself$_i$].
b.   *[John$_i$ expected [that the barber$_j$ would shave himself$_i$]].
c.   [John$_i$ expected [that the barber$_j$ would shave himself$_j$]].
d.   [They$_i$ looked at each other$_i$].
e.   *[They$_i$ believed [that John$_j$ looked at each other$_i$]].

Next, we turn to pronouns. Pronouns are such NPs as *I, me, you, he, him*
and so on. The basic assumption about the use of pronouns is shown in (3):

(3)   The well-formedness condition of pronouns
The pronoun and its antecedent (i.e. coreferential NP) must not
be clause mates.

Observe for instance the sentences below:

(4)   a.   [John$_i$ shaved him$_j$].
b.   *[John$_i$ shaved him$_i$].
c.   [John$_i$ expected [that he$_j$ would shave him$_i$]].
d.   *[John$_i$ expected [that he$_j$ would shave him$_j$]].
e.   [John$_i$ expected [that he$_i$ would shave himself$_i$]].

It should be noted that (3) does not prohibit such a case as when a pronoun
and its non-coreferential NP are clause mates, and in fact this is the case in
(4a) and (4c). Also, (3) does not prohibit such a case as when a pronoun
and its coreferential NP are not clause mates, and in fact this is the case in
(4c) and (4e).

Now, observe the following:

(5)   a.   John$_i$ wanted to shave himself$_i$.
b.   *John$_i$ wanted to shave him$_i$.
c.   John$_i$ wanted to shave him$_j$.

    d.   They$_i$ expected to look at each other$_i$.
    e.   They$_i$ expected to look at themselves$_i$.
    f. *They$_i$ expected to look at them$_i$.
    g.   They$_i$ expected to look at them$_j$.

At first sight, all sentences in (5) seem to be single, or simplex, sentences because of the distribution of reflexives, reciprocals, and pronouns. But it is reasonable to assume that they are complex sentences for the following two reasons, among others. One is that we have the same type of sentences as those of (5) except for the explicit appearance of NPs in the middle of the sentence, as shown in (6):

(6)   a. *John$_i$ wanted [Bill$_j$ to shave himself$_i$].
      b.   John$_i$ wanted [Bill$_j$ to shave him$_i$].
      c. *John$_i$ wanted [Bill$_j$ to shave him$_j$].
      d. *They$_i$ expected [Bill$_j$ to look at each other$_i$].
      e. *They$_i$ expected [Bill$_j$ to look at themselves$_i$].
      f.   They$_i$ expected [Bill$_j$ to look at them$_i$].
      g. *They$_i$ expected [Bill$_j$ to look at them$_j$].

In each of the sentences of (6), since the bracketed part is an embedded sentence, the entire sentence is a complex sentence. For the second reason, we are motivated to propose the following process called Equi-NP Deletion, which is eligible for complex sentences.

(7)   Equi-NP Deletion (Informally stated)
      [s NP$_i$ *want/expect* [s NP$_i$ *to*-infinitive ...]] ➔ [s NP$_i$ *want/expect* [s [NP Ø$_i$] *to*-infinitive ...]]

The effect of Equi-NP Deletion is this. Suppose that the verb of a matrix (or main) sentence is such a type of verb as *want*, *expect*, etc., and that the subject NP of an embedded infinitival sentence is coreferential with the matrix subject NP. In this case, the embedded subject NP must be deleted. For example, Equi-NP Deletion will apply to the underlying abstract structures in (8) below:

(8)   a.   John$_i$ wanted [he$_i$ to shave himself$_i$].
      b. *John$_i$ wanted [he$_i$ to shave him$_i$].
      c.   John$_i$ wanted [he$_i$ to shave him$_j$].
      d.   They$_i$ expected [they$_i$ to look at each other$_i$].

e. They$_i$ expected [they$_i$ to look at themselves$_i$].
f. *They$_i$ expected [they$_i$ to look at them$_i$].
g. They$_i$ expected [they$_i$ to look at them$_j$].

After the application of Equi-NP Deletion, the structures in (8) are all converted exactly to those in (5) with their grammaticality intact. Needless to say, when the subject NP of an embedded infinitival sentence is not coreferential with the matrix subject NP, Equi-NP Deletion will not apply. The latter case is the examples in (6).

Thus far, we have assumed first the well-formedness conditions (1) and (3), secondly Equi-NP Deletion (7), and thirdly the complex sentential structure for the matrix verbs like *want* and *expect*. All these assumptions combined, we will automatically explain the facts given above about the reflexives, reciprocals, and pronouns. We may rightly, then, conclude that sentences in (5) are all complex sentences in spite of their appearances.

6.8   Syntactic and Semantic Generalizations

In Chapter V, the chapter on syntax, we have observed a variety of cases where certain syntactic generalizations are possible over a substantive body of grammatical facts. There are, however, a number of cases where semantic generalizations are also possible over another area of empirical facts. This section is concerned with this type of phenomena.

6.8.1   Constraint

We have proposed Coordinate Structure Constraint to accommodate the cases where no natural explanation was conceivable without it. For example, when we want to exclude (1b) without recourse to Coordinate Structure Constraint, we have no way to prevent the generation of it because WH Movement (2) is applicable to (1a) with *Susan* replaced by *who*. Nor is it a sensible decision to complicate the formulation of WH Movement solely to prohibit (1b), because WH Movement as it is is sufficiently general and far reaching. Therefore we need Coordinate Structure Constraint (3) to block the application of WH Movement to (1a).

(1) a. John admired Mary and praised Susan.
     b. *Who did John admire Mary and praised ___ ?
(2) WH Movement (Informally stated)

$[_S$ X WH Y$]$ → WH$_i$ $[_S$ X $[_{WH}$ Ø$_i]$ Y$]$

(3) Coordinate Structure Constraint (Slightly modified)

No rule can move only one conjunct, or an element in this conjunct, out of the coordinate structure.

But consider the case where Coordinate Structure Constraint appears to be violated, as in (4):

(4) a. I went to a liquor shop and bought a bottle of wine.

    b. Here's the wine which I went to a liquor shop and bought
        ___.

This is a serious problem because (4b) has to have the structure of (5) at the moment WH Movement applies, which application is a stark violation of Coordinate Structure Constraint.

(5) Here's the wine which$_i$ $[_S$ I $[_{VP}$ went to a liquor shop$]$ and $[_{VP}$ bought $[_{WH}$ Ø$_i]]]$.

But the fact is (4b) is perfectly grammatical. This is the very point where a semantic generalization surfaces. From the viewpoint of our daily conventional activities, (4a) is virtually equivalent to (6a), and accordingly (4b) is virtually equivalent to (6b).

(6) a. I bought a bottle of wine at a liquor shop.

    b. Here's the wine which I bought at a liquor shop.

Notice that both (6a) and (6b) have no coordinate structure in their respective syntactic structures. In other words, the syntactic structure of (5), repeated below, is semantically generalized as having the structure of (7a), where $[_V$ went to a liquor shop and bought$]$ semantically corresponds to a single verb $[_V$ BOUGHT$]$ accompanied by a locative adverbial $[_{PP}$ AT A LIQUOR SHOP$]$ as shown in (7b). And this structure is immune from Coordinate Structure Constraint.

(5) Here's the wine which$_i$ $[_S$ I $[_{VP}$ went to a liquor shop$]$ and $[_{VP}$ bought $[_{WH}$ Ø$_i]]]$.

(7) a. Here's the wine which$_i$ $[_S$ I $[_{VP}$ $[_V$ went to a liquor shop and bought$]$ $[_{WH}$ Ø$_i]]]$.

    b. Here's the wine which$_i$ $[_S$ I $[_{VP}$ $[_V$ BOUGHT$]$ $[_{WH}$ Ø$_i]$ $[_{PP}$ AT A LIQUOR SHOP$]]]$.

Thus, we say that (4b) is the type of example where semantic generalization overrides the syntactic constituency. To be more specific, although
Coordinate Structure Constraint is a good example of syntactic generalization that will cover a wide range of facts, it is sometimes ignored when we
have a stronger semantic consistency.

As regards the other constraint we have proposed in the chapter on
syntax, i.e. Complex NP Constraint, we turn to it in §6.8.4.

6.8.2   *Tough* Construction

There is a construction called *Tough* Construction in English, which is
exemplified by (1) below:

(1)   John is easy to please.

Our analysis of (1) is such that the surface form (1) is obtained from the
abstract stages (2a) through (2b), where SOMEONE means an indefinite
person and it becomes phonetically null, i.e. not pronounced.

(2)   a.   [For SOMEONE to please John] is easy.
      b.   It is easy [for SOMEONE to please John].

(2a) is the Deep Structure, to which Extraposition applies with the result of
(2b). (2b) then becomes (1) with the process of the embedded object *John*
replacing the matrix subject *it*. This is the outline of deriving *Tough*
Construction and one of the characteristics uniquely attributable to the
construction is the type of *tough* predicates, of which, in addition to *tough*,
easy is an example. Other *tough* predicates include *difficult, hard, impossible* and others. Syntactically speaking, *tough* predicates are adjectives and
semantically, they are representing qualitative attributes ranging over the
easy-hard-impossible scale. Thus, we can show the surface characteristics
of *Tough* Construction as in (3), where TOUGH means a *tough* predicate.

(3) NP_i be [$_{Adj}$ TOUGH] [$_{VP}$ to V [$_{NP}$ $\emptyset_i$]]

The surface form of (3) is in a sense a syntactic generalization about *Tough*
Construction. But the problem is that *Tough* Construction is not confined to
the structure (3) alone.

Now, observe the sentences below:

(4)   a.   This book is a breeze to read.

b.   This book doesn't require any specialized knowledge to read.

The phrase "a breeze" in (4a) corresponds to [Adj TOUGH] in (3), which fact is a categorial inconsistency because "a breeze" is an NP and [Adj TOUGH], needless to say, an adjective. The phrase "doesn't require any specialized knowledge" in (4b) corresponds to "be [Adj TOUGH]" in (3), which fact is another categorial inconsistency because "doesn't require any specialized knowledge" is a structure of [Aux+Neg V NP] and "be [Adj TOUGH]," needless to say, a structure of [be Adj]. Despite the structural mismatch of this type, the sentences in (4) are all entitled to be called exemplars of *Tough* Construction. The problem here is that (3) is a syntactic generalization but it still fails to accommodate the cases in (4). Here surfaces the semantic generalization. The phrase "a breeze" metaphorically means something comfortable and easy, and the VP structure "doesn't require any specialized knowledge" can be reduced to mean, through the semantic interpretation of the phrase, some attribute that is common and easy. Therefore, both syntactic phrases are semantically generalized to mean qualitative attributes ranging over the *easy-hard-impossible* scale, which is nothing but what the *tough* predicate means. In this sense, sentences in (4) are good examples of semantic generalization in the case of *Tough* Construction.

N.B. There is a similar sentence (ia) to a *Tough* sentence (1) above, repeated here as (ib):
  (i)   a.   John is eager to please.
        b.   John is easy to please.
    The two sentences are constructionally different from each other. They mean different things, and the two readings are roughly represented as (iia) and (iib), respectively.
  (ii) a.   John$_i$ is eager [for John$_i$ to please SOMEONE].
        b.   [For SOMEONE to please John] is easy. (= (2a) above)
    The process to derive (ia) is not the same as that of *Tough* Construction. In (iia), the embedded subject is to be deleted through the process of Equi-NP Deletion. Therefore, though the two constructions appear to be alike, they are totally different from each other.

6.8.3   WH Question

As we saw in §6.3.13, the section on Presupposition, the content of a sentence, i.e. a declarative sentence, can be viewed as consisting of two major information units as in (1):

(1)   The propositional content of a sentence viewed from the perspec-
      tive of information structure:
      [s PRESUPPOSITION + ASSERTION]

Thus, from the viewpoint of information structure, a sentence is understood
as an act to assert something based on the information available at the
moment of speaking. Now, what is the act of WH questioning? It seeks
information not known to the speaker. Which part of information, then, is
not known to the speaker? The unknown information lies in [ASSER-
TION] part but not in [PRESUPPOSITION] part. The latter part should be
the information already known to the questioner, and therefore he or she
has no need to question any piece of information in there. So, WH
Question asks information in [ASSERTION] but never anything in [PRE-
SUPPOSITION]. Observe the contrast below:

(2)   a.   John will win the race.
      b.   It is John that will win the race.
      c.   Who is it ____ that will win the race?
      d.   *Which race is it John that will win ___?

The simple declarative sentence (2a) has a cleft-sentential counterpart as in
(2b), where the focus element *John* is asserted on the basis of the presupposed information that someone will win the race. Now, you can ask for
information as to who will win the race, as in (2c). But you cannot, or do
not, inquire into the information as to which race John will win, because
there is no need to do so since you should already know which race it is, as
the ungrammaticality of (2d) indicates. Notice that WH Movement should
derive both (2c) and (2d) because nothing structurally blocks the application of it. But the fact is only (2c) is grammatical but not (2d).

    There is another type of contrast with the same effect as in (2).
Observe (3) and (4):

(3)   a.   [That John will win the race] is likely.
      b.   *Which race is [that John will win ____] likely?
(4)   a.   It is likely [that John will win the race].
      b.   Which race is it likely [that John will win ___]?

Among the informational (or discourse) functions the grammatical subject assumes, that of representing old information is one case. For example, in (3a), the subject is old information and, therefore, the entire sentence of (3a) says something like this: that John will win the race is a presupposed topic, and what is asserted is that this propositional content is likely to happen. Thus, *which race*, which is part of old information, cannot be interrogated, i.e. asked about. On the other hand, in (4a), the entire sentence says something like this: what is presupposed is that something is likely, and what is asserted is such that what is likely is this propositional content "John will win the race." In this case, you can ask for information that is part of the assertion, as in (4b). Here again WH Question asks information that lies only in [ASSERTION].

There is a syntactic approach, however, that would manage to block the ungrammatical (3b) above, repeated below as (5):

(5)   *Which race is [that John will win ___] likely? (= (3b))

Namely, because it is impossible to extract an element from an NP subject as in (6), the same extraction is also impossible from a sentential subject, as in (5) above.

(6)   *Who is [the story about ___] fun?

But this analysis does not seem to accommodate the cases where the same extraction is possible from an NP object as in (7), as well as from a sentential object as in (8):

(7)   Who did John report [the story about ___]?
(8)   Who did John report [that Mary kissed ___]?

Examining an array of these facts, we conclude that the subject does assume a certain informational (or discourse) function that the object does not. And it is this function that is reflected in the process of WH questioning. Note that in a regular declarative sentence, the subject is presupposition and the sentence-final element is focused, i.e. asserted. Hence the grammaticality difference between one group of (5) and (6), and the other of (7) and (8).

It is true that WH Movement is a generalization about certain syntactic phenomena, but we have shown that WH Question can be generalized in semantic terms.

N.B.1 In (i) below, the subject is WH questioned, but still the result is perfectly grammatical.

    (i) Who ate the hamburger?

    This sentence is a WH counterpart of the following sentence:

    (ii) Jóhn ate the hamburger.

    In (ii), "Jóhn" has a focus stress and, therefore, it is asserted as new information. The rest of the sentence, i.e. "(someone) ate the hamburger," is presupposition.

N.B.2 In the case of yes-no question, what is questioned is the truth value of the proposition, i.e. whether the proposition is true or not. Thus you can question the entire sentence, be it a simple declarative, a cleft, or a pseudo-cleft, as in (i):

    (i) a. Did John eat the hamburger?

        b. Is it John that ate the hamburger?

        c. Is it the hamburger that John ate?

        d. Was what John ate the hamburger?

        (e. ?/*Was what John did eat the hamburger?)

Note that (ie) is somewhat odd because the purported subject "what John did" virtually corresponds to VP and VP is far away from subjecthood especially when it is to undergo Subject-Aux Inversion.

6.8.4   Semantic Island

Before we step onto Semantic Island, let us briefly review Syntactic Island. In §5.7.3, the section on Island, we have introduced a type of syntactic universal and explained what it is like. The universal is referred to as Island, which is defined as follows:

    (1) Island

        There is a kind of domain called Island such that no rule can relate an element inside this domain with another outside.

Let us call the prohibition on rule application dictated in (1) 'Island Constraint.' Island Constraint is indeed interpreted as a statement about certain syntactic processes. It should be noted, however, that the notion of Island itself is not so much a syntactic notion as a syntax-semantics neutral notion. One possible realization of the notion of Island was the syntactic phrase 'Complex NP,' which is, as expected, defined only by syntactic terms. There is also another possible realization of the notion Island. It is 'predicate,' which is essentially semantic in nature. Now observe the following sentences where each of the bracketed parts constitutes a predicate.

(2) a. John [kicked the bucket].
     b. John [took advantage of] Mary.

The reason we regard the bracketed parts in (2) as predicates is that they behave like verbs. As the paraphrase in (3a) shows, *kicked the bucket* simply means "died," which is nothing but a verb. As an object of a transitive verb can be passivized, so can the object of "take advantage of" be passivized as in (3b).

(3) a. John [kicked the bucket]. (= John [died].)
     b. Mary was [taken advantage of] by John.

Thus, it is quite reasonable to assume that though they are not single verbs, the bracketed parts in (2) are nothing other than predicates. Now, Island Constraint is at work on *kick the bucket* and *take advantage of* in (2). Observe (4):

(4) a. *What did John [kick ____]? ('*' as an idiomatic reading)
     b. *What did John [take ____ of] Mary? ('*' as an idiomatic reading)

Since the bracketed parts in (4) are predicates, i.e. Islands, no rule can relate an element inside this domain with another outside. This is the very effect of 'Semantic' Island Constraint.

Next, we can argue that Semantic Island is not confined to the cases of predicate, but that it has cases of another type. See the examples below:

(5) a. Who did you read [a story about ____]?
     b. *Who did you read [John's story about ____]?
(6) a. Who do you approve of [my seeing ____]?
     b. *Who do you approve of [John's seeing ____]?

This is an interesting array of facts in that the bracketed parts in all of the above examples are structurally of the same type but their grammatical behaviors are not the same. Therefore, we cannot but reason that the grammaticality difference does not lie in syntax but does in semantics. This leads to an analysis that the bracketed parts in (5b) and (6b) are Semantic Islands, and they happen to be NPs. Since the bracketed parts in (5b) and

(6b) are Islands, no rule can relate an element inside this domain with another outside.

N.B. The bracketed parts in (5) have the syntactic structure of [$_{NP}$ Det N [$_{PP}$ P [$_{NP}$ WH]], and those in (6) the syntactic structure of [$_{NP}$ [$_{Det}$ NP$_{(GEN)}$] V-*ing* [$_{NP}$ WH]]. The syntactically identical bracketed parts in (5) are semantically different from each other, and so are those in (6). But, linguists are in fact not unanimous in accommodating these facts. Some of the key terms employed by linguists in their analyses include [+/− definite], [+/− specific], and [+/− anaphoric], among others. They would say in effect that NPs with these features positively marked will become Islands, but that those with these features negatively marked won't, i.e. they are immune from Island Constraint. In any event, it seems reasonable to argue that grammaticality difference in both (5) and (6) lies not in syntax but in semantics.

Finally, there is one more interesting group of examples. One instantiation of the Island universal (1) was Complex NP Constraint shown in (7), and the constraint rules out the ungrammatical case (10b), which should otherwise be permitted. Note that the bracketed part of (9) is a simple sentence, while that of (10) is a Complex NP.

(7) Complex NP Constraint
No rule can move an item dominated by S that is dominated by the Complex NP out of this Complex NP.
(8) a. Bill kissed Mary yesterday.
  b. Who did Bill kiss yesterday?
(9) a. John believes [that Bill kissed Mary yesterday].
  b. Who does John believe [that Bill kissed yesterday]?
(10) a. John believes [the claim that Bill kissed Mary yesterday].
  b. *Who does John believe [the claim that Bill kissed yesterday]?

WH Movement (and Subject-Aux Inversion) will apply to a-sentences in (8) through (10) and the respective results will have to be the b-counterparts, though only (10b) is ungrammatical. The failure of deriving (10b) from (10a) is explained by assuming that Complex NP Constraint is operative during the derivation. That is to say, movement of *who* out of the bracketed phrase in (10b) is prohibited due to Complex NP Constraint. This is the outline of how Island Constraint (Complex NP Constraint in this case) functions in the field of English syntax. But, observe the examples below:

(11)   a.   John believed that Bill kissed Mary yesterday.
      b.   Who did John believe that Bill kissed yesterday?
(12)   a.   John believed [the claim that Bill kissed Mary yesterday].
      b.   *Who did John believe [the claim that Bill kissed yesterday]?
(13)   a.   John made [the claim that Bill kissed Mary yesterday].
      b.   OK/? Who did John make [the claim that Bill kissed yesterday]?

It is natural that (12b) is ruled out because the bracketed part constitutes an Island, i.e. Complex NP. But, surprisingly, (13b) is permissible, or sounds OK, for all its structural identity with (12b). This needs an explanation. And the explanation is that both sentences (13a) above and (14a) below have virtually the same meaning, and that (14a) is eligible for WH Movement as the grammaticality of (14b) shows.

(14)   a.   John claimed that Bill kissed Mary yesterday.
      b.   Who did John claim that Bill kissed yesterday?

Clearly, (14a) does not have a Complex NP, and therefore (14b) is immune from Complex NP Constraint. Thus, it is evidently the case that the syntactic structure "to make the claim that S" in (13a) is semantically generalized as having the same semantic structure as that of (14a), i.e. "to claim that S." And the latter semantic constituency imposed on (13a) overrides the apparent syntactic structure of (13a). Thus, we say that (13b) is the type of example where semantic generalization overrides the syntactic constituency. To be more specific, although Complex NP Constraint is a good example of syntactic generalization that will cover a wide range of facts, it is sometimes ignored when we have a stronger semantic generalization.

    Similarly, we have a pair like (15):

(15)   a.   John made [a suggestion that Bill should kiss Mary].
      b.   Who did John make [a suggestion that Bill should kiss]?

(15b) is another case of semantic generalization over syntactic structures in the sense that the phrase "to make a suggestion" is generalized to mean a single verb "to suggest": "to make a suggestion that S" is semantically equivalent to "to suggest that S," which is immune from Complex NP

Constraint.

EXERCISES

---

1.   There are types of colors called *pale blue*, *pale green* and *pale yellow*. Do you think such color terms as *pale white* and *pale black* make sense? If you think yes, explain why. If not, explain why not. (*Hint*: As for the key terms in your answer, you may choose from among such terms as compositional meaning, contradiction, componential analysis, reference vs. referent, family resemblance, and extension.)

2.   Of the sentences below, (iii) is becoming the common usage, or for that matter, (iv) is becoming not rare.
     (i)   Every student has to do <u>his</u> best.
     (ii)   Every student has to do <u>his or her</u> best.
     (iii) Every student has to do <u>their</u> best.
     (iv)   Every student has to do <u>her</u> best.
Why do you think it is so? (*Hint*: Answers may have vast possibilities. Among them, one may be related to sociological gender issue. There is another that is related to grammatical system: English grammatical gender system lacks a definite pronoun that refers to a gender-neutral singular person.)

3.   A regular prepositional phrase (PP) modifies NP, VP, and sentence, among others. But, as we see in (i), PP sometimes stands alone as a subject of a sentence, or as an object of a preposition.
     (i)   a. <u>Under the rug</u> seems to be the best place to hide rubbish.
            b. The cat appeared from <u>behind the curtain</u>.
Why do you think this is possible?

4.   When directed to a person who has never smoked in his/her life, the question below sounds bizarre, or the addressee has no way to answer it. Why is it so?
     "Have you stopped smoking?"

5.   There is a syntactic rule called Gapping, which deletes a main verb of
     the second conjunct, as is shown in the derivation of (ib) from (ia)
     below:
       (i)   a. John ate the hamburger and Bill ate the cheeseburger.
             b. John ate the hamburger and Bill the cheeseburger.
     Why do you think Gapping is applicable to (iia) to derive (iib) in spite of
     the fact that the second conjunct has no single verb to be deleted?
       (ii) a. John is ready to eat the hamburger and Bill is ready to eat the
                 cheeseburger.
             b. John is ready to eat the hamburger and Bill the cheeseburger.

Chapter VII

Pragmatics

7.1 Domain of the Study of Pragmatics: Sentence, Setting, and Participants

In Chapter V we defined the domain of the study of syntax as "a sentence," and in Chapter VI we also defined the domain of the study of semantics as "a sentence." The sentence was the utmost range of these studies. But now we are concerned with pragmatics. Pragmatics studies the intentions conveyed by the utterances that a speaker produces. The utterances themselves are embedded in the discourse. And the discourse is a body of linguistic tokens or materials that comprise grammatical sentences as well as ungrammatical expressions, sentence fragments, interjections, silence and others. So the question is: What is the domain of the study of pragmatics?

It is simply that the domain of the study of pragmatics is part of the discourse. And, as we have observed in the previous paragraph, this part of discourse is not necessarily "a sentence" but it may be "sentences" or "a certain amount of sentence fragments," which may well be called an utterance or utterances in pragmatic terms. Thus we may say that the target domain of pragmatics is our linguistic behaviors in the form of an utterance or utterances.

Once the domain of the study of pragmatics is delineated this way, the next question is: what do you study in the domain of pragmatics? As is clearly stated above (in the first paragraph of this section), pragmatics studies the intentions conveyed by the utterances that a speaker produces. In other words, while we know that semantics studies the "meaning" of a sentence, pragmatics studies the "intended or conveyed meaning" of an utterance, which "meaning" is the very notion called "intention," "implicature," or otherwise in pragmatic terms.

Now we know that we study speakers' intentions in pragmatics. What comes next is: how do you study such intentions? This is in fact the essential part of pragmatics. The speaker's intention is determined or calculated on the basis of the interaction of the following three parties: sentence, setting, and participants. This means that in order to know or infer what a speaker intends to communicate to a hearer, the hearer needs to have at hand the following types of information:

(1) Three types of information contingent in pragmatic inference
  a. the meaning of a 'sentence,' which is supposedly a grammatical counterpart of an utterance
  b. the environment in which an utterance takes place
  c. the type of the speaker and the type of the hearer, who jointly make up the communication environment

In other words, the three types of information in (1) are the semantic 'meaning' of a sentence, the pragmatic relevance of the setting, and the social attitude assumed or required of the participants, respectively. To understand how information of the types in (1) contributes to the pragmatic inference that a speaker intends to evoke in the mind of a hearer, let us take a simple example.

Suppose that there is a fragile lady and she says to a massive guy next to her something like "This trunk is so heavy." The addressee will then take the utterance to mean that he should carry it. Semantics gives the meaning of a sentence, and pragmatics calculates the "intention" on the part of the lady when she says that sentence on this very occasion. Below is a simple illustration of how pragmatic inference goes:

(2) Steps of how pragmatic inference goes
  a. the meaning of a 'sentence'
      "This trunk is so heavy" literally means "The trunk that the

lady is going to carry is very heavy."
　　b.　the pragmatic relevance of the setting
　　　　The lady is at a loss because she has so heavy a trunk that she
　　　　could not possibly carry it. She needs help. And beside her,
　　　　there is a man who looks dependable when asked to carry
　　　　such a hefty item.
　　c.　the social attitude assumed or required of the participants
　　　　If you see someone in need of help, you will be inclined to
　　　　lend him/her a hand since it is no doubt the case that humans
　　　　are disposed to be cooperative, or indeed philanthropic. In
　　　　this case, the lady is fragile and the man is vigorous.
　　d.　pragmatic inference
　　　　The man's inference proceeds:
　　　　(i)　the lady cannot carry the heavy trunk and needs help,
　　　　(ii)　there is no other man than him here,
　　　　(iii)　she is fragile but he is vigorous,
　　　　(iv)　she would be happy if he carries the heavy trunk,
　　　　(v)　her utterance could be interpreted as if to say, "Will you
　　　　　　help me carry this trunk?"
　　　　(vi)　he, being philanthropic, understands her intention and,
　　　　　　therefore, goes on to carry it.

Thus we understand that in order for the man to calculate the intention the
lady is trying to impart, he needs information not only of a sentence
uttered, but that of other resources, i.e. who said what on which occasion.
All this makes a pragmatic inference possible and available.

7.2　Grammaticality and Acceptability

　　Semantics and Pragmatics are, in a way, similar areas of study in the
sense that they both deal with 'meaning.' There are two notions that have a
lot to do with 'meaning' that appear to be similar and, therefore, we might
tend to think that there would be no defining features that could help to
discern their respective meanings. They are the notions 'grammaticality'
and 'acceptability.' But, strictly speaking, these notions are quite different
from each other. Grammaticality is the notion of how a given form is in
accordance with the rules of grammar. On the other hand, acceptability is

the notion of how you can succeed in interpreting a given form. Therefore, grammaticality is the notion of grammar, and acceptability is that of pragmatics. In §3.5 "Some Phonological Universals" in Chapter III, which is on Phonetics and Phonology, we touched upon the need for the four levels of abstraction in the study of linguistics. Grammaticality and acceptability have much to do with the two (or three) of the four levels: Grammar (or Language) and Data.

In the study of linguistics, we need to discern four levels of abstraction: they are Data, Language, Grammar and Linguistic Theory. Linguistic Theory is a theory about Grammar, Grammar is a theory about Language, Language is a theory about Data, and Data is a solid object, both concrete and observable. Data may sometimes be conceived of as a collection of acceptable and grammatical sentences. But the latter view is not correct. Let us explain this with examples. An utterance like (1) below may possibly be observed in our daily situations, i.e. (1) is an item in Data. Notice, however, that (1) is definitely not grammatical.

(1)   Wake up, boys, and you'll …, OK, breakfast isn't yet …, ah-ha, coffee?... cool!

The example (1) is a sequence of fragments and thus is not a full sentence or a sequence of sentences. Hence, this fact shows that Data is not always a collection of grammatical sentences. Next, observe (2):

(2)   John criticized the book before he read it.

The example (2) is authentically a grammatical sentence. But the related example (3) is not grammatical, though it is highly intelligible and, therefore, sounds acceptable.

(3)   *[John's criticism of the book [before he read it]] appeared last week.

The reason (3) is ungrammatical is that you cannot use an adverbial clause [*before he read it*] to modify the head nominal *criticism*, though an adverbial clause can modify the verbal element as it does in (2), where [*before he read it*] modifies the verb phrase [*criticized the book*]. Now, as a last example, observe (4):

(4)   The car the gentleman the young lady greeted with a smile owns

won the race.

The example (4) is really tough to interpret, but with the aid of paper and pencil, i.e. bracketing, it becomes intelligible: this construction is what linguists would call a "self-embedded construction" of relative clauses. See (4') below, where the symbol Δ indicates the site of the understood object.

(4') The car [(that) the gentleman [(that) the young lady greeted Δ with a smile] owns Δ] won the race.

Thus, although it seems it never happens that we utter sentences like (4) because of its incurable unacceptability, (4) itself is still grammatical. This means that (4) should not be an item found in the body of Data, but it nevertheless is an item that should belong to Language, which comprises grammatical sentences. Therefore, the examples (1) through (4) clearly illustrate the importance of the discernment of the notion grammaticality as distinct from the notion acceptability. In general terms, Language is in line with the notion 'grammaticality' of all its sentences, and Data with the notion '(un)acceptability' of all its utterances. Summarizing the discussion so far, we draw a cross-sectional table of grammaticality and acceptability.

(5) Cross-sectional table of grammaticality and acceptability

	grammatical	ungrammatical
acceptable	(2)	(1) (3)
unacceptable	(4)	"*The won car race the."

Now it should be clear that the notions grammaticality and acceptability are not the same: they are different from each other.

7.3 Speech Acts

Speech acts simply mean acts or attitude or behavior made possible through the utterances produced by a speaker. But what kind of "acts" do speakers perform when they put forth specific utterances? A variety of linguists attempt a variety of answers to this question. Broadly speaking, there are two camps of linguistics tradition that focus on the fields of study of their respective interest. One is what we call formal language approach and the other what we call ordinary language approach. We will see below what they are.

7.3.1   Formal Language Approach

If we try to characterize formal language approach in general terms, it would be such that the approach aims to construct a rigorous logical system of formal symbols through the use of which the linguists could envision the world of verbal behaviors without fail. Thus it seems reasonable to say that with the aid of such formal notions as 'inference,' 'premise, 'conclusion,' 'truth condition,' and others, formal language approach is trying to engage itself in assessing humans in their linguistic contexts. In this sense, formal language approach has an empirical side, which means that it is pragmatic in its broadest sense. But in a narrower perspective, it may well be semantic in its nature: it deals with sentences and their 'meaning.'

> **N.B.** Thus it is sometimes a regular practice to treat the analyses explained in this subsection as a kind of semantic analyses.

Let us take some examples. One of the topics that this approach deals with is 'valid inference.' Valid inference is indeed a piece of human activities. Examples in (1) are instances of valid inference.

(1)   a.   Aristotle is a man. All men are mortal. Therefore, Aristotle is mortal.
        b.   If a certain bird is a crow, it is black. This is a crow. Therefore, this is black.

The first and second sentences of (1a, b) are called premises, and the third is called conclusion. In (1), the conclusions are correct, which means that this inference is valid. But observe (2):

(2)   a.   Aristotle is a man. Some men are happy. Therefore, Aristotle is happy.
        b.   If a certain bird is a crow, it is black. This bird is black. Therefore, this is a crow.

Here in (2), it is clear that the conclusions are all incorrect, which means that inferences here are not valid. Notice that in (2a), Aristotle may or may not be happy, so you cannot say "Aristotle is happy": in (2b), this may or may not be a crow, so you cannot say "this is a crow." Thus, valid inference constitutes a part of humans' mental architecture and we argue that humans are disposed to make such valid inferences.

Another type of topic this approach is engaged in concerns the idea of whether a given sentence is true or false, which is ultimately a type of semantic calculation or processing in the field of 'from-form-to-real world' correspondence semantics. This area of study, we have actually observed it in chapter VI, especially in §6.3 on the Types of Meaning Properties and Relations. So, readers are to refer back to chapter VI.

7.3.2   Ordinary Language Approach

We produce words not only to make descriptions about the things we see in the world in which we live and descriptions about the state of mind we have when we see, read, or hear things that appear around us. But we also do produce words to try to actively engage ourselves in performing certain types of acts so that we could have interpersonal relationships with others.

Ordinary language approach is characterized in such a way as to say "Utterances in the ordinary linguistic context perform certain types of acts." There are said to be three types of acts performed: 'locutionary act,' 'illocutionary act,' and 'perlocutionary act.' Locutionary act is the act of locution, i.e. act of producing words. Illocutionary act is the act performed in saying something: in other words, an act implied by or deduced from the meaning of the utterance (= the locution). Perlocutionary act is the act that brings about a certain effect on the part of the hearer: in other words, an act that invokes something that involves the hearer as a result of hearing the utterance (= the locution).

> **N.B.** Etymologically, "locution" means 'speech, speaking, or utterance,' "illocution" is made of 'il-' (= "in-" (cf. *in* preposition)) + 'locution,' and "perlocution" is made of 'per-' (= "through") + 'locution.'

Suppose we make such utterances as "I will come tomorrow" and "Will you open the door?" Below are some examples of acts performed by producing these utterances:

(1) Types of acts performed by the utterance "I will come tomorrow."

    (i)   locutionary act: To utter this sentence.

      (ii) illocutionary act: To make a promise.

      (iii) perlocutionary act: To make the hearer happy, for example.

(2) Types of acts performed by the utterance "Will you open the door?"

      (i)   locutionary act: To utter this sentence.

      (ii) illocutionary act: To ask a question.

      (ii') indirect speech act: To ask a favor.

      (iii) perlocutionary act: To make the hearer obliged to open the door, i.e. to answer the request imposed by the speaker.

As for (1i), to say "I will come tomorrow" is to make a locutionary act. As for (1ii), by uttering this, the speaker makes a promise to the hearer such that the speaker will come tomorrow, which promise is nothing but an illocutionary act. As for (1iii), by producing this utterance under certain circumstances, the speaker makes the hearer feel happy, which is the result made possible through the use of this locution. In this case, the speaker's intention is calculated on the basis of the interaction of the three parties: utterance (= sentence), setting, and participants.

As for (2i), to say "Will you open the door?" is to make a locutionary act. As for (2ii), by uttering this, the speaker asks the hearer a question if the hearer will open the door. In this case, the hearer calculates the intention the speaker is supposedly making: the speaker wants a favor from the hearer such that the hearer shall exert his/her capacity to open the door. The latter act of asking a favor is called an indirect speech act. As for (2iii), this utterance, in a certain context, urges the hearer to do a favor for the speaker and eventually the hearer opens the door. In this case, the speaker's intention is calculated on the basis of the interaction of the three parties: utterance (= sentence), setting, and participants.

We have another type of utterances: they are called performative sentences, whose main verbs are also called performative verbs. Some examples are below:

(3) a. I agree with you.

     b. I apologize to you for the inconvenience.

     c. I promise you to finish the work by tomorrow.

     d. We name our daughter Mary.

In the examples (3a) through (3d), the utterances themselves are acts performed by the speakers: in other words, the locutions above are all illocutionary acts by themselves, i.e. act of agreeing, act of apology, act of promise, and act of naming, respectively. The performative sentences have a peculiar set of grammatical characteristics as shown in (4):

(4) a. The main verb is a type of verb called performative verb.
     b. The subject is the first person.
     c. The sentence is in the present tense.
     d. The sentence is in the active voice.
     e. The sentence is a declarative/affirmative sentence.

Thus, just as hitting a ball is a kind of act, so is producing performative sentences in the sense that these utterances constitute certain types of acts.

In this way, utterances are connected to the real world, which is essentially a pragmatic use of verbal behaviors.

N.B.1 A simple description of a state or event, as in (i), can be true or false.

(i) a. Aaron is in the office.
     b. Bob hit a home run in the first inning yesterday.

If these sentences are false, they can be denied: it is possible to say such negative sentences as in (ii):

(ii) a. Aaron isn't in the office.
      b. Bob didn't hit a home run in the first inning yesterday.

But performative sentences can never be true nor false: they are not the descriptions about the world but rather they are acts by themselves performed by the speakers. If the sentences in (3) above are negated, i.e. in the form of negative sentences as in (iii) below, they are no longer performative sentences nor performative acts, but rather they are simply descriptions or expressions of each of the speakers' state of mind.

(iii) a. I don't agree with you.
       b. I don't apologize to you for the inconvenience.
       c. I don't promise you to finish the work by tomorrow.
       d. We don't name our daughter Mary.

While the sentences we are concerned with in this section are called performative sentences, the sentences in (i) and (ii) are called constative sentences: constative sentences can be true or false.

N.B.2 The idea of this subsection is due to J. L. Austin, who is one of the trailblazers in the field of ordinary language pragmatics. What is outlined here is, for the most part, based on Austin (1962, 1975[2]).

7.4   Cooperative Principle and Implicature

7.4.1   Cooperative Principle

When we are having a conversation, we feel we have no difficulty in understanding the utterances produced by those who are on this occasion. In other words, we can easily understand the sentences that arise around us. A simple dialogue like (1) suffices to show that this is the case.

(1)   A: Hey, I'm Chris. What's your name?
      B: I'm David.

Here, the speaker A asks a question of the speaker B and the speaker B responds and answers the question. This is a fairly standard way of information exchange. But occasionally, things are not so simple as we expect them to be. Take, for example, the following dialogue:

(2)   A: I'm terribly thirsty.
      B: There is a drugstore around the corner.

In this case, the speaker A (hereafter, shortened to A) is simply reporting something about the physical condition he is experiencing, while the speaker B (hereafter, shortened to B) responds and says something only about the geographical information on the spot. On the face of it, the two parties appear to be exchanging no information at all. What B says seems to have nothing to do with what A says. But as far as informativeness is concerned, the fact is to the contrary: the dialogue of (2) is meaningful and A could receive a significant piece of information. But what and how?

In order to decipher the hidden dynamics of information exchange exemplified in (2), we need to have recourse to a certain kind of pragmatic principle, a principle called the Cooperative Principle, the essential part of which is briefly phrased as shown below:

(3)   The Cooperative Principle
      Participants of the dialogue should be cooperative in the sense that they contribute to the successful exchange of required information.

The Cooperative Principle is too general by itself to employ it as a yardstick when we do pragmatic analysis. Thus, we need some rules under the principle. We assume that the participants follow these rules, or from a different perspective, we assume that these rules govern the interactive behaviors of the participants of the dialogue. These rules are a kind of prescriptions about verbal behaviors, and we will call these rules maxims. There are said to be four categories of maxims under the Cooperative Principle: the four categories are 'Quantity,' 'Quality,' 'Relation,' and 'Manner.' The four categories and the maxims that fall under them are shown below:

> (4) Maxims under the four categories
>> a. Maxim of the category of Quantity
>> "Information given is to be no more or no less than required."
>> b. Maxim of the category of Quality
>> "Information given is to be true."
>> c. Maxim of the category of Relation
>> "Information given is to be relevant to the topic."
>> d. Maxim of the category of Manner
>> "Information is to be given in a perspicuous manner, i.e. being brief and orderly, and avoiding obscurity and ambiguity."

N.B. The idea of the Cooperative Principle in (3) is due to Paul Grice, who is also one of the trailblazers in the field of ordinary language pragmatics. Grice's formulation of the Cooperative Principle is as follows:

> (i) The Cooperative Principle
> Make your conversational contribution such as is required, at the stage at which it occurs, by the accepted purpose or direction of the talk exchange in which you are engaged. (Grice (1989: 26))

The four categories and the maxims that fall under them shown in (4) are, for the most part, based on Grice's article "Logic and Conversation," i.e. Grice (1989).

Now we go back to the problem we face when we try to interpret the dialogue in (2): the problem of indeterminacy such that although the participants of the dialogue appear to be exchanging no information at all, they are in fact trading meaningful messages if not latent.

In the dialogue (2), A says "I'm terribly thirsty," which literally reports the physical condition of A and is a candid expression of A's state of mind. This short utterance, or a sentence, conveys information that is no more or no less than required to describe what A is. Needless to say, A's statement is true. As a reply to A, B says "There is a drugstore around the corner," which literally means it is true that a drugstore is located at such and such a place. On the face of it, what B says looks as if it has nothing to do with A's thirst. But here, the Cooperative Principle is at work. B infers from what A says that A would be grateful if A should be given information regarding some drink to quench his/her thirst. B happens to know that there is a drugstore around the corner, where miscellaneous things are sold including food and drink. This means that A could buy some drink at the drugstore. In this sense, B's reply is relevant to A's need for something that is to be exploited to quench the thirst. In this way, the dialogue in (2) is made up of and organized with necessary and sufficient pieces of pragmatic information, where messages, if ever latent, are exchanged in accordance with the Cooperative Principle.

7.4.2 Implicature

There is a certain type of messages or information conveyed by the utterances the speaker produces. It is often called implicature. Implicature is not just what is said but rather it is what is implicated or implied by what is said. There are two types of implicature: conventional and conversational. Conventional implicature constitutes part of the meaning of the expression exploited by the speaker. To see what this is, observe the following:

(1) a. Eve started playing a computer game again.
     b. Fred managed to reach the top of the hill.

As for (1a), we know from the word "again" that Eve was once playing a computer game and that it is the second time that she played it. As for (1b), we know from the expression "managed to" that Fred actually arrived at the top of the hill but experienced a certain amount of difficulty before reaching there. One of the features of the conventional implicatures is that conventional implicatures cannot be canceled. So the examples below are all ungrammatical.

(2) a. *Eve started playing a computer game again for the first time.
     b. *Fred managed to reach the top of the hill with no difficulty.

As for (2a), the conventional implicature obtained from the word "again" cannot be canceled by the phrase "for the first time," and thus (2a) is ungrammatical. As for (2b), the conventional implicature obtained from the expression "managed to" cannot be canceled by the phrase "with no difficulty," and thus (2b) is ungrammatical. In short, (2a) is contradictory and so is (2b): both examples make no sense at all. Therefore, they are all ungrammatical.

Conversational implicature, on the other hand, is something that can be canceled. Observe below:

(3)   a.   George ate some of the apples on the table.
      b.   Harry didn't pass the exam.

As for (3a), what is conversationally implicated is that George did not eat all of the apples on the table, but this implicature can be canceled as is shown in (4a) below. As for (3b), what is conversationally implicated is that Harry took the exam, but this implicature can be canceled as is shown in (4b) below.

(4)   a.   George ate some of the apples on the table, but in fact he ate all of them.
      b.   Harry didn't pass the exam, but in fact he didn't take the exam.

In short, (4a) is non-contradictory and so is (4b): both sentences do make sense. Therefore, they are all grammatical.

7.5   Discourse and Conversation: Dynamics of Verbal Behaviors

We noted earlier in §7.1 of this chapter that while a sentence is the utmost range of the studies of syntax and semantics, pragmatics has as its research domain a discourse, i.e., the body of utterances produced by the people on the spot. This means that a discourse mainly consists of linguistic communications held by the participants of the dialogue. Linguistic communications held by the participants of the dialogue are, put simply, conversations between those who happen to be there. Thus in this section, we will focus on the structure and function of conversations: this structure and function is, we claim, what underlies the dynamics of verbal behaviors. In other words, this section aims to be a little showcase of certain verbal behaviors that could be seen, or analyzed, from a viewpoint of pragmatics.

7.5.1   Communicative Force

In an everyday conversation, we give out and receive various types of information, one type of which we may call communicative force: it is an intention that is directed from the speaker toward the hearer. As a way of realizing the types of communicative force, we often ask a question, ask a favor, give a command, make a request, make an apology, and so forth.

Now suppose you are in a room where it is very hot and stuffy. Suppose further that you want someone to open the window. In this case, there are several ways to express your own intention. See below:

(1)   a.   Open the window!
      b.   Will you open the window?
      c.   Would you be kind enough to open the window?
      d.   I would be very happy if you could open the window.
           (Examples (a) through (d) are from §6.2.4, Chapter VI.)

If we make grammatical descriptions about the sentences in (1) by means of purely syntactic and semantic terms, then all sentences in (1) are described as falling into totally different categories from each other: (1a) is an imperative sentence with the meaning 'command/order,' (1b, c) interrogative sentences with the meaning 'question/inquiry,' and (1d) a declarative sentence with the meaning 'statement or description of the state.' But if we look at those in (1) from a pragmatic point of view, we could see another scenery coming into view: all of them are acts that manifest the speaker's intention, with varying degrees, that someone should open the window. There is a cline, or gradience, of politeness here with regard to how directly or indirectly or politely the intention is expressed: (1a) is the most direct and (1d) the most polite. (1a) is a direct command/order, and (1d) a simple description of the speaker's state of mind, which is not a command or order by itself. But the latter indirectly invites the hearer to think about what he/she could do to get the speaker to feel comfortable in this hot and stuffy room. The hearer needs to be cooperative in order to keep a fair relationship with the speaker. The hearer would then conclude that he/she could make the speaker feel comfortably happy by opening the window. Thus the hearer would open the window for the speaker. In this case, the act of hearer's opening the window is not simply induced by the speaker's locutionary act (i.e. saying this sentence) or illocutionary act (i.e. describing the state of mind), but rather it is induced by the speaker's perlocutionary act such that the speaker indirectly/politely makes the hearer calculate the speaker's intention on the basis of the three parties here: the sentence meaning, the setting, and the participants involved.

As for the sentences of (1b) and (1c), they are placed in between the two poles of (1a) and (1d): (1b) being more direct than (1c), or (1b) less polite than (1c). The sentence of (1b), carrying the present tense, simply asks if you will open the window. The one of (1c), on the other hand, carrying the past tense, asks if you would be kind or not. This difference between these two sentences is entirely responsible for the difference of politeness. But note that though the two sentences are distinct from each other with respect to the degree of politeness, they are nonetheless pragmatically interpreted as the same expression of the speaker's intention, "the hearer shall open the window."

To cite another case for the communicative force in conversation, let us see the example below:

(2)   Do you know where the City Hall is?

The sentence in (2) is a syntactic interrogative sentence and the speaker of this sentence simply asks if the hearer knows where the City Hall is. At this stage, pragmatics comes into play. Since the speaker is asking for information about the location of the City Hall, the hearer calculates that the speaker does not know where the City Hall is. Now the hearer feels that he/she is obliged to tell the speaker where the City Hall is, and he/she would possibly eventually take the speaker to the City Hall. In this way, the sentence in (2) embodies a type of communicative force of asking a favor or making a request.

7.5.2   Negative Polarity Items (NPIs)

There are a certain group of expressions or phrases that are used only in the restricted contexts. Negative polarity items (sometimes abbreviated as NPIs) are one such type of expressions: they are used in the so called 'negative' contexts. A typical example of this group is "any" in the case of *some-any* alteration as shown below:

(1)   a.   We have some food in the refrigerator.
      b.   We don't have any food in the refrigerator.

This alteration of "some" and "any" can be viewed from a pragmatic perspective, or to be more precise, from the Cooperative Principle viewpoint.

   Suppose there was some food in the refrigerator, and suppose further that there is no food in there now. In this case, in order to negate the existence of food in the refrigerator, there is no need to negate the existence of the entire amount of food that was in there. Rather, it suffices to negate the smallest amount of food that is to be found there. This means that if there is nothing of the smallest amount of food in the refrigerator, then there must be no food in the refrigerator that is greater than the food of the smallest amount. Therefore we need only to negate the smallest portion, which is what we mean by saying "We don't have any food."

   The type of observation made just above regarding a negative polarity item "any" can be interpreted in the Cooperative Principle terms. That is to say, since information to be given should be no more or no less than required as far as the exchange of information is successful, when we want to mean that there is no food in the refrigerator as in (1b) above, we need only to say that there is not the smallest portion of it in the refrigerator. In other words, we need not accumulate such things as "We don't have one fourth of it," "We don't have one third of it," "We don't have half of it," "We don't have two thirds of it," and so on. But rather, we simply say "We don't have any of it," just in the way of (1b).

   N.B. The example of (1b) is given as an example of how and why "any," an NPI, is used. If we employ the negative particle "no," we simply say "We have no food in the refrigerator."

   There are some other cases where different types of negative polarity items are used. See for example the cases below, where "lift a finger," "move an inch," and "a red cent" in (2) through (4), respectively, are negative polarity items or expressions:

(2)   a.   Ivan didn't lift a finger to help Jane.
      b.   *Ivan lifted a finger to help Jane.
      c.   If Ivan had ever lifted a finger to help Jane, she wouldn't have changed her career.

(3) a. Don't move an inch.
     b. *Move an inch.
     c. Move an inch and I'll shoot you.
(4) a. Kevin didn't give us a red cent.
     b. *Kevin gave us a red cent.
     c. Lindy knows better than to give Mike a red cent.

The examples in (2a), (3a), and (4a) above all show that NPIs are allowed
in the negative context, and those in (2b), (3b), and (4b) above all
demonstrate that NPIs are not allowed in the affirmative context. But, if
we take a look at the examples in (2c), (3c), and (4c), we come to
understand that NPIs are also allowed in the 'apparent affirmative' context.
This means that NPIs are not only confined to the context of 'syntactic
negation' but they are also permitted in some semantically defined context.
So we may ask what this semantically defined context is, or how we can
characterize this context. The answer will look like (5), and if we try to
translate it into plain English, it is (6) below:

(5) The licensing context of NPIs
     An NPI is allowed in the context where the description is not true,
     in other words, the description is about a non-truth 'imaginary'
     world.
(6) The licensing context of NPIs (in plain English)
     An NPI is allowed when the paraphrase, or the interpretation, of
     the whole sentence has within it a syntactic negative context in
     which this NPI is supposed to occur.

A few more words are in order here to understand how NPIs in c-examples
in (2) through (4) are licensed, or approved. In (2c), the NPI "lift a finger"
is used in *if*-clause, which is a conditional clause. A conditional clause is a
description about a non-truth 'imaginary' world. In this case, the truth is
that Ivan did not lift a finger to help Jane and she changed her career.
Therefore, the NPI "lift a finger" is licensed. In (3c), the NPI "move an
inch" is an imperative sentence and this imperative sentence is coordinated
with "I'll shoot you," which is a kind of threat. In this case, the whole
sentence means "Don't move an inch, and if you don't move an inch, I
won't shoot you." Therefore, the NPI "move an inch" is licensed. In (4c),
the NPI "a red cent" is used in *than*-clause in the comparative construction.

The description of *than*-clause is not a fact but rather it is a description about a non-truth 'imaginary' world on which a comparison is made. In this case, the whole sentence means "Lindy is so sensible that she wouldn't give Mike a red cent." Therefore, the NPI "a red cent" is licensed.

In all examples in (1) through (4), NPIs to be negated represent the smallest portion of the entire entity that is to be negated. This use of NPIs is made possible, and can be explained, by the principle imposed on verbal communications, i.e. the Cooperative Principle.

> **N.B.** There are cases where "any" appears in some different contexts than those just mentioned above. Observe below:
>
> > (i)   Do you have any question?
> > (ii)   You may ask any question.
>
> We assume that there are at least two types of "any": one is "any" as an NPI as in (i), and the other is "any" as a universal quantifier as in (ii). The former is an NPI in the interrogative sentence, which constitutes the licensing context of (5) and (6): asking a question is something about a non-truth 'imaginary' world and the whole sentence of (i) could be paraphrased, or interpreted, as, for example, "I wonder if you have some questions or you don't have any." Looking at this paraphrase, we may well see that "any" in (i), being an NPI, is the "any" in the paradigm of, i.e. in the typical set of, *some-any* alteration.
>
> As for the case of (ii), however, we assume that "any" in this example functions as what logicians may call a universal quantifier. A universal quantifier is a theoretical concept that guarantees the existence of all entities of its designated quality. For example, the sentence in (iii) has a universal quantifier "all" in it and the logical interpretation of (iii) with this universal quantifier is shown in (iv).
>
> > (iii)   All men are mortal.
> > (iv)   For all x such that x is 'a man,' it is the case that x is mortal.
>
> Likewise, the logical interpretation of (ii) is (v):
>
> > (v)   For all x such that x is 'a question,' it is the case that you may ask x.
>
> Just in case for the additional knowledge about the terminology, we note that there is another type of quantifier called an existential quantifier. An existential quantifier is a theoretical concept that guarantees the existence of at least one entity of its designated quality. For example, the sentence in (vi) has an existential quantifier "some" in it and the logical interpretation of (vi) with this existential quantifier is shown in (vii).

(vi) We have some food in the refrigerator.

(vii) For some *x* such that *x* is 'food,' it is the case that we have *x* in the refrigerator.

7.5.3 Modals and Modality

Modal auxiliary verbs, or modals, are used to represent the speaker's mental attitude toward the state of the world that he or she is going to describe in the form of a grammatical sentence. This type of mental attitude directed toward what the speaker wants to render a grammatical characterization of is called modality. The choice of modals, or the type of modality the speaker is to represent, is sometimes determined, and can be explained, by the principle regarding the structure and function of conversations that underlies the dynamics of verbal behaviors: it is the principle imposed on verbal communications, i.e. the Cooperative Principle.

N.B. Modals include *must, may, might, can, could, will, would,* and so on. As for modality, there are among others two basic types of it.
  (i) Two basic types of modality and their subcases
      a. Deontic: Something is mandatory, obligatory, permissive, etc.
      b. Epistemic: Something is possible, probable, necessarily unavoidable, etc.

Now let us take a look at some examples. Observe the following dialogues:

(1) A: Do you think I must do it right now?
     B: No, you don't need to. /*No, you mustn't.

In (1), the speaker A (hereafter, shortened to A) asks the hearer B (hereafter, shortened to B) if B thinks that A's doing it is mandatory. B replies "No," which would literally mean that B's thought is such that A's doing it is not mandatory. However, if B really thinks that way, B should have said, "No, you mustn't." But that is not what B said. Instead, B said, "No, you don't need to." Here, we may ask why B's choice of modals has changed from "must (not)" to "(not) need." It is at this point where pragmatic inference comes into play. According to the Cooperative Principle, utterances should be relevant to the theme of communication. In (1), A asks B if A's doing it is mandatory, and then B responds that it is not. But what B said is not "you mustn't," which would have meant "it is mandatory that you do not do it." The modal "must" in this case, whether in the affirmative ("you must do …") or in the negative ("you mustn't do…"), has the effect of forcing the hearer to feel obliged to do things that the speaker has told him/her to do. This is such a mandatory order or command that the hearer would unavoidably have to do what he/she is told to do. This situation is rather odd from a sociable and friendly interpersonal perspective since the speaker is too demanding and intrusive for the hearer. Thus B in the dialogue of (1) did not employ the modal "must" and instead chose the modal "need (not)." This is because the interpersonal communication should be carried out in an amicable and congenial manner: therefore the speaker avoided such annoying and challenging wording as the one that includes "must" like that shown in (1-B) as the ungrammatical counterpart. Notice that the modal "need (not)" does not carry with it a demanding or annoying connotation any longer. This choice of modal is entirely due to the pragmatic principle such that people try to attain the relevant goal with as small amount of conversational load as possible. The latter pragmatic principle, we may conclude, is one of the manifestations the Cooperative Principle.

Next, let us see the dialogue below:

(2)   A: Paul must be a coward to say so.
      B: No, he cannot be. /*No, he mustn't be.

In (2), the speaker A (hereafter A) thinks that it is necessarily true that Paul is a coward, but the speaker B (hereafter B) does not agree with A. If B thinks that it is necessarily true that Paul is not a coward, he/she should have said "No, he mustn't be," which B did not say. But if B ever has said, "No, he mustn't be," it surely would offend A, since the latter comment by B is quite incompatible with A's appraisal of Paul's cowardliness. Therefore B chose to say, "No, he cannot be." That means that while B still thinks with less certainty that it is the case that Paul is a coward, he/she thinks with much more certainty that it is the case that Paul is not a coward. This is the meaning that the approved utterance of (2–B) "No, he cannot be" is purported to convey. Thus the choice of modals exemplified in (2) is in line with the modality that could best fit the speaker's mental attitude: while keeping good terms with A, B still tries to insist on his/her point without offending A too much. That way, choice of modals is an instance of realizations of pragmatic adjustments that make good use of conversational tactics, part of which surely involves the Cooperative Principle in the sense that communication is successful when we achieve the relevant goal with the smallest amount of conversational load.

As a third example of the dialogue, we will examine the following:

(3)   A: May I drive without a license?
       B: No, you mustn't. /*No, you may not.

In (3), the speaker A (hereafter A) is wondering if he/she is permitted to drive without a license, and the speaker B (hereafter B) says "No." It is generally acknowledged that driving without a license is not only permitted but also prohibited. So if B has only said, "No, you may not," this remark is both inappropriate and improper, since it fails to send the strong message of prohibition: the wording of "No, you may not" is equivalent to simply saying "No, you are not permitted," and no more. If B wishes to send a strong message so as to make A refrain from driving without a license, B should say, "No, you mustn't," which B actually chose to say. B's utterance "No, you mustn't" means a prohibition such that it is mandatory that A does not drive without a license. Hence, the modals changed from A's permissive *may* as in "May I ...?" to B's prohibitional *must not* as in "you mustn't ...." That way, again, choice of modals is an instance of realizations of pragmatic adjustments that make good use of conversational tactics, part of which surely involves the Cooperative Principle in the sense that communication is successful when we achieve the relevant goal with the smallest amount of conversational load.

7.5.4   Rhetorical Questions

As a final exemplar in the little showcase of certain verbal behaviors that could be seen, or analyzed, from a viewpoint of pragmatics, we consider rhetorical questions.

It is true that rhetorical questions wear a syntactic garment of 'question,' but in reality they are not questions: rhetorical questions are semantically equivalent to declarative sentences with the meaning of 'assertion.' But how can we arrive at this declarative assertive meaning? The answer is: Only through the pragmatic inference can we arrive at the interpretation of rhetorical questions as a version of assertion.

Now, observe below:

(1) a. Isn't it beautiful? — (It's beautiful.)
     b. Is it beautiful? — (It isn't beautiful.)
     c. Who knows? — (Nobody knows.)
     d. Don't you know I'm ten years older than you? — (I'm ten years older than you.)
     e. How many times have I told you this? — (I have told you this many times.)

All these examples above appear to be questions in their syntactic forms, but they are in fact declarative assertions in their semantic interpretations. Each of the sentences in (1) has a respective assertive meaning in the parentheses. The process whereby we obtain the assertive meanings from these rhetorical questions involves a system of conversational tactics, and its essential part at work is the Cooperative Principle.

As for (1a), for example, suppose that the speaker says, "Isn't it beautiful?" to the hearer right in the situation where the speaker firmly believes that it is beautiful and in reality it is indeed beautiful, and suppose further that the speaker wants the hearer to know this. Here the process of pragmatic interpretation of (1a) is as follows:

(2) a. In this context, it is definitely an obvious fact that it is beautiful and the speaker thinks so, too.
     b. The Cooperative Principle guarantees that what the speaker says is true.
     c. But the speaker asks the hearer if the hearer thinks it is not beautiful.
     d. The reality in front of both of them (i.e. 'it is beautiful') and the proposition embedded in the question of (1a) (i.e. 'it is not beautiful') should pose a total contradiction.
     e. The hearer understands that the speaker is not telling a lie.
     f. So, in order to solve this contradiction, the hearer finally arrives at the conclusion that the speaker is not just asking a question but rather is hoping that the hearer should agree with the speaker: in other words, the speaker thinks it is beautiful and is hoping for the hearer to say, "Yes, it is beautiful."
     g. All through the pragmatic steps of inference above, the hearer comes to acknowledge the fact that it is beautiful.

In addition to the detailed account of the rhetorical interpretation of (1a) shown above in (2), we may have another possibility. This possibility of accounting for the rhetorical interpretation is like this.

Suppose in (1a), once again, that the speaker says, "Isn't it beautiful?" to the hearer right in the situation where the speaker firmly believes that it is beautiful and in reality it is indeed beautiful, and suppose further that the speaker wants the hearer to know this. The process below is a different type of pragmatic interpretation of (1a) than that shown in (2):

(3) a. In this context, it is definitely an obvious fact that it is beautiful and the speaker thinks so, too.

b. But the speaker asks the hearer if the hearer thinks it is not beautiful.

c. The Cooperative Principle guarantees that what the speaker says is true.

d. Then, the hearer wonders why the speaker asks the hearer if it is not beautiful. For, the speaker should already know whether it is beautiful or not.

e. The hearer tries to solve this puzzle and arrives at the conclusion that the speaker is not just asking a question but rather is expecting that the hearer should agree with the speaker: in other words, the speaker thinks it is beautiful and expects the hearer to say, "Yes, it is beautiful."

f. All through the pragmatic steps of inference above, the hearer comes to acknowledge the fact that it is beautiful.

As regards other cases in (1), i.e. (1b–e), we could afford to offer several possible pragmatic approaches to the rhetorical assertive interpretations of these examples, but here we should point out one common feature that is shared among all of these interpretations. The common feature among them is as follows:

(4) In the situation where rhetorical questions are produced, the truth value of the proposition embedded in the rhetorical question and the truth value of the proposition that depicts the circumstance of the situation are incompatible: the former is false, and the latter true.

The speaker of a rhetorical question will, intentionally or unintentionally, make good use of this chasm between the two values and invite the hearer to jump over the rift and to land on the truth side of the divide. This is the very nature of the process in which rhetorical questions are interpreted. Below is a table of the truth values of the relevant propositions in (1).

(5) Table of truth values of the propositions

rhetorical question (RQ)	prop. embedded in RQ — (TV)	prop. depicting circumstance — (TV)
1a. "Isn't it beautiful?"	It isn't beautiful. — (F)	It is beautiful. — (T)
b. "Is it beautiful?"	It is beautiful. — (F)	It isn't beautiful. — (T)
c. "Who knows?"	Somebody knows. — (F)	Nobody knows. — (T)
d. "Don't you know I'm ten years older than you?"	I'm not ten years older than you. — (F)	I'm ten years older than you. — (T)
e. "How many times have I told you this?	I have never told you this. — (F)	I have told you this many times. — (T)

prop.: proposition   RQ: rhetorical question   TV: truth value   T: true
F: false

There is one thing to note here: in order for the communication to be successful, participants of the dialogue must be cooperative in exchanging pieces of information, i.e. keeping to the Cooperative Principle (one of whose maxims says, "Information given is to be true"), but sometimes they digress in that they embed false propositions into the questions directed toward the hearer. This is what rhetorical questions are: it is the type of construction that employs a false proposition in the utterance. That is essentially a rhetorical, or for that matter poetic, means to create an additional rich value to be given to the mere text interpretation of the material. In this sense, pragmatics contributes to literary understanding. As for another attempt to apply a linguistic method to literary understanding, see Nakazawa (2008).

N.B. The interpretation of (1d) in the table (5) is rather complex. When the speaker says, "Don't you know I'm ten years older than you?" the proposition embedded is (i):

(i)   You don't know that I'm ten years older than you.

The proposition (i) ultimately means or is virtually equivalent to the proposition (ii):

(ii)   I'm not ten years older than you.

Likewise, the interpretation of (1e) in the table (5) is complex. When the speaker says, "How many times have I told you this?" the proposition embedded is (iii):

(iii)   I have told you this a very small number of times.

The proposition (iii) ultimately means or is virtually equivalent to the proposition (iv):

(iv)   I have never told you this.

EXERCISES

1.   Suppose Professor John Jones told the students in the classroom the comment in (i):

(i)   Some of the students passed the test.

But the fact is that all students passed the test. Do you think the professor lied or not? If you think he lied, explain why you think so. If you don't think he lied, explain why you don't think so.

2.   Observe the dialogue below, and decide what Susan would do over the weekend.

Rick: Hi, Susan, let's go and see a movie this weekend.
Susan: I'm going to take the Italian Placement exam next Monday.

3.   What kind of question is it that Ursula uttered? What does it mean? Explain how you have arrived at this meaning.

Tom: I'm still wondering when to start.
Ursula: Why don't you start now?

References

Austin, J. L. (1962, 1975²) *How to Do Things with Words*, ed. by J. O. Urmson and Marina Sbisà, Cambridge, Massachusetts: Harvard University Press.

Grice, Paul (1989) "Logic and Conversation," *Studies in the Way of Words*, 22–40, Cambridge, Massachusetts: Harvard University Press.

Heine, Bernd and Heiko Narrog (eds.) (2010, 2015²) *The Oxford Handbook of Linguistic Analysis*, Oxford: Oxford University Press.

Jakobson, Roman (1968) *Child Language Aphasia and Phonological Universals* (Original title: *Kindersprache, Aphasie und allgemeine Lautgesetze*, translated by Allan R. Keiler), *Janua Linguarum, Series Minor*, 72, The Hague: Mouton.

Jakobson, Roman (1971) *Studies on Child Language and Aphasia, Janua Linguarum, Series Minor*, 114, The Hague: Mouton.

Jones, Daniel (1960⁹) *An Outline of English Phonetics*, Cambridge, England: Heffer & Sons. [There are some other editions and reprints of this book]

Kajita, Masaru (1997) "Some Foundational Postulates for the Dynamic Theories of Language," Ukaji et al. (eds.), 378–393.

Nakazawa, Kazuo (2002) "Epenthesis and a Mode of Extension," *Kiyo (The Bulletin)* 44, 39–46, The College of Literature, Aoyama Gakuin University. (Reproduced as Chapter 3 in Nakazawa (2018))

Nakazawa, Kazuo (2003) "Grammatical Naturalization and a Mode of Extension," *Tsukuba English Studies* 22, 273–278, Tsukuba English Linguistic Society, University of Tsukuba. (Reproduced as Chapter 4 in Nakazawa

(2018))

Nakazawa, Kazuo (2006) "Sango-fukugogo-no Rizumu-to Shushokubu-toiu Gainen (Stress Patterns of Three-Word Compounds and the Notion 'Modifier')," *Proceedings of the 78th General Meeting*, 29–31, The English Literary Society of Japan.

Nakazawa, Kazuo (2008) "The Role of Grammatical Dynamism in the Interpretation of Keats' *To Autumn*: Another Case for the Mode of Extension," Sano et al. (eds.), 87–99. (Reproduced as Chapter 5 in Nakazawa (2018))

Nakazawa, Kazuo (2010) "Koendori-to Honmachidori-no Kosaten: Eigo-Gairomei-no Keitairon (At the Crossroads of *Park Avenue* and *Main Street*: A Morphological Analysis of English Thoroughfare Names)," Hiroshi Yoshiba et al. (eds.), 11–24.

Nakazawa, Kazuo (2014) "Gentei-Shushoku-ni tsuite (On Attributive Modification)," *Studies in English Grammar and Usage* 21, 5–26, The Society of English Grammar and Usage.

Nakazawa, Kazuo (2018) *A Dynamic Study of Some Derivative Processes in English Grammar: Towards a Theory of Explanation*, Tokyo: Kaitakusha.

Nakazawa, Kazuo (2021) "Koishushokugo *Combined*-no Goho-to Bumpo: Dotekibumporiron-no Kanten-kara (The Grammar of the Postnominal Modifier *Combined*: A Dynamic View)," *Eibungaku Kenkyu* (*Studies in English Literature*) 98, 19–33, The English Literary Society of Japan.

Sano, Tetsuya et al. (eds.) (2008) *An Enterprise in the Cognitive Science of Language: A Festschrift for Yukio Otsu*, Tokyo: Hituzi Syobo.

Ukaji, Masatomo et al. (eds.) (1997) *Studies in English Linguistics: A Festschrift for Akira Ota on the Occasion of His Eightieth Birthday*, Tokyo: Taishukan.

Yasui, Minoru (1962) *Consonant Patterning in English*, Tokyo: Kenkyusha.

Yoshiba, Hiroshi et al. (eds.) (2010) *Current Studies for the Next Generation of English Linguistics and Philology: A Festschrift for Minoji Akimoto on the Occasion of His Retirement from Aoyama Gakuin University*, Tokyo: Hituzi Syobo.

Dictionaries

[Enclosed in square brackets are abbreviations]

Concise Oxford English Dictionary, Twelfth Edition [*COD*[12]] (2011), Oxford: Oxford University Press.

Oxford English Dictionary Online [*OED Online*], Oxford: Oxford University Press.

Random House Unabridged Dictionary, Second Edition [*RHD*[2]] (1993 edition),

New York: Random House. (A revised and updated edition of *The Random House Dictionary of the English Language, Second Edition, Unabridged*, New York: Random House)

Webster's Third New International Dictionary of the English Language [*Webster*³] (Principal Copyright 1961), Springfield, MA: G. & C. Merriam.

Data Sources

The British National Corpus (BNC) Online (Shogakukan Corpus Network).

WordbanksOnline (Shogakukan Corpus Network).

Index

A Short Introduction to the Structure of English

著作者　中澤和夫

発行者　武村哲司

印刷所　日之出印刷株式会社

2024 年 6 月 24 日　第 1 版第 1 刷発行©

発行所　株式会社　開 拓 社

〒112-0013 東京都文京区音羽 1-22-16
電話　03-5395-7101 （代表）
振替　00160-8-39587
https://www.kaitakusha.co.jp

ISBN978-4-7589-2408-5　C3082